The Economics of Production and Innovation

An Industrial Perspective

2nd Edition

Gerhard Rosegger

Frank Tracy Carlton Professor of Economics,
Case Western Reserve University

PERGAMON PRESS

THE ECONOMICS OF PRODUCTION AND INNOVATION

An Industrial Perspective

SECOND EDITION

OMEGA Management Science Series
Editor: PROFESSOR SAMUEL EILON

EILON, S.
Aspects of Management, 2nd ed.
Management Control, 2nd ed.
Management Assertions and Aversions

EILON, S., GOLD, B. & SOESAN, J.
Applied Productivity Analysis for Industry

GOLD, B.
Technological Change: Economics, Management and Environment

OTHER TITLES OF INTEREST

HAUSTEIN, H-D. & MAIER, H.
Innovation and Efficiency: Strategies for a Turbulent World
Innovation Glossary: A Handbook of Innovation Terms in English, German and Russian

LOWE, J. & CRAWFORD, N.
Innovation and Technology Transfer for the Growing Firm: Text and Cases

Pergamon Journals of Related Interest*

OMEGA
The International Journal of Management Science
Chief Editor: Professor Samuel Eilon
The purpose of OMEGA is to provide a vehicle for reporting developments in management, including research results and applications. Published material ranges from original contributions to review articles describing the state of the art in specific areas, together with shorter critical assessments of particular management techniques.

WORLD PATENT INFORMATION
The international journal for patent documentation, classification and statistics, of the Commission of the European Communities and the World Intellectual Property Organization. Published by Pergamon InfoLine Inc. at Pergamon Press.

Editor-in-Chief: V. S. Dodd, Room 458, State House, 66-71 High Holborn, London WC1R 4TP, UK

*Free specimen copy sent on request.

THE ECONOMICS OF PRODUCTION AND INNOVATION

An Industrial Perspective

SECOND EDITION

by

GERHARD ROSEGGER
Frank Tracy Carlton Professor of Economics
Case Western Reserve University
Cleveland, Ohio, USA

with a foreword by
BELA GOLD

PERGAMON PRESS
OXFORD · NEW YORK · BEIJING · FRANKFURT
SÃO PAULO · SYDNEY · TOKYO · TORONTO

U.K.	Pergamon Press, Headington Hill Hall, Oxford OX3 0BW, England
U.S.A.	Pergamon Press, Maxwell House, Fairview Park, Elmsford, New York 10523, U.S.A.
PEOPLE'S REPUBLIC OF CHINA	Pergamon Press, Qianmen Hotel, Beijing, People's Republic of China
FEDERAL REPUBLIC OF GERMANY	Pergamon Press, Hammerweg 6, D-6242 Kronberg, Federal Republic of Germany
BRAZIL	Pergamon Editora, Rua Eça de Queiros, 346, CEP 04011, São Paulo, Brazil
AUSTRALIA	Pergamon Press Australia, P.O. Box 544, Potts Point, N.S.W. 2011, Australia
JAPAN	Pergamon Press, 8th Floor, Matsuoka Central Building, 1-7-1 Nishishinjuku, Shinjuku-ku, Tokyo 160, Japan
CANADA	Pergamon Press Canada, Suite 104, 150 Consumers Road, Willowdale, Ontario M2J 1P9, Canada

First edition 1980

Second edition 1986

Library of Congress Cataloging in Publication Data
Rosegger, Gerhard.
The economics of production and innovation.
(Omega management science series)
Includes bibliographies.
1. Technological innovations—Economic aspects.
2. Production (Economic theory) I. Title. II. Series
HC79.T4R65 1986 338'.06 86-1450

British Library Cataloguing in Publication Data
Rosegger, Gerhard
The economics of production and innovation:
an industrial perspective. – 2nd ed –
(Omega management science series)
1. Technological innovations – Economic aspects
I. Title   II. Series
338+'.06   HC79.T4

ISBN 0-08-033958-1 Hardcover
ISBN 0-08-033959-X Flexicover

Printed in Great Britain by A. Wheaton & Co. Ltd., Exeter

TO PETER MICHAEL,
WHO WILL CARRY ON

Foreword to the First Edition

For some forty years after the end of World War I, the dominant focus of economists was on macro-economics—first on business cycles and later on economic growth—and the dominant concerns of industrial management centered around the problems of marketing and finance. Since then, however, there has been a steadily accelerating interest by both groups in the role of technology as the most promising source of continuing advances towards increasing the competitiveness of firms and industries in domestic and international markets and, more broadly, towards raising standards of living despite prospective resource stringencies.

As has been customary in all fields, newly recognized problems were tackled initially by resort to available concepts, theories, and tools, despite their having been developed for quite different purposes. Multiplying evidences of their inapplicability to urgent pressures on governmental policies and industrial decisions engendered an expanding array of research efforts and of analytical models more sharply focussed on the specialized characteristics of technological changes and on their distinctive role in determining managerial performance and modifying wider economic relationships.

The resulting literature has now burgeoned to quite substantial proportions. But there have been as yet few serious efforts to summarize the wide variety of findings and to relate them in an organized way to the general structure of economic and managerial thinking. This alone represents a valuable contribution of the present volume.

In addition, however, Professor Rosegger has also provided a careful examination of the gaps between widely accepted conceptions and beliefs and the emerging empirical findings, thus identifying some of the most significant obstacles to be overcome if extant theory and decision models are to be developed so as to encompass these later and more penetrating insights.

The issues dealt with in this volume overlap technology, management, and economics. A careful exposition of relevant theory is followed by consideration of a wide array of research and experimental findings. Alternatives are evaluated within a broad range of successively more aggregative frameworks, from individual operations through plants, firms, industries, and beyond. And technological changes are considered at every stage, from research and development efforts through application and diffusion. The result is a carefully integrated summary of the state of knowledge in this increasingly important area of concern to industry, government, and the public at large.

BELA GOLD

Formerly Professor of Economics and
Director, Research Program in Industrial Economics,
Case Western Reserve University;
now Professor of Economics, Claremont Graduate School

Preface

The first edition of this book was published in 1980, as an introduction to the economic analysis of production and technological change. The time seemed right for such a survey of the state of the art, not because most methodological and theoretical problems had been solved, but because of my belief that economics could contribute toward asking the right questions and thinking clearly about answers.

Developments since then have vindicated that judgment. Innovation and entrepreneurship are increasingly being recognized as the keys to maintaining an economy's health and international competitiveness. A veritable flood of writings testifies to the interest of managers, engineers, and public officials in what needs to be done to stimulate technological advance. And growing numbers of colleges and universities have decided to introduce courses in the subject. As a consequence, the gratifying reception of this book caused the Publisher to bring out a second edition.

The present version represents a complete revision of the original. Additions and deletions of topics reflect both, experience with the first edition and changing emphasis of scholarship. Where necessary, statistical materials have been up-dated and new findings incorporated. Like every author, I hope that the labor of re-ploughing familiar ground will be justified by an improved product.

The book assumes that readers have some familiarity with the principles of microeconomics. These principles form the basis for the development of a conceptual framework in which key topics in production and technological change can be explored. The "industrial perspective" in the title is meant to suggest not only a point of emphasis but also a firm belief that, in order to be useful, an introduction to the subject must at times go beyond the economist's traditional scope: technical, organizational, political and social considerations constantly come into play as one attempts to gain a better understanding of the innovative process. I have attempted to incorporate such considerations into my discussion, even at the price of giving up some of the seeming rigor of tightly-structured economic models.

More than other writers, the author who gets a second chance at a book has incurred intellectual debts that are beyond detailed acknowledgment. Of all the people who influenced my thinking and my work, Professor Bela Gold, now of the Claremont Graduate School, continues to occupy front rank. During his tenure as Director of Case Western Reserve University's Research Program in Industrial Economics he was an inexhaustible source of ideas, encouragement, and helpful criticism. Copious references to his work and to our joint efforts are but feeble signals of my gratitude.

Among my current colleagues, I owe special thanks to Professors Bo Carlsson (now Director of the Research Program), Asim Erdilek, and to that occasional and always congenial co-author, Bill Peirce. Former fellow-workers Professor Samuel J. Mantel, Jr. (University of Cincinnati) and Myles G. Boylan (National Science Foundation) contributed substantially to the shaping of my views. My friend and sometime co-author, Professor John H. Jensen, of Waikato University (New Zealand), gave me a greater appreciation for the historian's way of looking at economic and social change. During the academic year 1983–84, Professor Hans Hinterhuber, of the University of Innsbruck, provided me with a stimulating and friendly working environment at his *Institut fuer Unternehmungsfuehrung*. It was there that I began the task of writing and testing some of the new material for this edition. Professor Samuel Eilon, Editor of the OMEGA Management Science Series, has provided valuable guidance in the preparation of the first and of this revised edition.

Numerous friends from the technical and managerial ranks served as foils for my ideas and in turn gave me a better understanding of what it is like to be "on the firing line." In the process, they also instilled in me a proper sense of humility about the scope and power of economists' traditional models. By their critical questioning, several generations of engineering and management students accomplished the same purpose. One of the teacher's great rewards is to learn, often years later, that these students derived not only intellectual but also direct professional benefits from having studied the economics of technological change.

In keeping with the theme of this book, I also must acknowledge the contribution of new technology. The job of writing and re-writing would have been unthinkably tedious, and much slower, without my trusty *Macintosh*®. Its productivity was fully in tune with my own, it never sighed deeply when it was time for yet another set of revisions, it kept hours on demand, and it abstained from all suggestions on how I might improve my somewhat erratic working habits. In other words, it did all the things one would expect from a good and faithful servant. Nevertheless, the responsibility for errors of fact or interpretation remains mine.

No words can adequately express my gratitude to my wife, Clare.

Cleveland, Fall 1985   GERHARD ROSEGGER

Contents

List of Illustrations

List of Tables

CHAPTER 1

Introduction

This chapter deals briefly with the role of economics in the study of technological change. It presents an initial view of the innovative process, discusses the relationship of technology to other forms of knowledge, and defines some basic concepts. Finally, it outlines the book's overall plan.

1.1 An Economist's View of Technological Change

Historians, philosophers, anthropologists and—of course—engineers have long recognized that advances in technology play an integral role in the transformation of societies and their cultures. Therefore, we have an extensive body of literature on the subject, as seen from the perspectives of these various disciplines. Somewhat surprisingly, economists were relative latecomers to the study of innovative activity. As a separate field of study, "the economics of technological change" is not much more than three decades old.

To be sure, even the fathers of our science, from Adam Smith to Alfred Marshall, recognized the importance of innovation in products and in methods of production as a source of economic progress. Seeing all around them the results of the industrial revolution, they hardly could have failed to do so. And yet, a reading of the classical writers' works show that, while they recognized the importance of technological advances, they did not see them as an integral part of the economic process itself but as originating outside the economist's framework of analysis. Therefore, they regarded inventions and the resulting improvements in what was generally called "the industrial arts" as mere data for the study of production and distribution. Even Karl Marx, who argued that transformations in the structure of production determined all changes in social relationships, had nothing to say about the origins of such transformations.

The game of tracing who, among the great economists, first made technology and technological change an essential part of his theories, could lead one into many more or less obscure byways of the discipline's history. Nevertheless, the contributions of two men probably would be recognized as milestones. The first of these was Thorstein Veblen [1857-1929], an American economist. In two of his books, *Theory of Business Enterprise* (1904) and *The Engineers and the Price System* (1921), he stressed the importance of the interaction between men and their artifacts *within* the economic system. Technology was not an exogenous force, a given, for businessmen, managers, and workers, but rather a set of material and social relationships shaped by them and at the same time shaping their behavior and their values. To anyone living in the last quarter of the twentieth century, this may not seem like a stunning discovery. But in an era when the realization of a seemingly unlimited potential for technical progress was regarded as the domain of the inventor and of the engineer, pulling the two kinds of activity into a unified view represented an important step forward.

Credit for completing the task surely must go to Joseph Schumpeter [1883-1950], an Austrian who taught at Harvard University from 1932 until his death. In his *Theory of Economic Development* (1912, in German; English translation in 1934), he tied innovative activity directly and explicitly to the dynamics of economic growth. His theory starts with the assumption of an economy in *stationary equilibrium*, a concept entirely in line with classical thought, which viewed all economic processes as tending toward such an equilibrium. In this state, firms and households had settled into the optimal positions familiar from microeconomic theory. Then, however, Schumpeter departs from tradition: instead of regarding such equilibria as inherently stable, he sees them as the very conditions that invite disturbance from within.

The central role in bringing about radical transformation is assigned to the *innovator-entrepreneur*, the person who recognizes the opportunities for profit from "deploying existing resources in a different way" or "detaching productive means . . . from the [static] circular flow" and using them in a new fashion.[1] Taking advantage of these opportunities requires recognition of technological potentials, the ability to raise the necessary capital, i.e., persuading capitalists to take unusual risks. When innovator-entrepreneurs succeed in upsetting the existing equilibrium, they do so by producing what Schumpeter called *new combinations*:

1. The introduction of a new product or of a new quality of an existing product;
2. the introduction of a new production process;
3. the development of a new market;
4. the exploitation of a new source of raw materials; and
5. the reorganization of an industry.

The result of these activities, according to Schumpeter, was not just a disturbance of prevailing economic conditions, but a process of *creative destruction* which devalued existing market positions of firms and their stock of capital. Eventually, of course, competition would lead to the spread of the new combinations and the profits reaped by the pioneers would be eroded: The economy had reached a new equilibrium state—inviting new creative destruction.

Schumpeter's theory has received a lot of attention in recent years, especially as it became clear that the "economy of abundance" in which only the demand side mattered and which was postulated by many writers in the 1950s and 1960s had not yet arrived. And yet, the notion of an inherently unstable economic system is difficult to incorporate into traditional microeconomic thought. A flavor of the difficulty will be gotten even by readers of most modern texts on the principles of economics. There, in the typical chapter on economic growth, they will be told that technological advances provide the single most important explanation of increases in real output; but in the chapters on the economics of the business firm, they will find scant mention of innovation as an integral concern of decision-makers.

Despite the fundamental problem of reconciling the Schumpeterian view of economic dynamics with the more traditional one, a large amount of fruitful theoretical and analytical work in both veins has been done. While access to this literature is difficult because of its very diversity, some excellent summary reviews have appeared in recent years.[2]

1.2   Some Reasons for the Growth of Interest in Technological Change

The growing interest of economists in the subject matter of our book can be explained by a number of developments in industry and business since World War II. Among these, the following probably have marked the most important changes from an earlier era:

1. During the war, a heavy commitment of governmental resources to research and development demonstrated that massive, purposeful searches for technological solutions to specific problems can be organized, managed, and carried to success in relatively short order. Although corporations like DuPont and General Electric had long maintained their own R&D departments, the growth of in-house research groups pursuing particular "projects" in thousands of firms probably can be traced to the wartime experience.[3]

2. Once they had committed themselves to this kind of investment, firms learned quickly that innovating is a productive activity like all others, involving costly inputs, much managerial attention, fuzzy relationships between inputs and outputs, and—most important—unprecedented levels of risk. Efforts to understand why some organizations were successful in their innovative efforts, while others failed badly, provided a great stimulus to economic and management research.

3. With the rapid technological changes that characterized the 1950s and 1960s also came the recognition that their effects transcended the economist's usual measures of performance. For one thing, there was increasing concern about the impact of global industrial development on the availability of natural resources. And for another, the problems of the environmental effects of modern production and consumption became a matter for growing public attention.

4. In the case of the United States, at least, it seems clear that most of these concerns arose from the very success of the economic system in introducing

new products and processes. This country was the world leader in technology, production, and trade. To what extent the transfer of technology could aid other countries in developing their economies became a topic of great significance, especially because of this country's interest in political stability in the Free World.

5. More recently, however, the situation has been reversed: The spectacular accomplishments of the Japanese and Western European economies, as well as the rapid rise of a number of so-called Newly Industrializing Countries like South Korea and Taiwan, have led to a searching re-examination of the U.S. economy's performance. In the process, the managerial practices, production methods, and the innovativeness of American manufacturing industries have come in for a lot of criticism. Clearly, a fresh look at the system was called for, and a flood of writings on these topics testifies to public interest in the problem.

6. The seeming stagnation of the United States economy and of the traditional European industrial leaders has also given rise to a more fundamental question: Are there "laws" of technological and economic development suggesting that long spurts of innovative activity and rapid growth result in conditions of "maturity" that doom the original leaders to stagnation? Is being out-competed by newcomers to the global industrial economy a natural consequence of having been among the pioneers in technology and production? Whether there is such a thing as an "economic climacteric" remains a much-discussed issue.[4] Whatever the answer, no one disagrees that the secret to overcoming stagnation and decline lies in technological advancement.[5]

No doubt many other reasons could be cited for the growing interest among economists in problems of technology and production. It is interesting to note, however, that attention to these problems seems to come in waves. Thus, current concerns about the exhaustion of potentials for further advancement in traditional industries and, indeed, in whole economies have their antecedents in earlier periods of apparent stagnation.[6]

The economist's way of thinking and his analytical tools have made many contributions to a better comprehension of that major social force, technological progress. Yet we must conclude this brief introduction on a modest note: although the motives for initiating innovative ventures, the means for implementing changes, and the assessment of their direct effects are amenable to economic analysis, it should be obvious that economists do not have the last word on the subject. The rich interactions between technology and the social, political, and cultural characteristics of a nation transcend any one academic discipline's analytical competence. The observation should not stop us, however, from claiming that an understanding of the underlying economic principles is a necessary basis for wider-ranging explorations into the social and cultural meaning of technology.

1.3 Technology as a Form of Human Knowledge

Definitions are boring, but many of the words and concepts we need have been used so loosely in everyday discourse that we must establish their precise meaning at the outset.

To the economist, *technology is human knowledge applied in production*. It consists of information of how to convert inputs into outputs. This information is of two basic types: (1) The written recipes for production, e.g., blueprints, designs, manuals, operating instructions, product specifications, technical literature, and other documents; and (2) the unwritten know-how required to utilize the recipes productively. When an engineer speaks of *the state of the art* in a given field, he or she captures this dual nature of technology in a very descriptive fashion. In economic terms, the technology in existence at any given time determines what, and how much, total output can be obtained from the physical factors of production (land, labor, capital).

The emphasis on *application in production* sets technology apart from other equally important forms of human knowledge. Most importantly, it draws a distinction between two types of knowledge that have become totally confused in everyday language, because they are almost always mentioned in the same breath: science and technology.

1.3.1 *The Economist's View of Science and Technology*

While the essence of technology is application, science involves pure information, itself devoid of any practical uses, least of all in the conversion of inputs into outputs. *The objective of scientific activity is discovery; the objective of technological effort is productive results.*

For the economist, there exists a theoretically (and practically) significant line between these two types of knowledge: scientific knowledge is a *public good*, while technological information is a *private good*. A scientific discovery becomes a public good the moment it is publicized, because no one can be excluded from "consuming" it, and any one person's consumption does not impair the ability of others to consume it as well. In other words, scientific knowledge cannot be appropriated, and it is not subject to market transactions.

The rules of the scientific community reflect this economic characteristic. Information about a discovery must be disseminated as widely as possible, so that it can be submitted to the scrutiny of other workers in a given field.[7] Whatever economic rewards a scientist may receive for his or her work, its scientific worth is established through this process of dissemination and evaluation. By contrast, new technological knowledge can be appropriated. Indeed, the main motivation for the commitment of resources to innovative activity comes from the prospect of economic profit. The most obvious form of appropriation can be found in the property rights bestowed upon an inventor through a patent, but as we shall see in a later chapter, the benefits of ownership can also be secured without reliance on legal institutions. Furthermore, technological information can also be bought and sold in the market, although subject to certain inherent limitations of such contracts, that also will be discussed later on.

Inventors are often said to be interested in "fame, fun, and fortune." Of these, the last certainly is the most important driving force, especially in the case of business firms engaged in applied research. In fact, actual experience shows that unless the expected value of future returns justifies the investment in innovative activity, private economic units will engage in such activity only if offered some other economic incentive, such as a public subsidy.

1.3.2   Basic and Applied Research

In view of the distinction between scientific and technological knowledge, it is also useful to separate the search for new knowledge into two types of activity: basic and applied research. The National Science Foundation defines basic research as "the quest for fundamental understanding of man and nature, in terms of scientific observations, concepts, and theories;" on the other hand, applied research is aimed at "practical or commercial application.".[8]

Given this seemingly clearcut conceptual difference, we would expect basic research to be undertaken exclusively by such institutions as government laboratories, universities, and other non-profit institutions; and we would expect corporate research to be concentrated entirely on the applied side. In practice, however, no such neat distinction is possible. The following considerations tend to muddle a categorization of institutions: (1) Although publicly financed basic research may be aimed at scientific discoveries, the directions of such research frequently have a very pragmatic purpose. Thus, public and charitable support does not fall evenly, like snow, upon the scientific landscape but reflects a society's values and its concern with specific sets of problems. For example, ecology as a pure science did not receive much attention or funding until a whole host of environmental concerns suggested that a better understanding of ecological interactions might be useful for purposes of formulating public policy. (2) Many basic-research organizations, including universities, have found it increasingly rewarding to devote at least some of their efforts to the solution of very practical technological problems, especially when these solutions suggested themselves as "spin-offs" from scientific discoveries. (3) Private firms have committed resources to basic research when the existing scientific information seemed to pose barriers to the pursuit of technological objectives. Thus, no matter how basic in itself, the research typically has some potential for application as its ultimate goal. To the profit-seeking firm discoveries are but a byproduct of its quest for private gain.

One conclusion from these observations is that we must be properly cautious in interpreting official statistics on spending for basic vs applied research. With the dividing line between the two activities not always clear, the numbers may reflect no more than some casual judgments by the reporting organizations.

1.3.3 Inventions and Technology

An invention is an *idea* of how established scientific principles or existing technological knowledge *could* be turned into new and different applications. Practicality or economic feasibility are not essential ingredients of such an idea. Thus, inventions constitute a pool of information from which technology may draw. Most inventions, including the vast bulk of all ideas protected by patents, never get beyond the conceptual stage at all. Others may lie dormant for long periods of time, either because their implementation requires additional technological knowledge or because their development is not (yet) economically attractive.

A good example of an invention that had to await the solution of another technical problem before it could be developed is the use of oxygen in refining iron into steel. In the 1856 patent for the process named after him, Henry Bessemer claimed that oxygen would be a better refining agent than the atmospheric air that was actually used at the time. There existed no technique for producing oxygen in the quantities that would have been required in steelmaking. It was not until the late 1920s that the invention of fractional distillation of liquefied air made the production of bulk oxygen possible. Now experimenters took up Bessemer's idea and began work on a method of blowing oxygen into molten iron. A fully operative innovation did not occur until 1952.

The point is clear: Inventions as such do not produce any technical or economic results. They are a necessary, but not a sufficient condition for technological change.

1.3.4 Science and Inventions

A number of spectacular inventions of the recent past had directly traceable roots in scientific discoveries. But this fact should not obscure the broader historical record: the vast majority of all inventions was made in isolation from science. In many instances scientific explanations of the principles underlying the operation of successful technical ideas were provided well after the fact. The development of thermodynamics lagged behind the spread of the steam engine as a power source in industry. Aerodynamics did not become an interesting field of science until after inventors had proven that heavier-than-air flight was indeed possible. Man's technological efforts, of which invention is the first step, are aimed at making things work and not necessarily at understanding why they work.

There are, of course, many instances in which technological innovations and devices made possible the pursuit of scientific inquiry. Without the telescope, advances in astronomy would have been difficult to imagine. Without such giant machines as linear accelerators, the work of particle physicists would be severely constrained. In these and other cases, we see a feedback from technology to science, rather than the other way round.

In any event, the close interaction between science and inventive activity is a relatively recent phenomenon. It is reflected in the education of engineers and technologists, which has changed from an empirical, "hands-on" experience to one based on the notion of technology as "applied science." And it is firmly established in the cooperation of scientists and invention workers in research organizations. There can be no doubt that in many fields the pace of advancement has been speeded up by this integration of science and inventive activity and that in other fields advancement would have been impossible without it.

From the economic point of view, however, this development had an unfortunate consequence: people began to distinguish between "high" and "low" technologies, depending on whether inventions required a sophisticated scientific foundation or whether they were based on well-understood principles or on the clever re-combining of existing technological bits and pieces. In a competitive economy, only results make a difference. The measure of an invention is not its scientific brilliance nor its technical elegance. What matters is that someone thinks the idea sufficiently promising in economic terms to warrant its withdrawal from the reservoir of information and its development into an innovation.[9]

1.4 Innovating as an Economic Activity

Whatever the variegated forces that motivate the search for scientific discoveries and for inventions, the translation of new ideas into productive reality is a prototypical economic activity. It requires the *commitment of resources to the production of information* and, ultimately, to the act of innovating. An *innovation* is said to have occurred when a *new product or process has been incorporated into a regular production program.* It is also customary to speak of the "commercialization" of an idea. Therefore, innovating can be seen as the submission of a new product or process to the test of the market.

How are ideas converted into innovations? There are two ways in which one might attempt to answer this question. The first involves looking at technological change as a social process occurring in distinctive phases, and the second requires going "inside" the firm and examining the decision processes by which they go about the business of innovating. Here we shall deal with the first approach, reserving the micro-view for a subsequent chapter.

1.4.1 *A Stage Model of the Innovative Process*

When we look at technological change in the aggregate, as a social phenomenon, we are obviously forced to simplify an enormously complicated set of activities. In order to deal with this complexity, economists and other social scientists have found it useful to view the process as occurring in sequential stages. Figure 1.1 shows such a stage model, in which each of a series of well-defined activities produces a specific type of output which then in turn

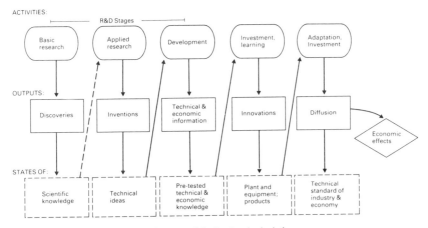

FIG. 1.1 Stage model of technological change.

affects the total pool of information at the various stages. Thus, basic research leads to discoveries which add to the state of scientific knowledge. Applied research produces inventions and adds to the pool of (untested) technical ideas. Some of these ideas are then selected for development, as we have already seen quite frequently with a considerable time lag. The pre-tested knowledge produced by the development process then forms the basis for investment in innovation. It is generally only as the innovation is diffused, i.e., spread among other users, that it exerts its economic effects. Therefore, the explanation of differences in diffusion rates is a particularly interesting task for economics.

Viewed as a whole, the process described in Fig. 1.1 involves the production of information, i.e., successive efforts to reduce uncertainty about the technical and economic characteristics of an idea. Many different methods for producing this information are involved: laboratory work, testing in pilot plants, the production of prototypes, cost studies, market research, checking on compliance with governmental regulations, and so on. At some point, enough information has been gathered to persuade an economic unit to make the investment in innovation. This does not mean that all uncertainty has been eliminated. The crucial question always is: how much information is required before a firm takes the risk of innovating? Clearly, there are hazards in both directions. If a product or process has not been sufficiently tested, dissatisfied customers or costly disruptions of production may result. If one waits too long in order to gather more information, competitors may get a headstart. Whatever the timing of the innovation, decision-makers know that it will be followed by a process of improvements in production and by the accumulation of market experience. In this connection, the term *learning* is used specifically to describe the ways in which production of a new product or utilization of a new process will be made to function more smoothly over time, resulting in better physical performance and in cost reduction. Information about the innovator and of other early adopters of a new product or process will also influence the decisions of subsequent adopters and thus will affect diffusion rates.

The stage model provides a very useful framework for the study of innovative activity, and we shall draw on it in organizing our later explorations. But it also has a number of shortcomings that must be mentioned at the outset: (1) Like all models that attempt to divide what is essentially an evolutionary process into neat phases, this one suffers from empirically fuzzy boundaries that often require arbitrary decisions on the part of the analyst. (2) The model is essentially unidirectional and does not take into account the numerous and complicated feedback mechanisms that influence observed phenomena at each stage. (3) The model is useful only for the description and analysis of major, visible innovations. But economists agree that these innovations probably account for no more than half of all observed technical and economic progress. The rest is the result of the hundreds of minor, incremental, low-risk adaptations and changes that are part and parcel of everyday life in industry.

1.4.2   The Risks of Innovating

Innovating clearly is a risky activity: technical and economic uncertainties can be removed only so far, and then the test of success or failure lies in the doing. But even after start-up or commercialization, the hazards of a mis-estimation of production capabilities and costs or of a lower than expected market response hover over projects.

Information about successes is easier to come by than data on failures, but the following findings provide some evidence on the riskiness of investment in innovation:

(1) In a study of 120 American firms it was found that at least 50 per cent, and often more than 60 per cent, of all R&D projects never resulted in commercially used products or processes.

(2) In a study of 50 firms, it was found that 50 per cent of their expenditures on product innovations were for products which proved commercially unsuccessful, and that 30 per cent of the products actually launched on the market turned out to be unsuccessful after some time.

(3) For the United States economy as a whole, it has been estimated that some 10,000 new products are developed each year, of which 80 per cent die in infancy; and that, of the remaining 2,000 new products, only about 100 incorporate significant technological advances as well as satisfying an economic demand.[10]

Individual cases of magnificent failures are usually reported only when they are dramatic enough to warrant media attention. Many a small firm might have been destroyed by an experience like Dupont's in the development of *Corfam*, a permeable plastic substitute for shoe leather. Despite the Company's experience and proven leadership in innovation, the new product turned out be be a commercial failure that resulted in a loss of approximately $100 million.[11] Sometimes, circumstances completely extraneous to an innovation can doom it to failure. In the early 1970s, the rotary-piston (Wankel) engine was hailed as a revolutionary automotive invention. Several companies committed themselves to producing rotary-engined cars and others, like General Motors, invested large sums in a development program. After the OPEC oil embargo of 1973-74, the new engines' comparatively poor fuel economy, which had been no consideration earlier, meant that demand for them dropped off almost completely. The original innovator, the NSU company of Germany, whose engine also suffered from frequent failures because of inadequate development, went out of business. The other early adopter, Mazda of Japan, made the costly switch back to traditional engines, although it continues to sell one expensive, rotary-engined model. The major manufacturers all abandoned their development efforts.

More recently, the spectacular exits from the small-computer field of several initially successful producers testify to the riskiness of being among the early innovators. They also illustrate a difficulty that we shall deal with in a later chapter—making the transition from a stage of new-product market development in which technical attractiveness is sufficient to a stage in which reliable mass production and marketing become the main criteria for competitive success.

Andrew Carnegie, the famous steel magnate, is reported to have said, "Pioneering don't pay." Experiences such as the above lend some support to his authoritative, if ungrammatical, pronouncement. If one considers that a strategy of pursuing technical innovations is only one among several paths open to firms, it is not surprising that many of them opt for alternatives, such as intensive marketing and advertising, diversification into other established lines of business, and seeking protection against their competitors from the government.

All the more remarkable that the prospect of high returns from just one success (and never mind the average number of failures) sufficiently motivates so many firms to keep trying for innovations, no matter how slim the objective probabilities for a solid winner! Confidence (or desperation), technical and commercial skill, sound judgement, an appropriate economic climate, and a substantial measure of good luck are among the requirements for success in technological innovation. At the same time, it is clear that innovating firms that operate from a substantial wealth position and who therefore do not have to stake all their resources on a single project are in a better position to survive in the competitive race than small enterprises unable to diversify their portfolio of technological ventures. Whether large, wealthy firms might not confront other obstacles to innovativeness is another question with which we shall have to deal.

1.4.3   Industrial Expenditure for Research and Development

The total resources an economy devotes to innovative activity are virtually impossible to estimate. Any reasonable guess would have to include not only direct expenditures for research and development, but also amounts committed to the education and training of research workers, the cost of experimentation in production, and a host of other outlays by government agencies, non-profit institutions, and business firms. There can be little doubt that the generation of technical and economic information makes up a substantial, if not the largest, part of what has been called the "knowledge industry".[12]

The production of information is, as we have seen, only the first step in innovation. The biggest commitment of resources occurs when firms invest in new plant and equipment in order to utilize an innovative process or to introduce a line of products. Thus, we might well look at the rate of industrial investment in an economy as one of the best indicators of its innovativeness. There is no assurance, of course, that all new investment will in fact represent up-to-date technology, but without the replacement of old capital and net

TABLE 1.1   Selected Indicators of R&D Activity, U.S. Industries, 1981

Industry	R&D expend's [10^6]	% of total R&D	% funded by Fed'l. Gov't.	Number of patents issued	% of all patents
Food & kindred prod.	719	1.4	n.a.	542	1.4
Textiles & apparel	124	0.2	n.a.	432	1.1
Lumber, wood products	167	0.3	n.a.	n.a.	—
Paper & allied products	570	1.1	n.a.	n.a.	—
Chemical & allied prod.	5,325	10.3	7.2	6,919	17.6
Of this: Industr. chem.	2,553	4.9	14.4	3,312	8.4
Drugs & med's.	2,000	3.9	0.7	1,308	3.3
Petroleum ref. & extr.	1,920	3.7	7.3	792	2.0
Rubber & plastic prod.	800	1.5	23.8	2,354	6.0
Stone, clay, glass prod.	470	0.9	n.a.	1,109	2.8
Primary metals	889	1.7	20.5	431	1.1
Of this: Ferrous metals	560	1.1	25.0	320	0.8
Fabricated metal prod.	638	1.2	12.5	5,400	13.8
Nonelectrical machinery	6,800	13.1	10.9	11,066	28.2
Electr. & electron. eq.	10,466	20.2	37.9	7,509	19.1
Of this: Communic. eq. & electron. comp.	6,396	13.5	33.9	4,196	10.7
Transportation equipment	5,089	9.8	13.8	2,245	5.7
Of this: Motor vehicles	4,929	9.5	n.a.	1,421	3.6
Aircraft & missiles	11,702	22.6	72.6	1,026	2.6
Prof. & scient. Instr.	3,685	7.1	17.3	5,404	13.8
Other industries	2,473	4.8	n.a.	n.a.	—
Totals	51,830	100.0	31.8%	39,224	100.0

Source: National Science Board, Science Indicators 1982 (Washington, DC: U.S. Government Printing Office, 1983).

additions to the capital stock, technological progress will not occur. In international comparisons especially, data on real investment in various economies give a better picture of their technological up-to-dateness than do other measures, such as expenditures on R&D. Taken by themselves, the latter reflect inputs only and do not tell anything about the output of innovative effort.

This is a matter with which we shall have to deal in some detail. For the present, however, our aim is more modest. We want to take a first look at direct spending for research and development by American industry. Table 1.1 shows some relevant statistics for a representative year. Substantial differences in expenditures are readily apparent. Not too surprisingly, the aerospace and the electrical and electronic industries are the leaders in R&D investment. These two industries also benefit most from governmental funding of their ventures. Equally striking are the differences in the extent to which industries rely on patent protection for their inventions. Patents play an insignificant role for the aircraft and missile industry, while they are obviously important in machinery, chemicals, metal products and scientific instruments.

The *research intensity* of industries has been measured by various indicators, of which R&D expenditure as percentage of sales is the most common. By this yardstick, the leader is once again the aerospace industry, which typically spends approximately 15 per cent of its sales on R&D, followed by professional and scientific instruments (8 per cent), electrical and electronic equipment (7 per cent), nonelectrical machinery (5 per cent), and chemical products (4 per cent).[13]

The statistics in Table 1.2 place industrial spending for R&D in relation to

TABLE 1.2   *National expenditures for R&D, by source, type, performer, 1981*

	Federal Government 10^6	%	Industry 10^6	%	Universities & colleges 10^6	%	Other nonprofit institutions 10^6	%	Total 10^6
By source:									
Basic research	6,220	67.7	1,597	17.4	905	9.8	466	5.1	9,188
Applied research	7,465	44.3	8,534	50.6	506	3.0	361	2.1	16,866
Development	20,067	43.6	25,766	55.9	101	0.2	130	0.3	46,064
Total	33,752	46.8	35,897	49.8	1,512*	2.1	957	1.3	72,118
By performer:									
Total	8,729**	12.1	51,830	71.8	9,269†	12.9	2,290	3.2	72,118

*   Includes State and local government sources.
** Federal intramural laboratories.
† Includes federally funded R&D centers administered by universities.
Source: National Science Board, *Science Indicators 1982* (Washington, DC: U.S. Government Printing Office, 1983).

total national expenditures. It can be seen that industry performs roughly 72 per cent of all R&D, as measured by expenditures, while providing about 50 per cent of all funding. The distribution of sources for the three types of activity conforms to what one would expect from our earlier discussion. Over two-thirds of basic research is financed out of public funds, with industry accounting for 17 per cent and universities for 10 per cent. The balance shifts in the case of applied research and development funding: over half comes from industry, although here, too, the federal government plays an important role in the financing of work in such industries as aerospace and electronics. The overall allocation of funds shows that $46 billion, or almost two-thirds of all spending, goes toward the development phase, while applied research absorbs less than one quarter and basic research approximately one eighth of expenditures.

These data suggest a number of questions: is there any correlation between investment in R&D and the actual production of innovations? Is there any correlation between the innovative activity and the profitability of industries? Are the R&D intensive industries more competitive internationally than the low spenders? Does the firm structure of industries and the level of intra-industry competition have anything to do with individual firms' R&D performance? Obviously, one year's statistics are not enough to answer these questions. We shall return to them in greater detail later in the book. Our only purpose here was to illustrate the great variety among industries, at least as reflected in financial inputs into innovative activity. We must recall once again that the number of patents produced is at best a partial indicator of the output of this activity and that other output measures are very difficult to come by.

1.5   Classifications of Technological Change

In order to bring some structure to the study of innovative activity, social scientists and historians have developed several useful ways of classifying the many-faceted phenomena of technological change. Since a number of these classifications and concepts will come up frequently in our explorations, we shall discuss them briefly at the outset.

1.5.1   *The Nature of the Innovation*

One of the widely used classifications deals with the nature of changes in historical perspective, identifying major themes of innovative activity that are thought to have dominated certain phases of long-term development. Thus, *mechanization* in the late eighteenth and in the nineteenth centuries involved the growing reliance on machine power instead of human physical effort. *Standardization* and *specialization* made possible the economies of scale inherent in mass production. The *automation* of production brought the feedback-control principle to mechanized manufacturing and reduced the degree of human judgment necessary to keep processes running smoothly. *Computerization* raised this principle to the level where the integration and coordination of sequential production stages became feasible. And *robotization* is said to represent the last step in this evolution, enabling whole factories to run according to pre-programmed instructions and without human intervention, except for the maintenance and occasional adjustment of equipment.

These familiar concepts illustrate an approach to the study of innovations that is probably more productive in the exploration of their broader social implications than in the somewhat narrower framework of economic analysis. For our purposes, we must first make a distinction between *process-oriented* and *product-oriented innovations*. The former involve all those changes affecting the methods whereby outputs are produced, whereas the latter are aimed at the outputs themselves. Clearly, these two types of innovation make different contributions to economic progress, and generally we have no difficulties in telling whether a given change is of one kind or the other. It is equally important to recognize, however, that in industrial practice one rarely finds a new product (or a new variant of an established product) that did not require changes and adaptations in process technology. Conversely, many process innovations do affect the nature of the final output in one way or another, even if only in the perceptions of potential customers. Thus, for example, we often find a prejudice against mass-produced merchandise, which, almost by definition, is supposed to be inferior in quality to certain "custom-made" products. Whether such prejudices are justified or not, they are certainly something that producers have to reckon with.

Another useful distinction is that between *primary (basic)* and *derivative (minor) innovations*. Although one can always argue whether a given change is basic or minor, we do recognize that there are some identifiable innovations that have generated clear discontinuities in the structure and behavior of industries and markets; and that there are yet other, even more important, innovations that give rise to whole new industries. As we shall see later, it is not unusual for a basic innovation to bring in its train a whole host of derivative, incremental innovations, some having to do with processes and some with products. In fact, variations in the growth of industries have been associated with the evolution and eventual exhaustion of the technical and market potential of individual basic innovations. But in order to keep such a view of industrial growth in proper perspective, one must remember that what may be a minor process innovation to a user industry may at the same time represent a major breakthrough for the industry turning out new process equipment.

For obvious reasons, such as their visibility and the availability of statistical data, major product and process innovation have received more attention in economic studies than has the sum of minor, perhaps equally significant, changes.

1.5.2   *The Innovation's Impact on Factor Inputs*

By definition, process innovations imply some change in the composition or in the relative quantities of inputs going into production. Economic theory distinguishes among *neutral, labor-saving, and capital-saving innovations*. A neutral innovation leaves the proportions of inputs the same while permitting a greater output for the same amount of inputs. The designation of the other two types of change is self-explanatory. We shall describe them more formally in Chapter 3, which deals with the microeconomic theory of production and technological change.

A second aspect of effects on inputs has to do with the way in which technological innovations bring about substitutions among raw materials and sources of energy. Evaluations of changes along these lines have become a major concern of economic analysis in recent years, as the threat of an exhaustion of certain resources seemed to pose absolute limits to future growth in output. Many of these prognostications tended to overlook an important fact: what we consider an economically useful resource is defined, first and foremost, by available technology. The statement that there exists some finite amount of a particular mineral, for example, is not very interesting from the economist's point of view. As we shall argue in the next chapter, what matters is whether the market gives proper signals to the participants in the economic game. When the (relative) prices of scarce minerals rise, these signals will trigger a search for substitutes and new technologies. The relevant question then is not whether an economy will "run out of " some resource but whether it is adaptable enough to come up with alternative solutions.

The concept of an innovation's effects on *factor productivity*, i.e. on the output achieved per unit of input, is one of the main concerns of economics. Most commonly, this is expressed in terms of changes in the output per man-hour, although a number of schemes for measuring the impact on labor and capital inputs have been developed. None of these is without limitations, because all inputs going into a production process form an integrated network in which simple substitutions among factors are but one of a variety of possible effects of innovations. This is a matter that we shall discuss in greater detail in Chapter 4.

Implicit in our discussion so far was the assumption that technological change is *embodied* in changes in the physical inputs, most importantly in capital, going into production. Quite naturally, one tends to associate innovations with new equipment, new machines, and various other physical manifestations of change. But economic progress also depends on *disembodied* technological advances. These have to do with improvements in the organization, coordination, and control of productive activity. One observer has referred to this type of knowledge as "metatechnology" and has claimed that, despite our economy's spectacular achievements in the development of new hardware, recent decades have been marked primarily by advances in our ability to manage, ". . . to trace actual or potential consequences and their interaction," and purposefully to pursue economic and social goals.[14] While this appraisal may be correct for some types of economic activity, a closer look at the many unresolved managerial and social problems may force us to take a less sanguine view of our progress in disembodied technical advance. There are others who have claimed that our material achievements with technology have in fact outrun our competence in managing the resulting systems.[15]

1.6   Economic Effects of Innovations

When we speak of the rate of technological change, we are using somewhat careless, if well accepted, terminology. To the purist, such change affects *the state of human knowledge*. But in the absence of any measures of advances in knowledge as such, we have to settle for a variety of quantifiable indicators of the effects of these advances.

To make this observation is not just to engage in a semantic exercise. Once we recognize that measures of technological change are more or less arbitrarily selected surrogates for the real thing, then we also realize that there is no one set of statistics that will adequately capture *the* effects of innovations. Furthermore, we are forced to admit that economics does not have a monopoly on observing and analyzing these effects. Historians, anthropologists, and sociologists may choose different variables for their analyses, but it would be difficult to argue that theirs are less relevant to an understanding of such a complex phenomenon. And the ultimate interconnectedness of technology with other aspects of the human condition may often be captured better in great works of fiction than in even the most carefully worked-out set of statistics.

Having thus conceded a lot of territory to others, we can retreat to the firmer ground of economics. But we understand that what we want to observe and measure is going to be determined by our particular interests: Are we looking at the effects of technological change in an economy over a long period of time? Are we attempting to trace the economic impact of one particular innovation? Are we concerned with technological advances in a given industry? Is our focus the adjustment of individual firms to changes in technology? Clearly, these and other equally sensible concerns will require different approaches and different sets of measures. Here we want to look only at a few major lines of inquiry that have characterized the work of economists.

1.6.1   *Aggregate Effects of Technological Progress*

If we accept increases in real output as a measure of an economy's growth, the question naturally arises: What has been the contribution of technological advances to this growth? Although everyone agrees that the contribution is substantial, it turns out that getting a more precise answer to the question is difficult.

What one would really like to know is how much of observed increases in total output resulted from innovations and how much from changes in other factors, such as increases in the stock of physical capital, investment in human capital, or the discovery of new natural resources. But how can one separate these other inputs empirically from advances in technology? The interactions among all the factors are so complex that statistical estimates depend very much on the assumptions underlying the initial specification of an analytical model. Not too surprisingly, then, studies of the aggregate effect of technological advances have come up with widely varying results, but they all concur in attributing the bulk of all growth in output (and income) over the long run to such advances.[16]

There is a second important question concerning the overall effects of technical progress: Granted that it has contributed in a major way to average income growth, what have been its effects on income distribution? The statistical evidence suggests that *increases* in real income were spread more or less proportionally across all segments of society, with the personal distribution of income changing very little over the long run. Obviously, technological advances have made the American poor of the 1980s substantially better off than the poor of the 1880s, but they have not solved the perennial social problem of income inequality. The claims of enthusiastic supporters of technical progress not withstanding, expecting technology to solve fundamental social problems may well be expecting too much. As we shall contend in a later chapter, the main argument for economic growth may well be that it enables societies to attack these problems with fewer frictions and conflicts than would result from such efforts in a stagnating economy.

1.6.2 *Microeconomic Effects of Innovations*

When we turn to an examination of the effects of technological change on plants, firms, industries, and markets, we immediately confront a fact on which we have commented earlier: These effects manifest themselves in a great variety of forms, and they do not stay invariant over time. First, we must distinguish between *physical effects* and *economic effects*. The former have to do with the changes in input–output relationships necessarily involved in product and process innovations, the latter with the consequences of physical changes for costs and prices.

Obviously, the success of innovations depends on the translation of the purely technical advances into economic benefits for the innovator. It is, after all, the expectation of such benefits that motivates innovative efforts in the first place. We must not, however, confuse motivation with results. Whether outcomes conform to expectations depends on a variety of factors: (1) The accuracy with which the economic consequences of even well-described technical changes can be predicted; (2) the speed with which an innovation's effects begin to spill over into the innovating firm's economic environment;

and (3) the speed with which the environment (suppliers, competitors, customers) responds to these initial effects.

Thus we may think of the economic impact of major technological advances as involving a series of wave-like ripples emanating from the original source. Over time, some or all of the following may be involved: (1) Lower costs per unit of output for the innovator; (2) new products opening up new markets for the innovator; (3) economic profit for the owners of the innovating firm; (4) higher wages for labor; (5) lower (relative) prices of the commodity or service affected by the innovation; (6) shifts in the relative prices of various resources going into production; and (7) increases in the general standard of living.

At first glance, even such a partial list of possible effects may look positively Utopian; but it represents the economic essence of all those phenomena which, in the aggregate, account for the output and income growth we have discussed above. The big question is not whether these effects occur, but how they are shared out over time among all the participants in the economic game. We may also think of this process as the absorption of technological changes by the economy by means of adjustments in input and output markets, in the flow of factors and final products, and in economic institutions. This view emphasizes that, whatever the effects of a given innovation, they do not show themselves in instantaneous, once-and-for-all transformations of the economic system, nor does the innovation itself remain unchanged in the process of being absorbed by the system.

For the innovating firm all this means that any initial economic benefits it may have reaped from a technological advance are bound to be eroded over time. In some instances, erosion may take place very quickly as competitors jump at the new opportunities opened up by the innovator. In other cases, a pioneering firm may manage to hold on to a lead position for prolonged periods, especially if it shores up this position through further innovative effort. One may contrast, for example, the rapidity of the small, electronic calculator's absorption with the slow erosion of the Polaroid Corporation's monopoly on instant photography. The dynamics of competitive adjustments to new technologies form one of the most interesting subjects in the study of the microeconomics of technological change.

1.6.3   *The Problem of Externalities*

Like virtually all other kinds of economic activity, technological changes produce some effects that do not enter into the cost-benefit calculations of their originators or their beneficiaries. These effects, generally referred to as externalities, have been studied extensively. Quite naturally, most of the concern has been with *external bads*, such as environmental pollution or occupational diseases. But we must not let this obscure the fact that technical progress has also resulted in a whole host of *external benefits*.

These two sides of progress have triggered endless debates about the relative weights of social costs and benefits. Since many participants to these debates bring to them their initial, ideological predispositions and their subjective assessments of the risks associated with specific technologies, it cannot be said that a great deal of enlightenment has been produced. This is not the place to attempt any kind of general assessment of the issues involved, but a few observations should be made at the outset of our study. First and foremost, it is easy to take the socially beneficial results of technological progress for granted, while focussing on external bads only. A balanced historical perspective would require us to take into account the great improvements in nutrition, the eradication of epidemic and endemic diseases, the reduction in the general meanness of existence, as well as the problems of air pollution or dirty rivers. As we shall try to show later on, there is little evidence that technological advances have made any of the external bads worse than they were in the much-heralded "good old days." On the contrary, a growing concern with these problems may well itself be a signal that advanced industrial societies have benefitted sufficiently from the direct, material effects of progress to be able to devote some of their resources to the eradication of undersirable, indirect consequences.

To state this is not to gloss over the seriousness of a number of contemporary concerns. Nor does it mean that we should expect technology to provide the answer to problems apparently rooted in human behavior. Thus, most economists would argue that the design of policies for dealing with undersirable externalities must take into account all factors that might lead individual agents to "internalize" externalities, i.e., to include them in their cost-benefit calculations as producers and consumers. Ill-advised policies may seemingly cure a problem while simultaneously creating others.

One example may suffice to illustrate the point. Only a very simple-minded person would blame the automobile itself, rather than the behavior of drivers, for road accidents. Indeed, accidents due to outright technical failures make up a small proportion of all mishaps. Other aspects of driver behavior aside, we also have incontrovertible evidence that a very unsophisticated innovation, the seat belt, has the greatest potential for preventing serious injury and saving lives in case of accidents; yet the majority of all drivers refuse to wear selt belts. Should we try to get them to change their obviously irrational ways or should we look for yet another technological fix for what is clearly not a technological problem? "Passive restraints," such as the air bag, are costly and will prevent injury only in a narrow range of possible accidents. They are clearly not the answer to the problem. Nevertheless, they continue to have many advocates who simply ignore all available evidence and expert judgment. As long as public policies are formulated in a climate of prejudice and emotionalism (or of narrow economic interest), we cannot expect to come to grips with these issues.

Most economists have no illusions that their way of looking at the problem of externalities will necessarily inform legislative and regulatory decisions. But their understanding of human behavior enables them to make some assessment of the likely success or failure of particular policy designs and of their benefits and costs. There are, of course, other areas of concern in which even scientists and technologists cannot agree on the actual nature and extent of external bads. In such cases it would be difficult for economics to make a great contribution. The same goes for situations in which the assessment of as yet unexperienced risks, like those associated with nuclear-power plant disasters, must of necessity be left to subjective judgments.

There is one other type of externality that will concern us at some length. We have touched on it already in our discussion of technology as a private good. To the extent that an innovator cannot *appropriate* all aspects of newly created technological information, external benefits are created. Thus, for example, employees may change jobs and take the essential know-how they have acquired in working with a new technique to another firm. Similarly, even the information contained in a patent may serve as a source of ideas for a competitor attempting to find some alternative to the idea protected by the patent. In a general way we observe that any advanced economic system is suffused by a network of such externalities and that all participants are likely to benefit from them. Nevertheless, the proper balance between these kinds of externalities on the one hand and secure intellectual property rights on the other is of obvious importance. Let the appropriation of the benefits of investment in innovation be too difficult, and the incentives for innovative effort are likely to be reduced. Prevent the dissemination of all new technical knowledge in the innovator's private interest, and progress is likely to be slowed down. At any given time, the actual balance is the result of legislation, regulation, judicial decisions, and more or less informal institutional arrangements. Basic innovations may upset this balance and require redefinitions of property rights. The recent cases of legal protection for computer software and of the copyright implications of videotape recording devices illustrate the point.

1.7 Outline of the Book

This book is intended as a guide through the most important topics in the economics of technological change. As the present chapter suggested, these topics are varied and in many instances not yet fully explored. Thus, the book as a whole reflects the state of the art in a relatively new field of inquiry. It was not written for the professional economist, who can inform himself through the specialist literature. Even a non-technical treatment must be scrupulously honest about what economists know. There are few generalizations without important exceptions; the empirical evidence is casual rather than comprehensive; the theorizing tends to be *ad hoc* and topical; and when it comes to questions of industrial strategy and public policy, the treatment has to be appropriately tentative.

We start with an examination of production (supply) in an aggregate view of the economic system and consider the contributions of labor, capital, and resources. We turn next to the standard microeconomic theory of production and technological change, and to the relationship between technology and the scale of productive units. This is followed by an outline of a framework for the empirical evaluation of firms' performance in production and innovation. From these essential preliminaries we move to the core topics, whose sequence conforms approximately to the stage model discussed earlier in this chapter. The economics of inventive activity, the role of the patent system, the process of development and innovation, and the diffusion of innovations are discussed in order. These matters are then looked at from the viewpoint of an individual firm's strategies in innovation, considering also the evolution of basic technologies over time. Next we move to an exploration of the effects of technological advance from several perspectives. Finally, we deal with a subject that has received increasing attention: the linkage between technology and international competitiveness and, more generally, the problem of international technology transfer.

Many of these topics would merit books in themselves, and such books have indeed been written. At the end of our survey, we present a small selection of samples from this vast literature. Our intent here was to give the interested general reader some guidance for further forays into the subject and not necessarily to select work that is theoretically brilliant or narrowly focussed on economic issues.

Special attention should be called to the Notes at the end of each chapter, which give sources for material referred to or elaborate on matters covered in the text. Where appropriate, chapter appendices contain additional, relevant information and illustrative case studies.

Notes

1. Schumpeter, J. A., *The Theory of Economic Development* (Cambridge, Mass.: Harvard University Press, 1934), pp. 68, 70.
2. E.g., Stoneman, P., *The Economic Analysis of Technological Change* (Oxford: Oxford University Press, 1983).
3. The following quote from the work of a professor of administration, published little more than three decades ago, reminds us just how much things have changed: "During the last five years there has been a popular move to establish research departments in industry . . . I have no adequate basis for expressing an opinion, but I suspect that some of these new research departments are window dressing, which will disappear as competition stiffens." Copeland, M. T., *The Executive at Work* (Cambridge, Mass.: Harvard University Press, 1951), p. 111.
4. The term seems to have been coined by Professor Charles P. Kindleberger, who raised the question whether there is an aging process for whole economies as well as for people. "An American Economic Climacteric?" *Challenge*, January-February 1974.
5. For an excellent discussion of current issues, see Ayres, R. U., *The Next Industrial Revolution; Reviving Industry through Innovation* (Cambridge, Mass.: Ballinger, 1984).
6. A classic paper along these lines, that foreshadows many present-day concerns is Kuznets, S., "Retardation of Industrial Growth," *Journal of Economic and Business History*, August 1929; reprinted in Kuznets, S., *Economic Change* (New York: Norton, 1953).
7. The imposition of restrictions on the dissemination of scientific information by governments

usually is justified by "security interests." Experience shows that such restrictions have not been very effective.

8. National Science Board, *Science Indicators, 1974* (Washington, D.C.: U.S. Government Printing Office, 1975), p. 51.

9. There are of course instances of a fascination with technology for its own sake, without regard to its economic implications. A well-documented example is provided by the development of rocketry in Germany during World War II: The V-1, a pilotless aircraft, cost about $600 to produce and delivered 1 ton of explosives over its target; the V-2, a ballistic missile, carried the same payload at a cost of $25,500 per unit. This spectacular innovation ". . . by its wholesale consumption of vital raw materials and labor, inflicted far more damage on Germany than it ever did on Britain." This and other cases are reviewed in Teich, A. H., ed., *Technology and Man's Future*, 2nd edn. (New York: St. Martin's Press, 1977), pp. 37-8.

10. Organization for Economic Cooperation and Development, *The Conditions for Success in Technical Innovation* (Paris: O.E.C.D., 1971), pp. 68-70.

11. Freeman, C., *The Economics of Industrial Innovation* (Baltimore, Md.: Penguin Books, 1974), pp. 103-4.

12. One of the first integrated analyses of this industry was presented in Machlup, F., *The Production and Distribution of Knowledge in the U.S.* (Princeton, N.J.: Princeton University Press, 1962).

13. National Science Board, *Science Indicators, 1982* (Washington, D.C.: U.S. Government Printing Office, 1983).

14. Simon, H., "Technology and Environment," *Management Science*, June 1973.

15. This view is expressed in particularly cogent and balanced fashion in Morrison, E., *Men, Machines, and Modern Times* (Cambridge, Mass.: M.I.T. Press, 1966), Ch. 8.

16. For a review of various models, see Stoneman, *op. cit.*, Ch. 12.

CHAPTER 2

Resources, Technology, and Production: An Aggregate View

We have defined technology as knowledge applied in production. Therefore, a closer look at the production side of an economic system is an appropriate way to begin our explorations. In the present chapter, we shall deal with the bases of production *in the aggregate,* as though the whole economy were a single mechanism for converting inputs into outputs. This approach will enable us to examine the interconnections between technology, technological changes, and the basic factors of production.

2.1 Two Familiar Descriptions of the Economic System

Among the many simple models used to describe the functioning of an economic system, two are particularly useful: the first emphasizes the role of markets in the circular flow of economic activity, and the second recognizes that this activity is constrained, at any given time, by the availability of inputs and by the state of technology. These models provide us with a convenient starting point.

2.1.1 *The Economy as an Exchange System*

Explanations of the working of a market system generally begin with a model of the *circular flow of economic activity.* In an abstraction from many real-life details, firms (producing units and demanders of inputs) and households (consuming units and suppliers of inputs) are seen as the key agents in a process whereby the factors of production (labor, capital, land) are converted into final goods and services. Emphasis in the model is not on how these conversions are effected but on the transactions by means of which factors and final goods are exchanged in the relevant markets. At least by implication, the emphasis also is on a system of defined property rights, because these are a prerequisite for market transactions.

Figure 2.1 presents a simple version of a circular-flow model. Real flows (i.e., the movement of goods and factors) and the corresponding flows of payments are shown. Households own the factors of production and sell them

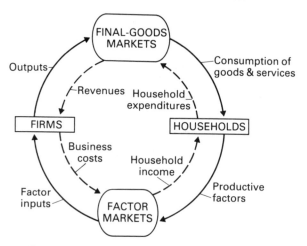

FIG. 2.1 Circular flow of economic activity.

to firms in the *factor markets*. Firms convert the factors into outputs and sell these to the households in the *final goods markets*. If allowed to work freely, both of these markets fulfill two essential functions: they *ration* out the currently available supplies of factors, goods, and services through the operation of the price system; and shifts in (relative) prices in turn *signal* to households and firms the advantages to be gained from adjustments in future decisions, i.e., reallocations of inputs and outputs.

The model tells us nothing about the nature of these decisions or about the conversion processes that take place inside the "black boxes," households and firms. It portrays the economy as a kind of perpetual-motion machine, mysteriously energized by the price system. But of course the very existence of prices points to the fact that there is a constraint to the volume of the circular flow—scarcity of the factors of production.

2.1.2 *Scarcity and Production Possibilities*

A second model recognizes explicitly that an economy's total capacity to produce goods and services is constrained, in any given period, by the availability of inputs and by the state of knowledge on how to combine these inputs—in other words, by technology. The model is based on the concept of a *production possibilities frontier* that defines the various combinations and quantities of outputs that might be produced under existing conditions. It says nothing about the mind-boggling task of choosing among the millions of possible combinations in a real-life economy. *Free markets* perform the task very efficiently. We must recognize, however, that a substantial and growing share of allocative decisions is made not in markets but through various *public choice* mechanisms, i.e., via the political process. In part, these decisions are

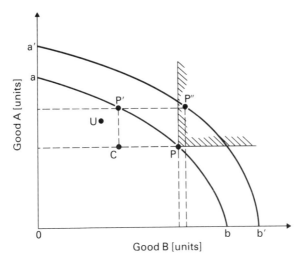

FIG. 2.2 Production possibilities frontier.

implemented directly through the taxing and spending power of governments, and in part they involve interventions into the operation of the price system . . . presumably in the interests of societal goals that override the market's efficiency criteria.

The model assumes, of course, that a choice has to be made only between two types of goods. Figure 2.2 shows the combinations of Good A (say, capital goods) and Good B (say, consumer goods) an economy is capable of producing. The resulting curve has negative slope, because producing more of one good implies producing less of the other. It is concave, because (a) not all inputs are equally good at producing either type of good and (b) the proportionality between inputs and outputs may change as more and more resources are devoted to the producing of one type of good or the other, i.e., there may be economies or diseconomies of scale [see Ch. 4].

When an economy is producing a combination of outputs that lies on the curve, it is operating efficiently. Production of a combination such as the one indicated by point U is inefficient, because not all available inputs are being utilized. In practice, we indicate such a state of affairs through our unemployment statistics, but it is clear that some part of other resources will also be idle at a point like U.

Assume that the economy is producing the combination of goods at point P, on the frontier. If market signals or public-choice decisions indicate a move to a new combination, P′, the economy has to give up the quantity CP of Good B in order to obtain the increment CP′ of Good A. In terms of the necessary reallocation of inputs, CP represents the *opportunity cost* of producing the extra amount CP′ of Good A. In the limit, the slope of a tangent at any point on the frontier reflects the trade-off involved in a shift in output combinations, i.e., *the marginal rate of transformation in production.* The lesson is obvious, though often ignored in public discussions of economic policy: when an economy is operating at capacity, the decision to produce more of any one output automatically means having less of another. All shifts in the composition of output involve resource costs as well as (presumed) economic or social benefits.

Why are these resource costs so often ignored or mis-estimated by decision-makers? There are two possible answers to this question. The first is that the *money costs* of a shift may not truly reflect opportunity costs because of distortions in prices. Such distortions may result from the non-competitive behavior of market participants or from governmental interferences with the price system. Whenever market prices are kept artificially above or below their equilibrium level, they will give the wrong signals, leading to the commitment of too many or too few resources to the production of a particular good.

The second answer is that there may be cases of *market failure*, i.e. markets may not give any signals at all with respect to certain resource costs. In the preceding chapter we touched briefly on the problem of externalities, which are of course the classic examples of market failure. When there exists no mechanism for forcing a firm to consider the social cost of, say, polluting a stream or river, it will underestimate the total resource costs of producing its particular output and therefore will produce larger quantities than it would if all costs had entered into its calculations. A discussion of policies encouraging firms and households to internalize all resource consequences of their decisions is reserved for a later chapter.

Here we want, finally, to look at *economic growth* as reflected in our model. This involves an outward shift of the production possibilities frontier to a new locus, such as a'b' in Fig. 2.2. This shift might have been the result of an increase in the available factors of production or of advances in technology. Now we can also be more specific about our earlier statement that reallocations are likely to be accompanied by less friction and conflict in a growing than in a stationary economy [Ch. 1, p. 18]. Note that under conditions of growth, an increase in the production of Good A, such as CP', can be achieved without having to give up any of Good B. This is shown by point P'' on a'b'. In fact, as long as the new output combinations on frontier a'b' lie inside the shaded quadrant, our economy will have more of both types of goods.

2.2 An Aggregate Production Model

The circular-flow model emphasizes markets and exchange; the production possibilities frontier describes the effects of resource constraints and technology on an economy's capacity to produce. Neither of them, however, sheds any light on the process of production itself. Therefore we turn now to a more detailed examination of the ways in which an economic system converts inputs into outputs. An *aggregate production model* is a useful device for this purpose. It will also form the base for our subsequent discussion of the factors of production. The model is an aggregate one, because it treats the whole economy as a single productive unit, ignoring the role of individual firms and households. For simplicity's sake it also assumes a *closed economy*, i.e., one without linkages to the rest of the world on either the input or the output side.

2.2.1 *Basic Inputs and Outputs*

Figure 2.3 shows the basic inputs into production on the left-hand side and outputs on the right-hand side. Reflecting the realities of a modern economy, the contribution of *labor* is seen as consisting primarily of *knowledge and skills*, with *human physical effort* playing a minor and declining part. The vast bulk of all energy inputs is derived from *natural resources*, which also provide the other raw materials and foodstuffs going into production. The model also recognizes the multiple contribution of *land*: it provides not only resources but also the *space* in which economic activity takes place, and it acts as a *sink* for the wastes resulting from production and consumption.

Central to the conversions effected by the production system is the stock of *physical capital*, which, for the economy as a whole, consists of plant, machinery, equipment, etc., as well as of public capital, such as roads, bridges, airports, and so on. Collectively, the stock of capital reflects the past commitment of resources to future production instead of to current consumption. The technology embodied in it, together with disembodied technology and the know-how of the labor force, will at any given time determine the economy's productive capacity.

On the output side, the model shows *final goods and services* and *intermediate goods*, i.e., those utilized in further production (including new fixed capital). As has long been recognized, a steady increase in the "roundaboutness" of production characterizes all advanced economies. In terms of the model, this means a growth of the intermediate-goods loop relative to the final-output flow.

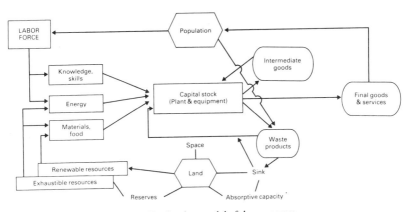

FIG. 2.3 Production model of the economy.

The *waste products* of our system range from the heat generated but not captured in energy conversion processes to the empty beverage cans thrown away at a campsite. The broken lines in the figure suggest that some of this waste is recycled immediately into production, but most of it goes into what we have called the "sink"—scrap yards, garbage disposal sites, slag piles, rivers and lakes. Eventually, portions may be reclaimed from the sink; the vast bulk becomes a burden on the land's absorptive capacity.

For obvious reasons, the model focusses on the conversion of physical inputs into final outputs of physical goods and services as the core of production. There are, of course, other types of productive activity that must not be overlooked: transportation, storage, communication, marketing and distribution, among others, form an essential part of any modern production system.

2.2.2 Production over Time

How does our aggregate production system change over time? Obviously, any changes in the absolute and relative quantities, as well as in the quality, of inputs will bring about such transformations, as will shifts in the composition of the outputs. Simplifying our production model somewhat, we may visualize the flow of activity along the lines suggested in Fig. 2.4. Here we show the economy's total output, Y, at any given time as a function of the inputs of labor (L), the stock of capital (K), and natural resources (R), with the ways in which these inputs are combined determined by the state of technology (T).

The composition of output in the current period (for example, the allocation of inputs to the production of consumer goods and capital goods) together with any changes in the inputs will then determine the size (and composition) of output in the next period, and so on. Each of these components carries along a more or less persistent heritage of the past. Thus, for example, the proportion of the population that enters into the labor force is influenced by previous economic and social conditions and, with the possible exceptions of major shocks like those of a full-scale war, will change only gradually. Similarly, the stock of capital incorporates plant and equipment of various ages, embodying

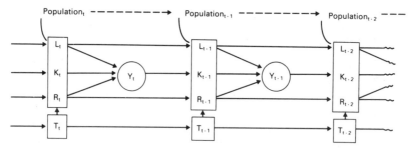

Fig. 2.4 Changes in inputs, technology and outputs over time.

the then prevailing technology. And, what we consider as natural resources is itself determined by changes in demand and technology.

In terms of Schumpeter's theory, which we discussed in the preceding chapter, the economy described by Fig. 2.4 might show steady growth in real output because of increases in demand (changes in population) or because of continuous, minor progress in technology. But without major innovations, introduced by entrepreneurs, the system would, as Schumpeter put it, move through time "with constant speed," in the process "simply reproducing itself." In other words, we would expect major spurts in output only on account of radical, discontinuous advances in technology. We shall return to the implications of this theory in several of our later discussions. Here we want to take a closer look at the components of the model.

2.3 Population: Labor Force and Mouths to Feed

As we have seen, the basic economic problem is *scarcity*, the fact that human wants seem continuously to outstrip the production system's ability to satisfy them. Therefore, economists and others have long recognized the need to view people in their dual role—as producers and as mouths to feed. From the dour prophecies of the Reverend Thomas Malthus in his famous *Essay on the Principle of Population* (1798) to the recent advocates of "zero population growth" and of "limits to growth," pessimists have worried about what looked to them like a growing gap between man's insatiable wants and his capabilities as a producer.[1] Utopians have proclaimed that, at least over the long haul, there was nothing to worry about. Their optimism is based either on the assumption that ever-accelerating technological progress will ultimately overcome the problem of scarcity, or on an abiding faith in the perfectibility of man, by which they apparently mean the reduction of his material requirements to a level that they consider adequate. At times, even otherwise somber economists have expressed such visions. Take, for example, the hope of John Maynard Keynes for a world in which the fundamental economic problem has been solved:

> "I see us free . . . to return to some of the most sure and certain principles of religion and traditional virtue—that avarice is vice, that the exaction of usury is a misdemeanor, and the love of money is detestable, that those walk most truly in the paths of virtue and sane wisdom who take least thought for the morrow."[2]

Let us be properly agnostic with respect to both extreme schools of thought until we have finished our own explorations. Here we want to concentrate on just two basic questions: (1) Interpreting "feeding" broadly, in the sense of providing a socially acceptable level of living, what is the relationship between the size of an economy's labor force and its population, and how do changes in technology affect this relationship? And (2) How has technological advancement influenced the quality of the labor force?

2.3.1   *Population, Labor, Leisure, and Production*

From the economic point of view, two facts about a population are of particular interest—its *size* and its *age composition*, where changes in the first obviously lead to changes in the second. Population growth is determined by the size of the existing population and by the interaction of births per year (fertility) and deaths per year (mortality or, conversely, life expectancy). That technological changes have affected these determinants is evident and needs no great elaboration. It has done so directly, for example, by advances in medicine, or indirectly, through such social transformations as increasing urbanization.

Our main interest is in the *labor force*, those members of the working-age population who are gainfully employed or actively seeking employment. The *participation rate* measures the percentage of the population that is in the labor force at a given time. This rate varies substantially among countries, and it changes over time in a given country. Does an economy's technological development have anything to do with these differences and changes? We intuitively suspect so.

Note, first of all, that the participation rate depends on our definition of the *working-age population*. But this definition in turn hinges on how many laborers it takes to provide adequate real incomes for households. In poor countries, there is nothing unusual about children working gainfully at a very early age and for old people to know no such thing as retirement. Our own child labor laws and changes in the legal retirement age are social reforms firmly grounded in advances in economic conditions. Conversely, changes in the age structure of the population may lead to revisions in concepts of who should be in the labor force. In the United States, does the fact that our population is growing slowly and developing a growing bulge at higher ages have anything to do with the rising entry of women into the labor force and with movements to give "senior citizens" the option of staying on the job beyond age 65?[3] We may certainly suspect so. Furthermore, individuals' decisions on whether to join the labor force may also be influenced by institutional factors, such as social-welfare legislation and the taxation of incomes; but this is a matter beyond our purview.[4]

An economy's production possibilities are determined not just by how many people are in the labor force but also by how much time they spend on the job. Changes in the length of the working day and of the average work week, together with conventions concerning the length of vacations, also are the result of improvements in labor productivity, i.e., technological advances.[5]

Let us deal with these observations in a more general fashion by saying that all of them reflect, in the aggregate, social decisions about the allocation of potentially available labor-time between actual *gainful work* and what, for want of a better term, we shall call *leisure*, in the broadest possible sense. Our analysis is restricted to the short run because, as we shall discuss in the next section, time not spent in current production may represent an investment that

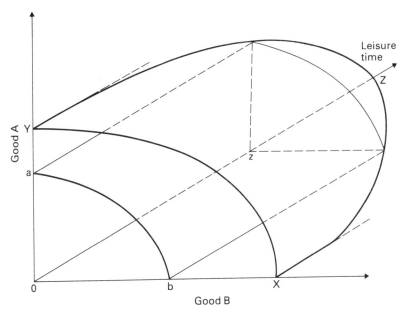

Fig. 2.5 Production possibility–leisure surface.

will lead to higher production in the future. In the absence of this caveat, students could object that they are certainly not engaged in a leisure-time activity!

Having made these points, we realize that the production possibilities frontier reflects an economy's productive capacity at a point in time, *after* decisions about the relationship between work and leisure. To incorporate these decisions into our earlier model, we can construct a *production possibility–leisure surface* of the type shown in Fig. 2.5. Here we have added a third dimension, leisure, to the conventional diagram. The heavy line yx represents the hypothetical "zero–leisure" output potential of the economy. An actual production–possibilities curve, such as ab, implies that the economy has also opted, collectively, for the amount of leisure 0z. By reducing this amount, the economy could presumably increase real output without any other changes. This might happen, for example, during an all-out push for more production in wartime.[6]

Note that the curves yz and xz are drawn so as to become parallel to the leisure axis 0Z, as they approach zero leisure. This is meant to suggest that giving up more leisure in the relevant range (adding more human inputs to the other inputs available in the short run) does not result in any increases in total output. In overpopulated, poor economies one may find that the total amount of labor input has been pushed beyond the limit where it produces any additional output. Such conditions are referred to as *underemployment*: People are scrambling for work to increase their money incomes, but it would be possible to reduce the total amount of labor without any reductions in real output. How to break this log-jam is one of the biggest problems of economic development.

One final observation must be made in connection with our labor–leisure model: We spoke above (p. 32) of the provision of "adequate real incomes for households" as a criterion for the allocation of time. This is of course an entirely subjective yardstick, with the aggregate outcome reflecting the individual decisions of millions of people. It seems clear that, regardless of their income levels, many families have a preference for additional real incomes beyond those determined by the socially accepted balance between work and leisure. Dual job-holding ("moonlighting") by individuals and job-holding by several members of a household testify to this fact. There probably are many explanations for this phenomenon, but an economic historian has pointed out that in the United States we may be ". . . approaching the plateau beyond which leisure time begins to become an 'inferior good'—a likelihood which may be increased by the high money cost attached to many leisure-time activities, such as foreign travel."[7] This observation becomes all the more persuasive when we consider that virtually all modern leisure-time activities involve substantial investments in equipment.

2.3.2   *The Quality of Labor—Investment in Human Capital*

In our discussion so far we have ignored the fact that the qualitative characteristics of a population will play an important role in determining productive performance. At a fundamental level, this quality is determined by such factors as the conditions of health and nutrition. Beyond this, however, economists agree that people's education and training, and with these their ability to come to terms with technological changes, are the keys to improvements in real output.

The concept of *investment in human capital* has been developed to account for this aspect of labor's contribution to production. From an individual's point of view, this investment involves all expenditures for formal education and training undertaken in the expectation of increased future income. For the economy as a whole, it also includes the knowledge and skills acquired by persons in the course of their actual work. Although the rates of return achieved by individuals from this type of investment may vary greatly, one fact stands out: International comparisons show that, in the aggregate, there is a striking correlation between a society's commitment to education and its ranking in terms of such performance measures as real output per capita.

This observation also sheds some additional light on the dilemma of poor countries: In the short run, the relationship between their productive capacity and the number of mouths to feed forces these countries onto a point on the production possibilities–leisure surface that leaves little time for the preparation of entrants into the labor force. Just as their low savings rates keep such economies from building up their stock of physical capital, so their low current incomes prevent them from achieving higher levels of investment in human capital.

There is no assurance, of course, that mere time spent in education will produce persons capable of performing satisfactorily in an advanced economy with rapidly changing technology. This fact lies at the root of many of the current criticisms of the American educational system. More fundamentally, however, we observe that in a society where few discoveries, inventions, and innovations are produced, education is in danger of becoming no more than the transmission of well-established, codified knowledge from generation to generation. Such a society may devote substantial resources to schooling, but the investment may result in nothing but a body of "learned men" who pass on a deteriorating stock of knowledge in the form of rules and myths.[8] The problem is accentuated when access to education is restricted to certain social classes or, worse yet, to men only. In such a setting, the prevailing culture tends to place greater value on people's remaining content with their station in life ("If my job was good enough for me, it ought to be good enough for my son") than on economic improvement and social mobility.

Obviously, many of these matters transcend the economist's traditional frame of reference. But we ignore them at the peril of developing purely mechanistic models of the relationship between technology, society, and production.

2.4 Capital: The Economy's Plant and Equipment

The term, capital, has several meanings in economics. For our purposes it stands for the *physical stock of capital*. This includes not only privately owned production facilities, but also public investment in the so-called *infrastructure* of the economy (roads, bridges, ports, etc.) and other government-owned capital (schools, fire stations, postal facilities).

For the economy as a whole, the two most important characteristics of the capital stock are its *size* and its age composition, which is generally referred to as the *vintage structure* of capital. The stock is increased each year by the amount of *gross investment*; this is determined in the aggregate by the *savings rate*, i.e. the proportion of income not spent for consumption.[9] The stock is reduced by the amount of capital that is worn out on account of its age and, more importantly, by the amount of capital that has become obsolete. By *obsolescence*, we mean the process whereby some part of the (technically still serviceable) capital stock becomes economically useless because of the competition from new equipment embodying more advanced technology. Physical wearing-out and obsolescence, therefore, determine the "mortality" of an economy's stock of capital. *Net investment* in any given year represents the additions to capital beyond those required simply to replace plant and equipment that have been pulled out of service.

Having made these seemingly straightforward observations about the determinants of the capital stock's size, we confront an empirical dilemma: We have no really satisfactory way of measuring this quantity. The amount of money invested in the past less the usual accounting depreciation tells us little about the current productive value of capital. The *book value* of our total assets reflects the market prices of plant and equipment at the time they were acquired as well as more or less arbitrary conventions about depreciating these assets. Alternatively, we might try to define the capital stock in terms of its capacity to produce a certain amount of real output, but we know already that this capacity is jointly determined by many factors, such as society's work–leisure decisions and the quality of natural resources. There are statistical techniques for trying to determine the total economic value of our fixed capital, but just like our "national wealth," this value remains a somewhat elusive concept.

For purposes of our study of technological change, we can extricate ourselves from these empirical difficulties by observing that bygones are forever bygones and that, therefore, the *aggregate value* of the economy's stock of capital is of limited interest. Understanding why particular industries made particular investments at a certain time will be more helpful in our efforts. Whatever lessons there may be in history come from an examination of the nature and the outcomes of strategic decisions.

In the analysis of the dynamics of innovative activity the focus is on *changes in the stock of capital*. What causes firms to bid for resources which are to be allocated to facilitating future production? Presumably it is the expectation that a given project will earn sufficient income over its useful life to provide a satisfactory return on the invested funds. This expectation will be influenced by many factors, among them the performance of a firm's existing plant and equipment, the current prices of the relevant capital goods, the prevailing rate of interest, estimates of future operating costs, and estimates of the future demand for the firm's products. As should be evident from everything we said in Chapter 1 about the nature of innovations, investment decisions involving new processes or new products are always made under conditions of great uncertainty. Such commitments generally involve judgments that cannot be cast into the framework of a more or less precise rate-of-return calculation. Rather, they will reflect the judgment and the venturesomeness of the people and organizations who make these decisions.[10] Insistence on the quantification of all benefits and costs of alternative investment projects will tend to produce a bias in favour of "sure things," i.e., of more or less well-tried technologies and of near-term, rather than farther-off, benefits. Some critics have claimed that this kind of insistence by American decision-makers has been one of the reasons for many established industries' difficulties in international competition, because it has resulted in a stock of capital that does not sufficiently embody up-to-date technology.[11]

The validity of such claims must await later evaluation. Here we want to do no more than to state the problem confronted by managers in familiar economic terms: The rules for *short-run* decision-making say that a firm should utilize its existing plant and equipment as long as its output can be sold at a price that covers average variable cost and makes some contribution to fixed cost ("overhead and profit," to use the accountant's language). By this criterion, it does not matter how old the stock of capital is or what technology it embodies. But in the *long run*, adherence to the rules of short-run rationality can lead to all sorts of trouble. Increases in input prices may find firms unprepared to deal with the resulting changes in the cost of production. Downward pressure on output prices by foreign competitors or producers of substitutes may suddenly invalidate the assumptions on which investment decisions had been based.

With the wisdom of hindsight, judgments about managerial decisions concerning a firm's plant and equipment are easy to make. We will be interested in the question what current conditions, rooted either in the structure of the firms themselves or in their technical and economic environment, influence these decisions. Rapid technological advance in an industry depends on the replacement of the stock of capital. Why was it that at one time an observer could describe "American practice" in the iron and steel industry as follows?

> "The principle . . . was to destroy anything from a steam engine to a steel works whenever a better piece of apparatus was to be had, no matter whether the engine or works was new or old, and the definition of this word 'better' was confined to the ability to get out a greater product. Such a course involved the expenditure of enormous sums of money, it involved the constant return of profits into the business, it involved mistakes, but it produced results, and the economies from the increased output soon paid for the expenditure."[12]

What circumstances caused this principle to be abandoned somewhere along the way? Did markets change? Conditions of technological evolution? Managements' assessments of the future results of investment? Governmental policies? Developments in other countries? These are the kinds of questions we shall have to try to answer if we want to get a better understanding of the role of investment decisions in our economy's aggregate performance.

2.5 Land: Space, Resources, Sink

Readers may recall that basic economic theory treats land in a rather austere fashion. The *theory of rent* focusses on one main characteristic of the factor: it is in perfectly price-inelastic supply. While many important implications for the working of the market system can be derived from this feature, we want briefly to probe beyond it. As suggested by our production model, land makes three distinct contributions to economic performance. First, it provides the *space* in which productive activity takes place. Although the interactions between technology and space use had much to do with the shaping of our society, their consideration would go beyond the scope of our explorations. The fields of location theory and economic geography deal explicitly with the spatial aspects of production, exchange, and consumption. We shall refer to these only occasionally, such as when we discuss the possible reasons for the regional agglomeration of certain types of industrial activity or the possible connections between technological development and the relocation of industries. Second, land furnishes the *natural resources* which become food, raw materials, and energy inputs. And third, land acts as the *sink* for all the non-recoverable or non-marketable wastes of production and consumption. We assigned key roles to these latter functions in our aggregate production model, and we shall now discuss them in somewhat greater detail.

2.5.1   Natural Resources, Technology, and Production

Natural resources are those components of the land that can be gathered, harvested or extracted and converted into factors of production, given current demand (prices) and technology (costs). This seemingly obvious notion deserves special emphasis, because it is so often overlooked in public discussions: What constitutes a resource is defined not just by the biological or physical characteristics of the item in question, but also by human tastes and by human knowledge about cultivating, searching for, collecting, and converting them.

Man, not nature, determines what is a resource at any given time, in a given set of economic and social circumstances. One observer has put the matter very bluntly: "Resources are not finite, for the simple reason that they are not natural. Resources are created by technology. They are now, always have been, and will likely continue to be so."[13] He also points out that, from the economist's point of view, the finiteness of what we currently call resources is not an interesting question. If any of them become increasingly scarce, their (relative) prices would rise. In fact, however, the opposite has been true for at least the past century: decreasing costs can be found in agriculture and in virtually all extractive industries. In historical perspective, technological change has more than compensated for the decline in such factors as the ready accessibility of high-grade ores or naturally fertile land. Whether one believes that it will continue to do so obviously depends on one's faith in man's ingenuity and in the ability of human institutions to deal with impending shortages. Some classifications may help in gaining a better understanding of the problems involved.

Renewable resources are those regenerated by natural processes over shorter or longer periods of time. Such regeneration may involve the expenditure of labor and capital or it may occur without human intervention. It is in any event neither inevitable nor independent of society's rate of utilization of a resource. There exists a *maximum sustainable yield*, which reflects the need to balance the use of renewable resources against nature's regenerative potential. What this yield is in a particular case may be subject to disagreement, but no one would deny the economic threat of over-cutting forests, over-fishing certain species, or misusing the locally available supplies of pure water. The difficulties of achieving agreement on sustainable yields are most apparent in situations where property rights to a resource are undefined and therefore individual decision-makers perceive the resource to be available for the taking. Under these conditions, the development of techniques for the large-scale exploitation of resources, such as modern fishing vessels, has often contributed to the problem, but it is hardly the villain of the piece.[14]

Exhaustible resources are those that are used up, once and for all, in the process of extraction and conversion, with any possibility of regeneration well beyond the human time scale. The prime resources of this type are of course minerals. Since concerns about minerals availability have been in the forefront of discussions about the possibility or desirability of continued technical progress and economic growth, it is important to have an understanding of what is meant by availability and how this is affected by technological and economic forces.

Figure 2.6 illustrates the concepts necessary to such an understanding. Two dimensions determine the availability of a mineral at any given time: the probability that a deposit exists, and the economic feasibility of extracting and converting the mineral. We define as *reserves* those known and identified deposits that can be exploited under the prevailing cost-price conditions. Reserves are distinguished from *conditional resources* purely by technical and economic criteria. Let the market price of the mineral rise, or let the cost of extraction and conversion be lowered through innovations, and the line between conditional resources and reserves will shift.

The distinction enables us to make an additional observation: From the viewpoint of individual economic units, identifying resources and holding them against the possibility of future demand requires substantial investments.

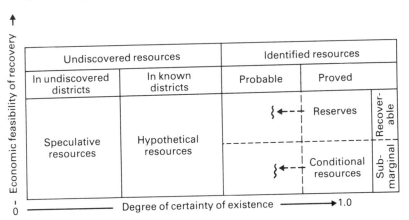

FIG. 2.6 Classification of mineral resources.

Therefore, it is not surprising that the statistics for many minerals show long-run stability in the relationship between the rate of exploitation and the "inventory" of proven supplies of a mineral. No rational decision-maker will invest in conditional resources or in the development of technology for creating additional resources without the expectation of a pay-off within a reasonable planning horizon. Thus, for example, the anticipation of further sharp increases in crude-oil prices triggered a variety of ventures, such as the exploitation of oil shale and coal liquefaction. In the face of declining prices for natural crude oil, most of these projects have been abandoned. They may be started up again at some future time, but for now investment in them cannot be justified.[15]

Hypothetical resources and *speculative resources* are mineral deposits whose existence is assumed with varying degrees of certainty. The development of new geological theories and of technologies for searching would be required to obtain more information. Investments in the latter again will take place only if prospective market conditions promise an acceptable return on the investment. Thus, none of the dividing lines in our diagram is fixed. Rather, the relationship among the physical characteristics of the resource, the available technology, and the expected development of demand will determine the availability of specific minerals. Furthermore, what is regarded as a valuable resource in one kind of economic setting may be strictly submarginal in another.

For all these reasons, most economists tend to be properly agnostic with respect to the validity of long-range forecasts of mineral supply and demand. The number of variables impinging on actual developments is simply too large for us to achieve any degree of accuracy. Besides, any prediction must include, implicitly or explicitly, a general technological forecast that considers not only the resource in question, but also the development of substitutes and complements. In some ultimate sense, every particular exhaustible resource is in finite supply. Inappropriate private strategies or misguided governmental policies can always create shortages at prevailing prices. But in terms of developing alternative solutions to "resource problems" over the longer term, the test of an economic system is how well it can adjust to changing availability, technology, and prices.

2.5.2 *Land as a Sink for Wastes*

Our natural environment must absorb, temporarily or permanently, all the technically non-recoverable or non-marketable byproducts and waste products of economic activity. The emphasis on technology *and* markets once again reminds us that what is "useless waste" depends not only on the physical characteristics of the substances involved, but also on the price system.

The aggregate production model shows that some byproducts become new inputs almost immediately. Heat recovered and utilized in production or home scrap recycled in iron and steel manufacturing are examples. Others are withdrawn from the sink only after some time, if economic conditions change. Thus, automobile hulks and old farm machinery will be collected and processed only if the prices obtainable for this type of scrap justify the costs incurred. Similarly, low-tenor supplies of an ore may have been set aside in unsightly piles as long as high-grade ore was plentiful; they may be utilized when the price of the metal in question has risen. Nevertheless, large quantities of wastes are consigned to the sink forever.

We may think of an upper limit to the ability of any given area of land to hold such wastes in terms of its *absorptive capacity*. But this capacity, too, appears to be determined not only by basic physical or ecological factors, but also by a society's demand for what it considers a desirable environment. Further complications arise when wastes that were thought to be harmless are later discovered to present a danger to human health or lives. Without belittling this consideration, we may suspect that the level of demand for satisfactory environmental conditions, much like a society's preference for leisure over additional output, is strongly influenced by levels of economic development. A concern with this particular aspect of what has become known as "the quality of life" seems to be the mark of economies with a reasonably high standard of living. By contrast, many less-developed countries have argued that their willingness to tolerate various forms of environmental disruption gives them an essential cost advantage in their efforts to expand industrial production. For this reason they have been reluctant to subscribe to any global agreements on environmental standards, arguing that these would of necessity contain the wealthy societies' definitions of absorptive capacity and would therefore be just one more means of curbing the competitiveness of developing countries.

One other point must be made in this connection: the generation of whatever we consider as undesirable wastes and pollutants is the result of industrial production itself and not of the particular economic system in which production and consumption take place. In other words, our earlier observations about the failure of markets to induce consideration of externalities must not lead us to believe that economies placing less reliance on private entrepreneurship and on the market system have been more successful in dealing with problems of the environment. If anything, the evidence suggests the opposite: environmental disruption from industrial activity tends to be an even more serious problem in centrally-planned, socialist economies.[16] In view of our earlier discussion of the importance of property rights in conserving resources, this should be no great surprise.

More generally, however, the issue confronting all societies is the same: what is an acceptable trade-off between the production of goods and services and the use of land as a sink for wastes? And, assuming that some consensus on the trade-off has been reached, what are the technological means and economic incentives most likely to achieve the desired targets?

2.6   A Final Look at the Aggregate Production Model

In the process of looking at the main components of our production model we should have become impressed by an additional fact: even in its greatly simplified form, the model portrays a *system*, in the original meaning of that much-abused term. "Everything is connected with everything else," no one part can be changed in a significant way without affecting other parts, and these effects may show themselves directly and transparently, or they may appear in the form of very subtle and often unpredictable feedbacks. This is particularly true for major changes in technology; like stones dropped into a pond, they create ripples of effects that will transform economic and social relationships.

2.6.1   *Markets, Products, and Services*

The responsiveness of the system to major innovations and its speed in adjusting to new economic relationships created by them will play a key role in determining economic performance—the ability efficiently to convert inputs into outputs in response to private and social demand. A high level of responsiveness is one of the main features of a market system with its decentralized decision-making mechanisms. In the risky game of technological innovation, the system also implies that mistakes are decentralized and their costs thus kept within bounds. Commitments to particular new technologies through central planning or by government fiat, on the other hand, tend to maximize the economic consequences of errors.

Of course there may be situations in which, for example because of a lack of competition, market participants do not respond optimally to technological advances, just as in other situations the very speed of their responses may itself create some undesirable side effects. But when this has been said, the fact remains that the market system does the job of resource allocation and output distribution under conditions of technological change in a manner that has not been duplicated successfully by other institutional arrangements. Actual or anticipated changes in relative costs and prices signal decision-makers that they must take some actions: substitute one resource for another; change the nature of their products; reorganize productive activity; search for new technologies; and defend themselves against the inroads of competitive goods and services.

When we try to assess the actual performance of modern market economies, two developments complicate the picture. The first has to do with the rapid growth of service, as contrasted with commodity, production. Since we have no unequivocal measure for most of the service sector's outputs, we are somewhat at a loss in evaluating its efficiency as well as the effects of technological advances on the quality of services. To be sure, in the production of some kinds of services, efficiency criteria are not relevant at all. We would not judge the performance of an orchestra by how loud or fast it can play a

Beethoven symphony, nor would we expect its violinists to replace their instruments according to modern depreciation procedures! But there are large service sectors in which our inability to define relevant output measures raises serious problems for economic evaluations. One example is provided by what has become known as the health-care industry. In most advanced economies, the total costs of medical care, including expenditures for R&D, have risen to where they account for 10 per cent or more of gross national product. Have the resulting benefits kept pace with this increase in expenditures? We cannot really be sure.

A second set of problems arises in connection with the steady growth of the public sector in most economies. Here again we are dealing with activities whose output is difficult, if not impossible, to measure. Therefore, the usual concepts of efficiency are not very useful operationally; indeed, many analysts have argued that efficiency criteria have little to do with how the public sector evaluates its own performance.[17] If it is true that bureaucratic organizations (including no doubt certain private organizations) operate under completely different rules, then this has clear implications for our economy's overall performance. When larger staffs, larger budgetary allocations, or higher levels of investment in physical facilities are regarded as desirable goals in themselves, then output, however measured, may not determine success or failure, and the adoption of technological innovations may be subject to criteria having little to do with efficient resource use. These problems have received greatest attention in connection with technological decisions in the area of national defense, but they probably exist in less visible form wherever a branch of the public sector produces non-marketable outputs.

2.6.2   Size and Economic Performance

Our production model raises one other question: What is the influence of an economy's total size on its productive performance? Is it easier for a large country to generate and digest the technological innovations that lead to increased output per capita than it is for a small one? The empirical evidence is mixed. On the one hand, there can be little doubt that the size of the United States economy (in terms of land area, resource endowments, and markets) has been an important factor in determining the direction and the outcomes of technological advances. And furthermore, this size has made possible a diversity of economic activities at a scale that is beyond the reach of smaller countries. On the other hand, there are many examples of small economies that have managed to do very well in the international division of labor, either by specializing on a narrow range of outputs or by exploiting some other advantages.[18] The past successes of Sweden and Switzerland, as well as the much-admired rise of Japan as an industrial power demonstrate that countries can come to terms with contraints of size and resource availability.

But small economies do appear to pay a price for their accomplishments, as compared to larger economic units. A high degree of specialization and heavy dependence on international markets leaves them more exposed to the vagaries of technological changes and of shifts in demand. Consider, for example, the Swiss watch industry, which once dominated the world market for all but the cheapest mass-produced time pieces. The development and rapid diffusion of inexpensive but precise electronic watches rendered Switzerland's advantage in the manufacture of high-quality mechanical watches obsolete, putting the industry under severe pressure and forcing its complete reorganization. The consequences for the Swiss economy obviously would have been less severe if its industrial structure had been more highly diversified.

Without international markets, small economies have few opportunities to exploit the advantages of large-scale production. These markets also may help to stimulate internal competition, because they make possible the existence of a larger number of firms than could survive on the basis of the domestic market alone. It could be argued, however, that exposure to global competition is in any event sufficient to stave off the complacency and technological conservatism that are often attributed, rightly or wrongly, to national monopolies or oligopolies.

A consideration of these issues is beyond the scope of our study. We must, however, conclude this discussion with an observation that we believe to be especially important at a time when the imitation of other economies' organizational arrangements and governmental policies is frequently advocated as *the* solution to American industrial problems. We believe that the concepts by which a large country like the United States guides its industrial system, its policies toward competition, and even its management–labor relations, are rooted in a heritage that is unknown to smaller economic entities. This suggests that there is little in the way of lessons for the United States that could be lifted from the entirely different economic, social, and cultural context of smaller countries. We may, for example, decide that our antitrust laws are out of tune with the requirements for inter-firm cooperation in the development of new technologies, but we would probably fail if, instead of relying on our own institutional innovations, we tried to imitate the Japanese system of cooperation under strong governmental guidance.

Notes

1. Of recent studies in this vein, a computer simulation conducted for the Club of Rome by a group of researchers at Massachusetts Institute of Technology has received the greatest attention; see Meadows, D. H. *et al.*, *The Limits to Growth* (New York: Universe Books, 1972). The study triggered a host of extensions as well as some highly critical responses. For an economist's reasoned critique of continuing output increases, see Mishan, E. J., *Technology and Growth: The Price We Pay* (New York: Praeger, 1970).
2. Keynes, J. M., "Economic Possibilities for Our Grandchildren." in Essays in *Persuasion* (London: Macmillan, 1972), quoted in Gendron, B., *Technology and the Human Condition* (New

York: St. Martin's Press, 1977), p. 15. It is worth noting that, had Keynes had any grandchildren, they would probably be grandparents themselves in the 1980s.

3. The labor force statistics include only women who are gainfully employed. But according to one study, the work of housewives contributes to one half of the average family's real income. See Gronau, R., "Who is the Family's Main Breadwinner?—The Wife's Contribution to Full Income," Working Paper No. 148, National Bureau for Economic Research, September 1976; cited in Posner, R., *Economic Analysis of Law* (Boston: Little, Brown, 1977), p. 108.

4. For some examples of how such institutional arrangements might influence labor–leisure decisions, see Rosegger, G., "Enforced Leisure—Some Further Conundrums," *Omega*.

5. Economic historians have shown that long working hours were a byproduct of the industrial revolution. In earlier times, the debilitating effects of poor nutrition and endemic diseases generally kept men from putting in what was considered a "normal" work week. See, for example, Freudenberger, H., and Cummins, C., "Health, Work, and Leisure before the Industrial Revolution," *Explorations in Economic History*, **13**, 1-12 (1976).

6. Wartime efforts to maximize output are not strictly comparable to peacetime production, because so many members of the labor force are drawn into military service. Nevertheless, it is significant that during World War II any number of industries were reported to be producing annual output in excess of 100 per cent of their rated capacities.

7. Rosenberg, N., *Technology and American Economic Growth* (New York: Harper & Row, 1972). Causation does not run in one direction only; the average American household's increased leisure has given rise to a whole range of industries producing entirely new goods and services.

8. An interesting example is provided by the history of China. During the first fourteen centuries A.D., Chinese technology was well ahead of European developments. Then stagnation set in, even though education, in a formal sense, continued at a high level. In a relatively short span of time, China fell behind the West in the utilization of new knowledge, and, indeed, some old knowledge seems to have been forgotten.

9. Part of the current consumption foregone does not, of course, involve voluntary savings decisions; rather, it reflects taxes collected by the government and spent for public investment.

10. In the face of otherwise inexplicable decisions, John Maynard Keynes referred to the "animal spirits" of investors, that presumably overrode rational calculations. See *The General Theory of Employment, Interest, and Money* (New York: Harcourt, Brace, 1936). Joseph Schumpeter would have found nothing puzzling about such behavior, because it is entirely in keeping with this definition of the innovator-entrepreneur. A managerially oriented evaluation of the judgmental element in decisions to invest in innovations is provided in Gold, B., "The Shaky Foundations of Capital Budgeting," *California Management Review*, Winter 1976.

11. For a particularly strong example of this type of criticism, see Hayes, R. and Abernathy, W., "Managing Ourselves into Economic Decline," *Harvard Business Review*, August 1980.

12. Campbell, H. H., *The Manufacture and Properties of Iron and Steel*, 4th ed. (New York: McGraw-Hill, 1907), pp. 470-71.

13. DeGregori, T. R., "Technological Limits to Forecasts of Doom: Science, Technology, and the Sustainable Economy," *Technovation*, **2** (1985), p. 5.

14. Consider, for example, the response of nations to the realization that large-scale commercial fishing on the high seas was rapidly depleting certain species. The need for an international agreement concerning sustainable rates of exploitation became obvious; but before beginning negotiations, most states expanded their claim of sovereignty beyond the traditional three-mile limit in order to exclude the more efficient fishing vessels of other countries from their shores or to subject them to unilateral regulation.

15. A brief but incisive discussion of this problem can be found in Ayres, R. U., *The Next Industrial Revolution* (Cambridge, Mass.: Ballinger, 1984), Ch. 5.

16. See, for example, Goldman, M. I., "The Convergence of Environmental Disruption," *Science*, **2** (October 1970).

17. This point is made, and substantiated by a number of case studies, in Peirce, W. S., *Bureaucratic Failure and Public Expenditure* (New York: Academic Press, 1981).

18. An excellent collection of essays on the relationship between size and economic performance can be found in Robinson, E. A. G., *The Economic Consequences of the Size of Nations* (New York: St. Martin's Press, 1960). A more recent work dealing directly with issues of technological change is Ergas, H., *Why Do Some Countries Innovate More than Others?* (Brussels: Centre for European Policy Studies, 1984).

CHAPTER 3

The Microeconomic Theory of Production and Technological Change

In this chapter we shall undertake a review of the elementary theory of production and technological change. Like all general theories, it abstracts from many real-life considerations. Indeed, one might argue that, despite its name, the theory's main intent is not to explain production as such. Rather, its assumptions, postulates, and conclusions establish certain logically consistent rules for the behavior of firms in input and output markets. Whatever the theory's predictive content, it is focussed on the reactions of firms to market signals under conditions of certainty. The implication of this statement is that, given rules of rational behavior and the necessary information, a firm is no more than a decision-making automaton.[1]

3.1 The Production Function and Technical Efficiency

The concept of the *production function* forms the basis for a description of input–output relationships in a firm. If we assume homogeneous factors of production and a single output, as well as full information about existing technology, we may think of the function as the set of all "recipes" (to use an analogy we introduced in Chapter 1) by which this output can be produced. More properly, we can say that the production function shows the maximum output that can be achieved by combining various quantities of inputs.

The algebraic form in which the function is generally presented in the theory of the firm is

$$Q = f(K, L),$$

where Q stands for the quantity of output (measured in appropriate physical units), K is the number of "service-units" derived from homogeneous physical capital (for example, machine-hours), and L is the number of labor-service units (man-hours) employed—all of this for some specified period of time. The restriction to two basic inputs obviously represents an abstraction from real life, but it enables us to deal with the theory in diagrammatic form. The assumption that these inputs can be measured in terms of a single dimension, such as hours of service, also bypasses many operational problems, such as differences in the quality of labor. But as we shall see, a greater level of realism would not add substantially to the insights yielded by the theory.

3.1.1   *Production with a Single Technique*

Let us start by assuming a state of technology such that there is only one known set of input proportions for producing a certain output, i.e., that there exists a single *technique* or *process*. If, for example, this technique requires that 1 unit of K always be combined with 2 units of L, we can show the relationship between inputs and output in three-dimensional perspective, as in Fig. 3.1.a. A mapping of the relationship on the input plane results in the diagram of Fig. 3.1.b. The line OP is called a *process ray*. It shows the proportionality of inputs required under the single known technique. Note that here we have to label points on the ray in order to indicate output quantities, i.e., the vertical distance of these points from the plane.

We have drawn this example so as to show that there exists proportionality between inputs and output: a doubling of inputs results precisely in twice the output. When this relationship holds, we speak of a *linear process* or of *constant returns to scale*. As Figs. 3.2.a and 3.2.b suggest, however, there are other possibilities. If output rises more than proportionally as a result of increases in inputs, our technique exhibits *increasing returns to scale*. If output rises less than proportionally, we have *decreasing returns to scale*. In either case, the mapping of the process ray will still result in a straight line, but the *scale effects* of increases in inputs (i.e., in the size of the production system) would show up in the labeling of the resulting output quantities. The concepts of scale effects and of economies of scale will be discussed in Chapter 4.

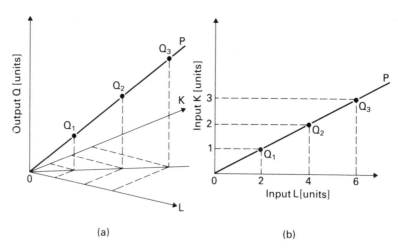

(a)   (b)

FIG. 3.1 Input–output relationships, single technique

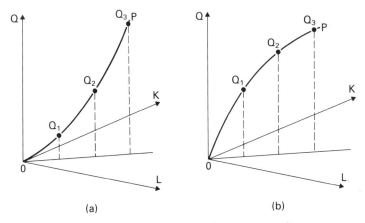

FIG. 3.2 Increasing and decreasing returns to scale.

3.1.2 *Multiple Techniques and Technical Efficiency*

Let us assume now that an inventor has come up with an idea for a new process, shown as OG in Fig. 3.3. We could dismiss this invention without further investigation, because for any given output quantity it uses more of both inputs than does our original technique, OP. We call any process that requires at least the same quantity of one input and more of the second input than another process, *technically inefficient*. The regions of technical inefficiency, relative to the original technique, are suggested by the vertical and horizontal lines originating from the output points on process ray OP.

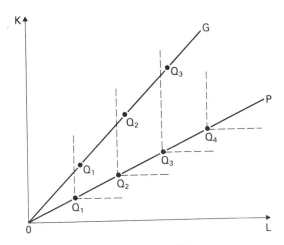

FIG. 3.3 Technically inefficient process.

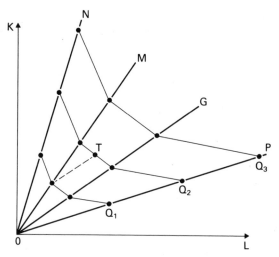

FIG. 3.4 Isoquants; combination of processes.

In Fig. 3.4 we show four different processes for producing our output, each of which is *technically efficient*. We connect equal-output points on the rays and obtain lines that indicate the same vertical distance from the input plane. Such lines are called *isoquants*. They are analogous to the contour lines on a topographic map, which show points of equal elevation above sea level. When there exist several technically efficient processes, a firm would not have to commit itself to just one of these. It could, for example, produce output Q_1 by using technique OM and the incremental output Q_2–Q_1 by relying on technique OG. This combination of processes would result in total-output point T, as shown in the diagram. Note that throughout these examples we have assumed a linear input–output relationship, i.e., constant returns to scale.

3.1.3 *Isoquant Maps*

When technology permits an infinite number of substitutions between the inputs, our isoquants become smooth curves with negative slope, as shown in the *isoquant map* of Fig. 3.5. The isoquants drawn represent an arbitrary selection of vertical distances (outputs) from the *production surface* which they describe; here the analogy with the contour lines of topographic maps is even more apparent.

The requirement that isoquants have negative slope throughout is explained by our earlier definition of technical efficiency: any positively-sloped segment would indicate that there are processes which use more of both inputs to produce the same quantity of output. The slope of a tangent to any isoquant would indicate the *marginal rate of technical substitution* between the two inputs, at the point of tangency. Note also that a particular technique, like ON, can still be shown as a process ray in an isoquant map.

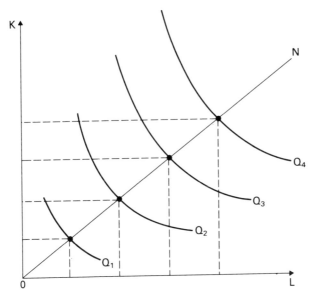

FIG. 3.5 Isoquant map.

Under the assumptions we made at the outset, we may think of the isoquant map as a complete description of the technology for producing some homogeneous output. A *change in technology* might involve an extension of the isoquants toward the capital or the labor axis, or it might result in a different shape of the production surface and therefore an entirely new set of isoquants. A movement from one point on an existing isoquant to another point is called a *change in technique*. These two types of changes should not be confused. In practice, full information about all possible points is not likely to exist in all firms; therefore, from the viewpoint of an individual firm even changes in technique may involve considerable adaptation and learning.

When there exist many technically efficient techniques, an optimal choice among them obviously requires information about the relative prices of the inputs. This is a matter to which we shall turn in the next section. Here we want to make just one additional observation about the concept of technical efficiency: Only if we assume that the firm's decision-makers have perfect knowledge about techniques and that all agents in the firm behave in optimal fashion, will production actually be "on the isoquant" for a given output. Other kinds of inefficiency, such as slack in management or coordination, may mean that actual input combinations used for producing that output may lie anywhere in the region above (to the northeast of) the particular isoquant. When real-life firms engage in what is often called belt-tightening (laying off redundant inputs) without any effect on total output, this shows that they were not on an isoquant, in the theory's sense.

3.2 Input Prices and Economic Efficiency

The production function contains information about feasible and technically efficient input combinations. In order to select the input combination which involves the lowest total cost for a given level of output, a decision-maker also needs information about the prices of the inputs.

In order to simplify our analysis, let us assume that the firm confronts a perfectly price-elastic supply of inputs. This assumption implies that our firm is one of very many competitors for the inputs in question and that its decisions on the actual quantities to be purchased do not influence prices in the factor markets. While the concept of an explicit price for an hour's worth of labor services raises no great difficulties, the hourly price for a unit of capital services is a somewhat more elusive notion. Let us extricate ourselves from the problem, for the time being, by assuming that the firm can also hire (e.g., rent) capital equipment on a short-term basis. Later on, we shall drop this assumption for a more realistic one, but we shall also see that the notion of hiring an hour of capital services is still a useful guide, even if the firm is the owner of the capital in question. Let us also assume that we are dealing with a single-plant firm.

Once we know the relevant input prices, selection of the *economically efficient technique* becomes a straightforward decision. The actual task might be presented to the designers of the firm's plant in two logically equivalent forms:

(1) Design a plant that will produce some target output, Q_0, at the lowest possible total cost; or

(2) given some budget, B_0, for a given period, design the plant that will produce the largest possible output.

For purposes of our illustration, we shall initially solve the second of these tasks, and we shall then show that the approach to solving the first would have been exactly analogous. Let us present the designers' problem in a somewhat more formal way:

Maximize $Q = f(K, L)$,   i.e., output, under the technical conditions that are specified by the production function,

subject to the constraint
$B_0 = rK + wL$,   where B_0 is the allowed total cost, K and L are the quantities of capital and labor purchased and r and w are their respective unit prices.

The graphic solution to the problem is presented in Fig. 3.6. Let us concentrate first on the budget (cost) constraint, shown by the dotted *isocost lines*. These are derived by the following reasoning: Assume that the designers decided to spend the total budget on capital services only; then they could

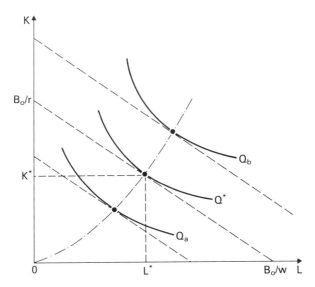

FIG. 3.6 Selection of the optimal technique.

acquire a total of B_0/r units of capital. Similarly, if only labor services were purchased, the number of labor units would be B_0/w. These two quantities establish the limits along the capital and labor input axes. Since, by assumption, the prices of the inputs are given and invariant with the actual quantities bought, the total budget could also be spent on any combination of inputs that lies on a straight line between these limits. Various (parallel) isocost lines imply different levels of total expenditure.

Now, in order to meet the criterion of economic efficiency, our designers will select the technique that lies on the highest possible isoquant, while still satisfying the budget constraint. In our example, this is output Q^*, whose isoquant is tangent to the isocost line B_0, and which calls for the optimal input combination K^* and L^*.

Production of a quantity like Q_a would have been feasible, because it meets the budget constraint, but this quantity also could have been produced at a lower total cost. On the other hand, quantity Q_b lies outside the constraint and could not be achieved within the given budget. Generalizing, we can say that any input combination inside the *feasible region* described by the triangle B_0/r, B_0/w, O, could have been selected, but that only the combination K^*, L^*, is optimal in terms of the task set.

Let us now turn to the first version in which the task might have been posed, the design of a plant with a given capacity at minimum total cost. If, for example, that output was to be Q^*, we would have to search for the lowest isocost line just tangent to the relevant isoquant. In our geometric presentation, we could have drawn any isocost line and then, since all isocost lines must be parallel as long as *relative* input prices remain the same, shifted it until it was tangent to Q^*.

A line drawn through the tangency points of isocost lines with successively higher isoquants is called the *expansion path*. It shows the economically efficient input combinations for various levels of output. The expansion path depends on the configuration of the isoquants, i.e. the shape of the production surface they map. In our diagram, it clearly is not a straight line, reflecting the (quite realistic) assumption that production systems of varying size would not necessarily use the same technique. More labor-intensive techniques are economically efficient at lower levels of production, while the optimal techniques at higher levels become more capital-intensive.

3.2.1   *Changes in the Optimal Technique*

As long as the production function does not change, i.e., technology remains constant, shifts in the relative prices of the inputs will cause moves to a new optimal technique. Assume, for example, that the price of a unit of labor has increased while the price of capital has remained the same. In Fig. 3.7 the isocost line I represents the original conditions, with input combination P economically efficient. Isocost line II reflects the change in relative prices. The new optimal technique for producing output Q_0 is P'. The move from P to P' involves two effects. First, some of the now (relatively) cheaper factor, capital, has been substituted for some of the previously used labor. And second, total

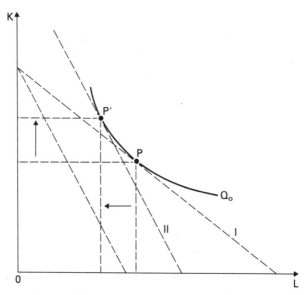

FIG. 3.7 Change in optimal technique due to an increase in labor cost.

cost has risen, since output Q_0 could no longer be produced with the original budget, indicated by isocost line I.

Under our initial assumptions, such a change in technique means that a firm has moved from one perfectly known region of technology to another, equally well known one. As we have suggested already, however, the shift to a new technique—even if this technique is already utilized by other firms—may involve more than straightforward imitation.

A further consideration we have set aside so far is that substitutions between inputs typically cannot be accomplished without substantial costs. In our discussion above (p. 52) we stated the initial problem in terms of "designing a plant." While firms may be free to hire varying amounts of labor input on short notice, their decisions about the number of capital service-units to be acquired involve a commitment to plant and equipment of a certain capacity. In other words, once such decisions have been made, a firm operates under the well-known *short-run* conditions, in which at least one input is fixed.

3.2.2   Consequences of a Fixed Input

The capacity of its plant and equipment, and the technology embodied in it, is a constraint with which the firm has to live in the short run. What period of chronological time is meant by the short run clearly depends on particular circumstances. In some instances, capacity expansions may involve no more than purchasing a piece of machinery, installing it, and starting operations. In others, several years of planning and construction may be involved.

The implications of a short-run capacity constraint for our two-input production function are illustrated in Fig. 3.8. Here we assume that the plant was built so as to produce output Q_2 with the optimal combination of capital and labor. K_0 units of capital services (per time period) have been put in place. We refer to Q_2 as the *design capacity* of the plant, i.e. the output at which unit costs (average total costs) are at a minimum.

Other quantities within the capacity constraint, such as Q_1 or Q_3, can be produced, but unit costs will be higher than at design capacity. The maximum possible output is at Q_4, the isoquant tangent to the constraint line K_0K_0. This the *physical capacity* of the plant. No matter how much of the additional variable input (labor) we add beyond quantity L_4, we cannot produce any more than that.

The plant's *short-run total product curve* can be derived from the isoquant map, as is shown in the lower half of Fig. 3.8. Here we plot short-run output on the vertical axis and units of the variable input on the horizontal axis. We may also think of this curve as a vertical slice through the production surface, along the line K_0K_0. With fixed costs per time period determined by the commitment to plant and equipment, and given the assumption of a perfectly price-elastic supply of labour, the plant's short-run total cost curve and its average and marginal cost curves could be derived in a straightforward

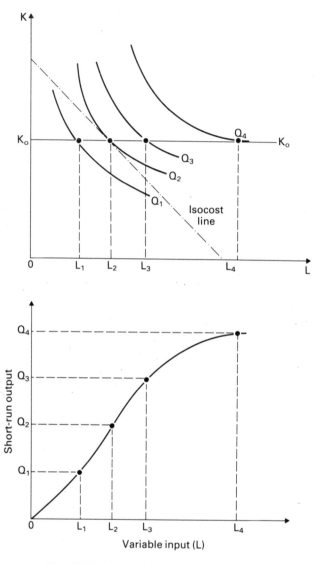

Fig. 3.8 Derivation of the short-run total product curve.

manner. The average cost curve would have its minimum at the design capacity. This is an exercise with which we need not be concerned here. The relevant material can be found in any elementary economics text.

Greatly simplified as our model is, it nevertheless helps us to explain an otherwise puzzling real-life observation: At any given time, an industry includes plants embodying techniques other than the currently optimal one. Each plant will follow the rules of short-run profit maximization. Profitability will vary from plant to plant, reflecting technical conditions and capacity. If managements could build a new plant right now, they would choose the currently optimal technique and capacity. But as long as revenues from the sale of output are sufficient to cover all variable costs and make at least some contribution to fixed costs, even short-run losses are less than would result from a complete shut-down.

Therefore, shifts in the relative prices of inputs will not trigger immediate adjustments on the part of all firms in an industry. From the individual firm's viewpoint, such adjustments represent long-run, *strategic decisions* which are influenced by a host of factors other than current cost and price conditions. Chief among these are expectations about future changes in technology.[2]

3.3   The Microeconomic Theory of Technological Change

Our model of production and costs has been helpful in exploring the behavior of firms under given conditions of technology. Its very generality, however, limits its power in explaining the nature and implications of changes in technology beyond some very elementary statements.

For *product innovations*, the model can say no more than that these involve entirely new production functions, i.e., previously unknown combinations of inputs. This substantiates our previous observation about the somewhat artificial dividing line between product and process innovations, although the degree of "newness" of production functions will of course depend on how radically new a product is. Therefore, we have also referred to major (basic) and minor (improvement) innovations. The ultimate test for new products is provided by the market. Success or failure are determined not by some objective criteria for the quality of the product but by economic results.

The theory of pure *process innovations*, i.e. those assumed not to affect the nature of the output, has been worked out in very elaborate fashion, within the constraints imposed by the basic concept of the production function. Here we shall deal only with the theory's main features[3]. Most generally, a process innovation is defined as a change in input–output relationships that results in lower unit costs for the (unchanged) output, with current input prices constant. Thus, whereas a change in technique is triggered by shifts in relative input prices and involves a move to another point on an existing production surface, a change in technology is motivated by the expectation of cost savings through the combination of inputs in a previously untried manner.

The characteristics of the new combinations will be influenced also by the innovators' expectations about the future behavior of the relevant input prices. Therefore, it is customary to classify process innovations according to their effects on the (relative) quantities of inputs demanded. The basic possibilities are shown in Fig. 3.9, where we use shifts in a single isoquant to illustr   is classification. Different writers have used varying assumptions about the

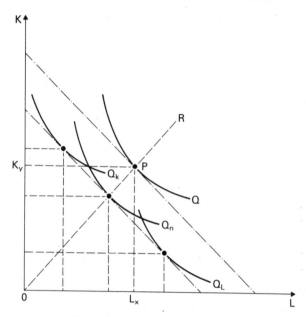

FIG. 3.9 Types of process innovation.

detailed effects of the shifts on the factors of production, but for purposes of our survey the concepts shown in the diagram are sufficient.

Isoquant Q represents the initial conditions of technology. The optimal technique is given by the isoquant's tangency with the isocost line at P, and the relevant process ray is OR. The amounts of inputs utilized are OK_y and OL_x, respectively. Now consider a process innovation that moves the isoquant to the new position Q_n. The new optimal input combination still lies on the process ray OR. The change resulted in a proportional reduction in capital and labor requirements, but the economically efficient technique has remained the same. Such a shift is referred to as a *neutral technological advance*. Instead of producing output Q at reduced total cost, the firm could have obtained a larger output with the original budget, in which case we would have to re-label isoquant Q to reflect this fact.

Take next the possibility illustrated by the new isoquant Q_k. Here the new optimal input combination lies above the original process ray. The labor input has been reduced and the capital input increased. We are dealing with a *labor-saving advance*. Note that any shift of the original isoquant to a tangency point above the old process ray but below K_yP would have meant that less capital was used as well, but the dominant effect still would have been a shifting of the isoquant toward the capital axis. By analogous argument we can show that the new isoquant Q_L represents a *capital-saving advance*.

Even this simple classification of technological changes raises some interesting questions. We assumed that our individual firm had no influence on input prices. But what if the innovation is diffused among many firms? We may expect that relative input prices will change and that this will affect the further decisions of firms that have not yet adopted the process innovation. Obviously, this kind of dynamic adjustment process could take many different directions and therefore cannot be analyzed in a simple model. Furthermore, what will be the effect of non-neutral advances on the income shares of the factors of production? Again, this depends on many variables that lie outside the scope of our model. And finally, how will the economic results of the innovations just undertaken influence the attitudes of decision-makers toward further possible advances, i.e., their future strategic decisions?

These and other questions arise, but they must remain open unless one expands one's view beyond the framework of the microeconomic theory of process innovations. No wonder that one critic has referred to this theory as "nothing more than a hodge-podge of suggestions."[4] In our efforts to gain a better understanding of innovation, we shall have to go beyond the structure of worked-out models. We hope to make up for the resulting loss in neatness and apparent precision by being able to gain at least some grasp of the complexities of industrial decisions involving changes in technology. Here we shall take just a few initial steps in this direction.

3.4   Theory and the Industrial Setting

Nothing would be gained by constructing a lengthy checklist of the assumptions of microeconomic theory that are unlikely to hold for real-life firms. As the late Professor Fritz Machlup argued very persuasively, different analytical goals demand different definitions of the firm as a decision-making entity.[5] Given our observation at the beginning of this chapter that the microeconomic theory of production is aimed more at explaining the market behavior of firms than their internal input–output structure, we are justified, however, in asking the question: "Do firms behave in input and output markets in a fashion that conforms to the predictions of the theory?"

The answer to this question, with all due allowances, has to be affirmative. Regardless of how production and innovation decisions are made and carried out inside what, for the theory, is no more than a "black box," firms on the whole and on average do react in expected ways. When relative input prices change or are expected to change, firms will attempt to make the appropriate substitutions within the framework of existing technology. Certainly, industrial responses to sharply rising energy prices in the 1970s illustrate this point. When total costs change relative to the revenues that can be obtained at prevailing prices, firms will make the necessary short-run adjustments in output. When prices are kept from tending toward their equilibrium levels, decisions of firms on techniques and outputs will result in inefficient allocations of resources. And market signals will have a strong influence on the strategies of firms with respect to the nature and direction of technological changes. In all these respects, then, the microeconomic theory is quite powerful.

We know, however, that in striving for technical and economic efficiency, firms encounter problems which lie entirely outside the structure of the theoretical models. Some of these problems arise from the environment in which firms have to operate and about which they never have the kind of full information we have postulated so far. Others are inherent in the firms' own organization, decision-making procedures, and in the *technological specificity* of their existing operations. By this term we mean the more or less unique way in which each firm, as a going concern, incorporates plant and equipment of differing vintages, different production flows, different product mixes, and different levels of experience with technology.

3.4.1   *The Problem of Uncertainty*

Only rarely do decision-makers in firms think that they have all the information they need for a decision. In some cases, decisions may be taken under conditions of *risk*, in the technical sense of that term, i.e., where there exists a statistical record sufficient to indicate the probability of certain outcomes. For example, short-run production targets may be set, based on accumulated data on what proportion of total output meets certain quality standards and what proportion will have to be rejected. We shall not be concerned with problems of this type.

Virtually all of the decisions we shall deal with are taken under conditions of *uncertainty*. Uncertainty does not mean ignorance! Rather, it involves information that is piecemeal, qualitative as well as quantitative, and based on experiential judgment as much as on formal analysis. This kind of decision-making is not, in other words, a matter of plugging known data into well-established formulae. In fact, what we have already called *strategic decision-making* always involves uncertainty in this sense. Moreover, it may even involve *conflict*, i.e., situations where a firm might expect its own moves to be met by the targeted counter-moves of a competitor.

Information-gathering itself is an economic activity. If this activity were guided strictly by the usual criteria of rational behavior, managements would decide to make decisions at the point where the marginal cost of obtaining additional information is equal to the expected marginal benefits of this information. But such a view of the problem of uncertainty ignores the fact that the generating and processing of information in an organization is subject to a host of influences, not the least of which are the personal goals and interests of the people involved. In the realm of technological innovation, particularly, we would expect these intra-firm factors to play a major role. Whether a given project is carried to success or not will depend to a considerable extent on the willingness and ability of top decision-makers to live with ambiguity and to overcome resistance to change within their organizations.

In the face of these characteristics of the decision process, one school of thought has hypothesized that firms do not, in fact, try to optimize on anything—output, or sales, or profit, or techniques. Instead, managements settle for what has been called "satisficing," the achievement of standards of performance that will assure the long-term survival of the firm, under the constraint that the owners (shareholders) earn an acceptable rate of return on their investment.[6] While this hypothesis contradicts the assumptions of traditional microeconomic theory, it has received a lot of attention from economists who are interested in what goes on *inside* that black box, the firm. Whether he or she believes that satisficing provides a complete alternative explanation, the student of the economics of innovation certainly cannot be very comfortable with profit (or rate of return) maximization as *the* explanation of how decision-makers in complex organizations evaluate alternative courses of action.[7]

3.4.2   *The Cost of Change*

Even if all necessary information were available, changes in an ongoing production system would involve considerable costs. For example, any major shift in technique will mean discarding old equipment and acquiring new. It may also mean disruptions in the flow of production and modifications in other parts of a firm. It is not surprising, therefore, that managements frequently show a preference for minor and incremental improvements in processes and products, rather than for major innovations. In many instances the cost of change may extend over long periods of time, as in situations where *learning* is required before the full economic benefits of new capital equipment can be reaped. We may think of learning in this connection as the process of acquiring the know-how required to make a new operation function smoothly.

Innovations and changes in technique often involve a second type of explicit and implicit costs, which are borne by individuals in an organization. Most obviously, people may fear that their jobs or their current level of incomes are threatened by a change. Equally serious, however, may be perceptions of losses in responsibility and status, even if these have no monetary implications. As we shall see in our later exploration of the diffusion process, overcoming resistance to change within a firm can be a major problem.

3.4.3   *Heterogeneity of Inputs*

Firms do not acquire essentially uniform "service-units" of inputs. They hire workers of varying abilities, not man-hours. They purchase materials, such as coal, steel or rubber, which only to an outsider look like homogeneous inputs, but which in fact come in hundreds of different specifications. And when firms invest in production equipment, they have to choose among various kinds of "machine-hours," each with its own characteristics.

It is interesting to note, however, that once such decisions have been made, managers, plant superintendents and shop foremen are generally evaluated by how well they can make these inputs perform *as though they were homogeneous*. Thus, for example, a competent foreman who runs a shop with machines of different vintages and capabilities will assign the most experienced workers to the oldest machines and the least experienced to the newest. As a result, output per man-hour among workers may not differ as much as one might expect on the basis of their varying skill levels. An economist stated the more general position very succinctly: " . . . an efficiently managed firm employing out-moded capital equipment may achieve lower operating costs than a poorly managed firm using modern equipment."[8]

When it comes to the acquisition of new capital equipment, firms are confronted by a host of trade-offs. General-purpose machinery may offer great flexibility, but it will also require careful tending and control. Highly product-specific machinery offers great productivity, but it becomes obsolete when major changes in the product are required. For example, it was little consolation to American automobile manufacturers that they had the world's most highly specialized and therefore most efficient plants for producing V-8 engines when market demand changed to smaller, four- and six-cylinder engines.

A given new machine may have capacity well beyond that of the rest of a plant, but it may be cheaper to carry along this excess capacity than to make piecemeal additions later on, if output has to be increased. Is it cheaper completely to rebuild an old machine than to buy an up-to-date one? Can we adjust materials flow in such a way as to utilize the capabilities of a machine with high production rates? What are the costs and benefits of installing two smaller units instead of one large unit? Are there technological advances in prospect that make it advisable to wait a while before buying any new equipment?

These and many other questions have to be addressed before decisions on capital investment can be made. Even if all other inputs were more or less homogeneous, the aggregate effects of these decisions over time would still create substantial differences in the performance of plants and firms. While our concept of the choice of techniques is valid in such a setting, this choice clearly involves many more variables than could be included in any generalized model. Nevertheless, the theory of production enables us better to understand the complexity of decision-making in the industrial setting.

3.4.4   *Levels of Effort and Performance*

In specifying a relationship between inputs and outputs, the production function abstracts from the question at what level of effort activities are carried out. In actual practice, however, this is an important concern of management. Regardless of how we define effort, the maintenance of some sustainable rate of operations is generally regarded as preferable to erratic fluctuations in

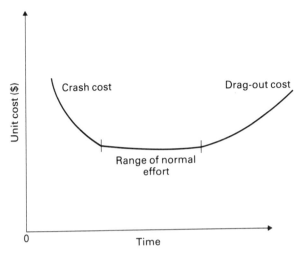

FIG. 3.10 Effect of task time on unit cost.

intensity. This is true not only for manufacturing operations themselves, but also for all other aspects of productive activity. Here we want to discuss just a few illustrative examples.

(a) *Effort and Unit Cost.* We cannot meaningfully assess the resource costs of producing a certain quantity of output in terms of the quantities of physical inputs only, because the time allowed for production is another influence on these costs. Figure 3.10 shows the relationship, for a given level of output, between unit costs and the time taken to produce this output. The unit costs resulting from "crash programs" are typically higher than the costs of producing at what might be considered a more normal level of effort. On the other hand, unit costs will increase again when a job is dragged out too long. Ideally, then, managements would like to plan all activities such that they can be accomplished in the normal-effort range. But things do not always work out that way. When there are unexpected delays in the delivery of input materials but production deadlines have to be met, it may well be necessary to intensify efforts beyond the normal range. When one of the firm's best customers demands, as the saying goes, "delivery yesterday," there may be no choice but to incur the additional cost of satisfying him. When a manufacturing problem requires completion of an R&D project for its solution, crash costs may be no consideration.

(b) *Managerial Effort and Production Flows.* Maintenance of a steady flow of activity requires that all necessary inputs be available at all times. For example, inventories of materials and semi-finished products can uncouple successive production stages, so that an interruption at any one stage does not cause others to come to a halt. But holding inventories involves an opportunity cost, because part of the firm's financial resources is tied up in these stocks of work in process. More careful planning and coordination may well eliminate some of this investment. In fact, inventories have been called a substitute for management: in a perfectly-run system, no more materials and parts would be on hand than are required to keep the pipeline of production filled. Such perfection may be difficult to achieve, but recent advances in production management, like the much-discussed Japanese "just-in-time" delivery system, show a recognition of the trade-off between planning and coordination on the one hand, and cost-effective production flows on the other.

(c) *Effort and Learning.* We have already defined learning as the acquisition of know-how through experience in production. Here managements confront yet another trade-off: If the tasks of individuals are narrow and highly specialized, little effort may be required to become proficient at these tasks, and the effects of learning (e.g., in higher output per hour) may show up quickly. But highly specialized, routine work may also lead to boredom and indifference, with the result that higher output rates are offset by declines in quality. Less narrowly defined jobs may require prolonged periods of learning, but better quality control and greater worker satisfaction may be the pay-off. These problems have been very much in the forefront of managerial attention. For example, many mass-production firms have watched the outcome of the Volvo Experiment, in which teams of workers are given the job of building whole automobile engines instead of having each worker perform one routine task on an assembly line.

We could add more examples of the relationship between effort and performance, but the point is made: Managements have a lot of influence on the economic results achieved within the framework of a particular set of techniques by designing systems that encourage satisfactory levels of effort from everyone concerned. In addition to these issues in the design of production methods and production flows, performance will also hinge on such psychological factors as motivation, job satisfaction and the firm's "work climate", but these are beyond the industrial economist's purview.

3.4.5 *Heterogeneity of Firms and Outputs in an Industry*

We may think of an industry as a group of firms relying on the same basic technology to produce recognizably similar outputs. While this definition may sound somewhat vague, it is adequate for our purposes. In each specific case, we can probably agree on what we are talking about when we speak of the aircraft industry, the shoe industry, or the food-canning industry[9].

By this definition we also recognize that individual, multiplant firms may be members of several industries. Although this fact may pose problems for other purposes, including statistical classification, it will not cause us any difficulties in our investigations of technological change. The "similar outputs" of the members of an industry are of course not the same as the homogeneous output assumed by the theory of production. Therefore it is not surprising that firms of varying size, using greatly different processes in the manufacture of differentiated products, can co-exist and prosper in the same industry. Their economic success is determined not only by their choice of techniques and by their costs, but also by their ability to satisfy a demand for some particular combination of product characteristics. If this were not so, we would have great difficulty in explaining why countries would be simultaneously exporting and importing products in the same industrial category, such as automobiles or machine tools. It would also be hard to explain how a manufacturer like Rolls Royce can hold its own in the market against mass-producers of automobiles.

To us, the interesting question is by what strategies, technological or other, firms manage to succeed in this kind of setting. At the same time, we want to understand how the evolution of technologies influences their behaviour. Competitive survival in an industry whose technology is relatively mature, such as the automobile industry, would seem to require strategies different from those in a young and technologically turbulent industry like minicomputers. These are matters to which we shall return in considerable detail.

In order to complete our initial survey, we must mention one additional feature of real-life industrial production and competition: In production theory, the assumption of a homogeneous product means that the firms in each industry compete for a market defined by that product. But if we recognize that the products of several industries can satisfy the demand for a given set of characteristics, we note the possibility of interindustry as well as intraindustry competition. Thus, for example, the past decade has seen a fierce struggle among several industries for the beverage-container market. The basic functional requirements for such containers are met by tin cans, aluminum cans, glass bottles, plastic bottles, and paper products. Firms in each of the respective industries have invested heavily in research and development in order to gain a larger market share. And firms not yet in the market may be preparing themselves for entry. Clearly, if we want to understand the nature of technological innovations in any one of these industries, we have to look at developments in the relevant market.

This brief list of real-life factors we must consider in our study suggests that many of the observations probably cannot be put into the neat diagrams of production theory. Nevertheless, the theory provides us with some very useful concepts and with a basic framework for our analyses. Beyond this, there begins the difficult and grubby work of dealing with the actual behavior of firms and industries in the face of changing technologies and shifting markets.

Notes

1. Only under these assumptions can we speak of *the firm* as a decision-making unit. In fact, of course, *people in firms* make decisions, and their views of what is rational may vary.
2. As we shall see in our discussion of the diffusion of innovations, firms making a change to a new technique frequently modify or adapt the technique in ways that lead to a transformation of an innovation over time.

3. For an excellent summary, see Blaug, M., "A Survey of the Theory of Process-Innovations," *Economica*, February 1963; reprinted in Rosenberg. N., *The Economics of Technological Change* (Baltimore, MD.: Penguin Books, 1971).

4. *Ibid.*

5. Machlup, F., "Theories of the Firm: Marginalist, Behavioral, Managerial," *American Economic Review*, March 1967.

6. The satisficing hypothesis, although elaborated by many writers, was first proposed by Professor Herbert Simon. See his *Models of Man* (New York: John Wiley & Sons, 1957) and "Theories of Decision Making in Economics," *American Economic Review*, June 1959.

7. A growing number of economists have argued that useful insights into the decision-making of firms can be gained only be going *inside* these organizations instead of treating them as monolithic entities. See for example, Leibenstein, H., "A Branch of Economics is Missing: Micro-Micro Theory," *Journal of Economic Literature*, June 1979.

8. Salter, W. E. G., *Productivity and Technical Change* (Cambridge: Cambridge University Press, 1960), p. 88.

9. Most government statistics organize data on industries according to the *Standard Industrial Classification* (SIC). This is a scheme that assigns approximately 5,000 products of the manufacturing sector to the industries primarily responsible for their output. The classification is by numbers and goes from the 2-digit level (Major Industry Groups) to 3-digit Industry Groups and then to 4-digit Industries. Thus, for example, the Industry 3541 – Metal-cutting Machine Tools – belongs to the Industry Group 354 – Metalworking Machinery – and again to the Major Industry Group 35 – Machinery, except electrical.

CHAPTER 4

Returns to Scale, Scale Economies, and Technological Change

In the preceding chapter we emphasized the fact that the choice of technique and capacity by a firm generally involves more than a transitory selection of economically efficient input combinations, which can be changed readily in the face of shifts in relative input prices or in demand for the firm's output. In the vast majority of cases, this choice will mean a commitment to a certain type and size of production system, which typically is defined by investment in fixed capital.

In this chapter, we shall explore the implications of the decision to build or acquire plant and equipment of a certain size, embodying specific techniques. In order to do so, we shall first look at the nature of *returns to scale* or *physical scale effects*, i.e., changes in input–output relationships as a result of variations in the size of systems; then we turn to what economic theory has to say about *economies of scale*, i.e. the cost effects of size, and we shall consider the nature of these effects in the industrial setting. Finally, we show that changes in the scale of operations are intricately connected with changes in technology.

4.1 Basic Concepts

Economists have long been interested in problems of bigness in industrial production and its consequences for plants, firms, industries, and markets. Originally, concern was mainly with efficiency gains that might result from large-scale operations, such as the advantages of specialization. Later on, the apparent tendency for modern firms to become larger and larger triggered an interest in the effects of this tendency on competition. More recently a number of additional issues have moved to the forefront, among them the following: the effects of large production units on resource use; the environmental impact of heavy concentrations of industrial activity; the often seemingly greater safety risks associated with large units; the ability of big systems to respond flexibly to changes in technology or in competitive conditions; and the effects of industrial giants on international economic and political relations.

In the context of these varying concerns, the term, bigness, is used in several meanings. Here we want to concentrate on just one of these, the size of production systems and its effect on costs. For our purposes, it will be useful to distinguish three levels of analysis:

(1) The size of a *production unit*, i.e. a single machine, pipeline, container, or other such device;

(2) the size of a *plant*, which we define as a purposeful, integrated arrangement of production units of various types; and

(3) the size of a *firm*, an entity controlled by some central decision-making body, but which may encompass more than one plant.

One's specific interests determine how one uses these concepts. In analyzing scale effects in commercial air transportation, for example, one may wish to consider each airplane as analogous to a plant, while total scale economies may be more properly observed at the level of an individual firm, since such factors as the selection of routes and the scheduling of flights will have a substantial effect on the actual size of the business. Conversely, an integrated steel mill may look like a single large plant, but for analytical purposes it is often treated as though it consisted of a separate blast-furnace plant, a steel-making plant, a rolling plant, and a finishing plant.

Technology and size interact in different ways at each of these levels. In the case of production units, a large machine is not simply a blown-up version of a small machine performing the same basic function; rather, the large machine is likely to embody different techniques. At the level of the plant, different sizes frequently imply different levels of *integration*, different ways of arranging the flow of materials and semi-finished products, and different methods of coordination and control. We have already referred to the uniqueness of each plant in this respect as its *technological specificity*. Finally, for multiplant firms relationships between technology and size will be reflected in the degree of specialization of individual plants in the same line of business on the one hand, and in the disembodied techniques of managing such more or less complex systems, on the other.

We have distinguished already between *returns to scale*, a technical concept, and *economies of scale*, a cost concept. The two need not go hand in hand or work in the same direction. For example, an improvement in the physical input–output relationships as a result of size increases may be offset by increasing operating and control costs. By contrast, economies of scale may also result from factors other than the technical advantages of bigness; if a large, multiplant firm can purchase inputs at quantity discounts, it will enjoy purely *pecuniary economies*.

We may further differentiate between *internal scale economies*, i.e., those connected with the size of a plant or firm, and *external economies*, which may result from such phenomena as the clustering at one location of several plants belonging to the same industry. In this situation, separate firms may provide services of various types to all plants at a lower cost than if each of them had to provide its own. Internal and external scale economies have their counterpart in *diseconomies of scale*, i.e., cost penalties attributable to bigness beyond a certain level.

4.2   The Theory of Scale Effects

In Chapter 3 (p. 48) we defined *constant, increasing, and decreasing returns to scale* for the case of a single technique. Although we restricted our definition of a technique to two inputs, we can say more generally that these concepts describe *what happens to output when all inputs are increased together*. Therefore they are also, by definition, *long-run* concepts—they deal with strategic decisions of the firm concerning plant size and technology.[1]

In Fig. 4.1, a–d, we illustrate the various scale effects, extended to the case of multi-process technologies, i.e., the production surface. Each of the possible configurations is shown as a perspective drawing of the input–output space, with the resulting isoquant maps added.

In economic theory, production systems with constant returns to scale have received the greatest attention. In mathematical terms, constant returns mean that we are dealing with linear homogeneous production functions, which have properties that make them relatively easy to manipulate algebraically. There is, of course, no reason to assume *a priori* that real-life technologies exhibit this characteristic. Whether they do or not is strictly an empirical question. Actual observation suggests that the variable-rate case may be the most common, i.e., that production systems enjoy increasing returns to scale up to some size, after which decreasing returns set in. On theoretical grounds alone one could cite *three basic reasons for increasing returns to scale*: specialization, dimensional effects, and indivisibilities.

The effects of *specialization* are readily seen. When productive tasks are broken down into smaller and smaller components of the overall job as plant size increases, we would expect output to increase more than proportionally with the increase in inputs. In terms of our production function, labor hours and machine hours are still combined according to a given technique, but in reality the nature of the labor and capital inputs is changed as the system becomes larger.

Dimensional effects explain why one large unit of capital might produce disproportionately more than a smaller unit. The notion derives from the simple physical fact that the capacity of certain types of equipment—vessels, containers, pipelines, and so on—will increase as a multiple of their exterior dimensions (and of the materials required for their manufacture). While these effects apply to individual components of a plant, we must not assume that they also automatically hold for the plant as a whole. We cannot derive general rules about increasing returns to scale, for example, from the geometric laws that govern the relationship between the surface and the volume of a container. This is a point to which we shall return in a later section.

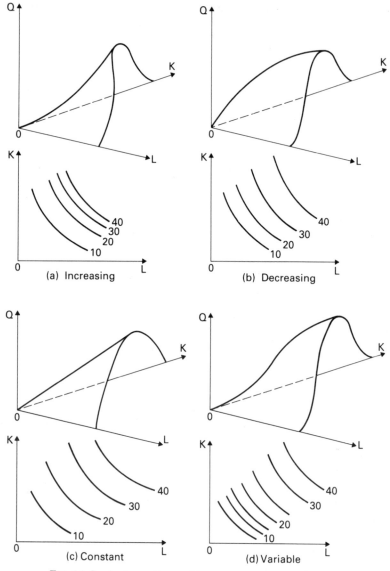

Fig. 4.1 Production surfaces and isoquants—returns to scale.

Indivisibilities are said to exist when certain inputs are available only in certain minimum sizes. One cannot buy half a fork lift or half a turret lathe, even if that is all that would be required for the current size of the rest of a plant. Therefore, if plant size is increased, no more of these essential inputs will have to be acquired; instead, the ones already in the system will now be utilized more fully. The British economist, Joan Robinson, provides a picturesque description of the concept:

"If all the factors of production were finely divisible, like sand, it would be possible to produce the smallest output of any commodity with all the advantages of large-scale industry. But actually, the factors consist of men, money capital, which is finely divisible like sand, but must be turned into instruments of production each of which, for technical reasons, must be of a certain size . . . in every case where increasing returns are found there must be some point in the process of production at which a single unit of a factor is engaged."[2]

The most obviously indivisible input is management. A manager may be able to run a larger plant just as easily as a smaller one. Beyond some size, however, he or she will have to delegate authority and responsibility; at this point, the consequences for managerial productivity are no longer clearcut. In fact, economic theory generally assumes that the increasing complexities of planning, coordinating, and controlling very large production systems are the most plausible explanation for *decreasing returns to scale*. As we shall see below, however, decreasing returns may also be explained by technological factors.

4.3 Economies of Scale

If we continue to assume that all inputs are in perfectly price-elastic supply to a firm, then the physical scale effects will be reflected in the position of the short-run average cost curves associated with various plant sizes. In other words, under this assumption and the assumption of a homogeneous product, decision-makers are able to choose among plants in terms of cost criteria only.

4.3.1 Economies Derived from Physical Input-Output Effects

Consider the problem illustrated in Fig. 4.2, where we show the short-run average cost curves for three plants, A, B, and C. Assume that each plant is

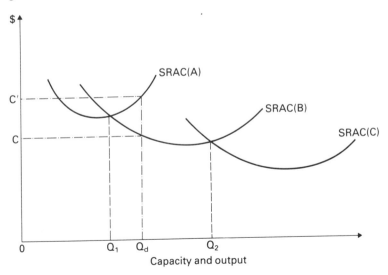

FIG. 4.2 Short-run average cost curves for three plant sizes.

capable of turning out the same product, by standard techniques. If decision-makers estimate that sales during the life of the plant are going to be in the range OQ_1, they would select Plant A, with cost curve SRAC(A). Plant B would have the lowest unit costs in the range Q_1–Q_2, and Plant C beyond Q_2.

Assume for example, that Plant A had been chosen, but that information about future demand was faulty and the quantity sold turns out actually to be OQ_d. In this case the plant would incur unit costs that are higher by amount CC' than they would have been if Plant B had been built. Clearly, for each discrete plant size, there exists a range of output and sales for which this plant has a short-run cost advantage over all others.

Assuming that there exists an unlimited number of possible plant sizes, up to some maximum, we can draw an envelope curve around the (infinite number of) short-run average cost curves (Fig. 4.3). This envelope is referred to as the *long-run average cost curve* (LRAC). Although this label has a long tradition in economic theory, it is somewhat unfortunate: the curve does not really show what happens to costs in the long run; rather, it reflects the cost structure resulting from the selection of various possible plant sizes, i.e. a *commitment for the long run*. Since the selection has to be made at a point in time, with a view toward future output requirements, the term *planning curve*, which is also used for the envelope, seems more appropriate.

Be that as is may, note that there is only one plant, the one with minimum short-run-cost output (i.e., design capacity) OQ^*, that represents the *long-run optimal plant size*. This concept may seem rather abstract unless one considers the conditions under which a given constellation of technology, optimal plant size, and market demand for an industry's output may raise the question as to how many such optimal plants there is room for in the market. The question assumes special importance in the case of the so-called *natural monopolies*, situations in which one firm (plant) can satisfy total demand in a given market at lower unit costs than could several smaller firms. The economic argument

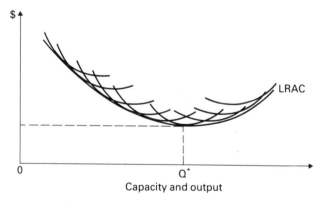

FIG. 4.3 Long-run average cost (planning) curve.

for granting a monopoly franchise to public utilities, for example, is based on this consideration.

The problem becomes more complicated if we take the argument just one step further: what if a firm has reached something approaching long-run optimal size and therefore has come to dominate a given market because of its own technological innovativeness? How does one balance the merits of competition against the apparent cost-efficiency of a proven leader? What assurance does one have that the leading firm will not take undue advantage of its monopoly position, once the smaller (less innovative?) competitors have been forced to exit from the market? These are questions with which economists and, more important, the courts have had to deal more frequently in recent years.[3]

4.3.2   Pecuniary Economies of Scale

Returning to Fig. 4.3, we would be able to explain the entire shape of the planning curve strictly in terms of the physical input–output effects we discussed in Section 4.2, above. In the variable returns to scale case, short-run costs would first decline with increases in plant size and then rise again as decreasing returns set in. However, we have already referred to the fact that large firms (or plants) also may enjoy purely *pecuniary economies of scale*. If such economies exist, we obviously have to drop the assumption that the firm can acquire all inputs at a given price, regardless of how many of them it acquires. When suppliers give quantity discounts on large orders of materials, when the firm can use its size to negotiate favorable contracts for the acquisition of capital goods, when it can obtain financial capital at a lower rate, or when it can pay lower wages to employees because it offers greater job security, then it will enjoy lower unit costs than smaller firms, even if its production system is no more efficient in input–output terms. In real life, of course, we would expect both types of effects to occur simultaneously.

4.3.3   Diseconomies of Scale

What can be said about the factors that cause the planning curve eventually to take on positive slope? We have mentioned already the possibility of *diminishing returns to management*. The argument here is that, no matter how variable all other inputs may appear to be in the long run, the planning, coordinating, and control of production in very large systems can become so difficult that inefficiencies and therefore increasing unit costs are the result. The existence of diminishing returns to management is entirely plausible if one assumes that an entire firm is run by an owner-entrepreneur; in a very large firm, he or she will eventually lose some measure of control over operations. One may suspect, however, that the same problem can exist as well in large publicly-held corporations with their teams of managers, layers of authority, and decision-making by committee. In such situations, minimization of unit costs for a given level of output may no longer be the overriding objective of anyone. Furthermore, cost data may well understate the managerial input into large systems, because (salaried) employees contribute working time well beyond what we have called the normal-effort range [see Chapter 3, p.63].

More generally, it is possible to argue that every one of the factors that is assumed to give rise initially to economies of scale may, beyond a certain plant size, result in diseconomies. Increasing specialization can mean that machines become so narrow in function that the breakdown of any one of them will bring production to a halt. To avoid this contingency, management may want to have stand-by equipment (i.e. excess capacity) on hand. Alternatively, the firm may have to buy components from outside suppliers at prices higher than its own costs. Or it may maintain large safety stocks of work-in-process, which serve to uncouple successive production steps and thus help to prevent stoppages in case of breakdowns. Increasing routinization of work may mean lessened worker performance, greater absenteeism, or a lower proportion of acceptable output. The consequence of all these possibilities would be a rise in the minimum short-run average costs of plants larger than the optimum. Finally, it may turn out that current technology is not sufficiently developed to permit size increases beyond a certain limit. Firms that push beyond such technological scale frontiers pay a price for their venturesomeness, in the form of higher unit costs. This is a matter to which we shall return in a subsequent section of this chapter.

4.4   Scale Effects in the Industrial Setting

Plausible as the theory of scale economies is, its conclusions have been difficult to verify in straightforward empirical fashion. There are two reasons for this state of affairs. First, the theory's assumptions about the nature of input–output relationships at varying plant sizes turn out to be overly narrow; some aspects of industrial operations that greatly complicate the picture are discussed in this section. And second, firms' cost accounting systems, designed for a host of other purposes, simply may not reveal the existence of scale economies. We shall not concern ourselves with these empirical problems, but it is worth mentioning that statistical studies generally have had to restrict themselves either to industries for which relevant data are available, such as electricity generation and other more or less transparent types of production, or to certain components of overall costs. In the latter category, interest has been focussed especially on *unit investment costs*, i.e., the behavior of fixed cost per unit of capacity with variations in the size of production units and plants.

When economists turned to general explanations of observed industrial behavior, they had to modify the restrictive framework of the theory and introduce additional factors that might contribute to economies or diseconomies of scale.[4] In a recent, comprehensive investigation of two dozen industries, Pratten[5] found that scale effects can take on the following "dimensions," as he calls them:

(1) The total output of particular products through time;
(2) the duration of production runs — the period through which a distinct product is made or produced before switching to the processing of another product;
(3) the rate of production of particular products per unit of time (the size of batches being determined by the duration of production runs and the rate of production);
(4) the extent of standardization of products;
(5) the capacities of units of plant, machines, and production lines within plants.
(6) the total capacity of individual plants;
(7) the overall size of a complex of plants at one site;
(8) the extent of vertical integration of a plant;
(9) the quantity (proportion) of output sold to each customer;
(10) the geographic concentration of customers; and
(11) the size of consignments (shipments) to each customer.

Not all of these dimensions are within the scope of the scale concept we have used. Thus, the duration of production runs may influence unit costs either through the number of units over which fixed costs are distributed at a given time, or through the effects of learning, i.e., the accumulation of know-how through experience in production over an extended period. The latter is important, but it has little or nothing to do with the size of facilities as such. Nonetheless, Pratten's list illustrates how complex the concept of scale becomes once one moves into the world of actual industrial performance. Despite this complexity, however, there are some empirically-based generalizations that should help us better to understand the behavior of firms and industries.

4.4.1 Product Differentiation

Unit costs are only part of the variables that determine a firm's profitability; the other part is the prices it obtains for its output. Therefore, if a small firm with high unit costs can differentiate its products in ways that permit it to charge a much higher price for them, then it would suffer no disadvantages of small scale. On the basis of this fact alone we can explain what would otherwise seem to fly in the face of the theory of scale economies — the profitable co-existence in the same industry of firms and plants of greatly varying sizes. In order to analyze industries in which we can observe such a divergence of sizes, we may have to introduce the notion of *strategic groups* of firms, i.e., groups whose members are in fact engaged in head-on competition. Thus, unit costs may be a key factor in competition among mass producers of furniture, but these producers would not consider custom cabinet-makers as their direct rivals, even though the latter belong to the same industry.[6]

4.4.2   Different Inputs and Techniques

Only rarely do large plants in an industry employ anything like the techniques used by smaller members of the same industry. The notion of some number of "capital services units," and with it the concept of techniques defined by capital-labor ratios, becomes very fuzzy. To be sure, one can imagine the theoretical possibility of a large plant that is no more than a multiple assemblage of the same types of labor and machinery to be found in a small plant, but in industrial reality such a situation would be difficult to find. There may be scale advantages even to assembling craftsmen, such as silversmiths, in one plant, but such "factories" surely are the exception in the modern industrial setting. Associated with each scale of production are equipment and labor skills most appropriate to that level of operations.

This observation also accounts for the fact that efforts at technological innovation are not necessarily aimed at larger and larger scales of equipment but may also try to reduce unit costs at plant sizes much lower than the alleged optimum. In the United States, for example, the deregulation of commercial air transport and the subsequent entry of new short-haul firms into the industry have stimulated the development of cost-efficient smaller aircraft than those traditionally used by trunk-line operators.

4.4.3   Wide Ranges of Efficient Output

To the extent that short-run average cost curves are not U-shaped, as shown in Fig. 4.2 above, but are essentially flat over considerable ranges of output (capacity utilization) there exist equally wide ranges of efficient output for plants of a given size. To a considerable degree, the shape and position of a plant's short-run cost curve are themselves the result of managerial decisions as well as being influenced by the particular technological characteristics of production.

To be sure, there are some processes, especially in the chemical and metallurgical industries, that will not function at all except within a narrow range of a plant's design capacity. In such instances, the short-run cost curve would be a very narrow U. But in many other cases, plant designers have considerable discretion: general-purpose machinery may not operate at the same low unit cost as highly product-specific equipment, but it will enjoy essentially level costs over a wide range, whereas the latter will quickly incur the penalties of operation below capacity. An automotive assembly line built to turn out 70 cars an hour would face totally unacceptable unit costs if it were run at the rate of 35 cars an hour! So-called flexible manufacturing systems, in whose development there has been much interest recently, are aimed precisely at reducing such technological constraints on cost behavior.

4.4.4 Imbalances among Production Stages

The theory of scale effects postulates that indivisibilities are the result of inherent technical characteristics of machinery and equipment. But in a vertical sequence of production stages within one plant, imbalances in the capacities of individual stages may be the result of deliberate managerial decisions. This is most obvious in cases where there has been piecemeal replacement of capital equipment over some period. However, even production units in a brand-new plant are frequently designed so that there exists excess capacity at certain stages. The key consideration here is a comparison of the expected costs of future additions to capacity with the cost of carrying the excess right from the beginning. Thus, in-plant storage facilities, cranes, paint shops, etc., may well be built in anticipation of eventual overall capacity expansion.

The point is best made with a practical example. Consider the four-stage plant illustrated by the flow diagram in Fig. 4.4. Each of the stages involves a unit (say, a certain type of machine) of the indicated capacity per time period. Obviously, this production system is out of balance. With one additional unit at Stage 1 and two more units at Stage 4, plant capacity could be increased to 600 units of output, with further excess capacity remaining only at Stage 3. With each of these expansions, the plant could be expected to achieve some scale economies, assuming no offsetting increases in other costs. Simple arithmetic shows that in our hypothetical plant the full effects of the (deliberate) indivisibilities could be absorbed only in a plant of 4200 units capacity.

Looked at in another way, the example also illustrates why the existence of "bottlenecks" in production seems to be such a frequent fact of life in industrial plants. Thus, there always are obvious places where an investment in additional equipment or a technological innovation improving existing equipment will yield increases in overall plant capacity. Conversely, it also shows why even a major process innovation affecting a given stage of production would be of no current interest to the management of a plant in which the stage is not a constraint on higher levels of output.

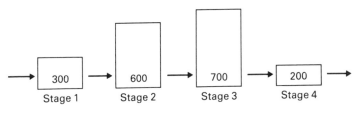

FIG. 4.4 Multi-stage production with different unit capacities.

4.4.5   The Role of Product Mix

As we mentioned at the outset of this discussion, the notion of a plant's total capacity also becomes ambiguous when we take changes of product mix into account. Such changes will most commonly be triggered by customers' orders or by shifts in the relative profitability (contribution margins) of a plant's various products. Therefore, a plant design that gives managements flexibility in responding to market opportunities is frequently preferred to one promising the lowest unit costs, but only at one particular product mix.

As a consequence, one often finds increasing amounts of what looks like excess capacity at production stages close to the finished-product end of a vertically integrated system. This enables decision-makers to shift semi-finished products into several types of finishing operations, not all of which will be fully utilized at any one time. Here, too, the concept of an optimal scale is confounded by managerial perspectives that go beyond the consideration of short-run costs associated with production units and plants of a given size.

4.4.6   Uncertainty and Rules of Thumb

Managerial decisions on technology and capacity are not made on the basis of hard data alone, nor are they always the result of intricate engineering calculations. Uncertainty is the rule in industrial decision-making. Thus it is not surprising that managers' receptivity to proposals for increases in equipment or plant sizes is often influenced by a basic faith in the technical and economic advantages of bigness.

Such a faith may be supported by supposedly tried-and-true rules of thumb, which can be applied in the absence of more specific information. An example is the often-encountered "power rule" for the rough estimation of the cost of new plants, especially in the materials-processing industries. Its origin has been explained as follows:

> "The rule has been adduced from the fact that for such items of equipment as tanks, gas holders, columns, compressors, etc., the cost is determined by the amount of material used in enclosing a given volume, i.e., cost is a function of surface area, while capacity is directly related to the volume of the container. Consider a spherical container. Its cost . . . varies as the capacity [raised] to the 2/3 power . . . If the container is cylindrical, then . . . cost varies as capacity raised to the 1/2 power if the volume is increased by changes in diameter, and if the ratio of height to diameter is kept constant, cost varies as capacity to the 2/3 power."[7]

Logical as application of this rule may be for certain types of production unit, there is no economic reason why it should apply to entire plants. Whether costs vary with size, and in which direction, depends on many factors having nothing to do with these purely dimensional effects. Nevertheless, to the extent that such rules of thumb are widely accepted, even if only for the proverbial "back of the envelope" calculations, they may reinforce decision-makers' belief in the intrinsic merits of bigness.

There is, however, one additional reason why a firm may build very large plants, without regard to implications for short-run costs: By having unutilized capacity in place, the firm hopes to discourage its competitors from considering expansion of their facilities. In the struggle for what are hoped to be growing markets, such *pre-emptive investment* may be an important strategic weapon.[8]

4.4.7 An Operational Definition of Scale

In our preceding discussion of the possible meaning of scale economies in the industrial setting, we have moved well beyond the description of these economies by means of a well-defined planning curve. At best, this curve may in fact be a wide band covering vertical as well as horizontal size-cost relationships. Nevertheless, it is a useful conceptual device, a kind of short-hand symbol for these relationships.

At the core of all the different dimensions of scale lie decisions with respect to the ways in which individual plants achieve targeted size-cost relationships through various designs for sub-dividing and organizing the work to be done. This fact is best captured by a proposed definition of scale as ". . . the level of planned capacity which has been determined by the extent to which specialization has been applied in the subdivision of component tasks of a unified operation."[9]

Note that according to this definition an increase in plant size need not insure an increase in scale. Conversely, such a scale increase could come about not just through the expansion of physical facilities, but also through changed organization and coordination, or through the allocation of plant resources to a different range of products. We conclude that the question as to which of the many dimensions of scale are relevant in a particular case cannot be answered except by reference to the economic and technological characteristics of the entity to be analyzed. The general theory of scale can give us no more than rough guidance in this endeavor.

4.5 Technological Change and Scale Effects

Everything we have said about the nature of scale effects in the industrial setting supports a conclusion that might not be obvious from the pure theory of scale: Large machines are not simply blown-up versions of small machines doing the same job, and large plants involve different techniques, different levels of specialization, and different modes of organization than do small ones. Therefore we want to consider the possible interactions between technological changes and changes in scale. Empirical observation suggests that causation works both ways. Efforts by firms to push out into previously untried levels of capacity raise technical problems and therefore stimulate invention and innovation. And technological breakthroughs may suddenly open the door for the design and construction of much larger plants than had previously been considered feasible, or they may push down unit costs at much lower capacities than had previously been thought economically viable.

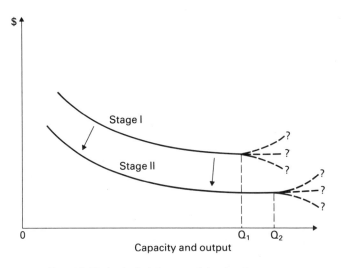

FIG. 4.5 Technological change and the planning curve.

If we deal with these interactions between technological advances and scale changes in terms of the planning curve (with all our reservations about the concept in mind), we can conceive of two types of effects. Figure 4.5 illustrates them in stylized fashion.

The first effect consists of an extension of the known *scale frontier*, i.e., a pushing out of the planning curve to the right. The second effect results from technological efforts at *scaling down* operations, i.e., a downward shift of the planning curve at capacity levels lower than the currently feasible optimum. A third possibility, not shown here, might be that the whole curve becomes flatter as a consequence of innovations, thus extending the range of capacities at which plants have essentially identical unit costs.

In our diagram, the Stage I planning curve terminates at capacity OQ_1, the capacity of the largest plant then in existence. The three dotted extensions of the curve are meant to suggest that beyond this scale frontier lies unknown territory. Whether further extensions of scale will result in economies or diseconomies is not known. In Stage II, technological progress is assumed to have affected plants of all sizes by reducing their unit costs. At the same time, the curve now extends to plants with a capacity as large as OQ_2. Beyond this, there is once again uncertainty about the behavior of unit costs.

To show these effects as occurring in identifiable stages is only an aid to our understanding. Most frequently, scale changes occur through a continuous nudging of the planning curve in both directions. Occasionally, however, we have examples of how a given level of technology poses definite limits to size increases and penalizes those firms who try to go beyond these limits through decreasing returns to scale. Such constraints can be broken only through major innovations which do create clear discontinuities (phase transitions) in development.

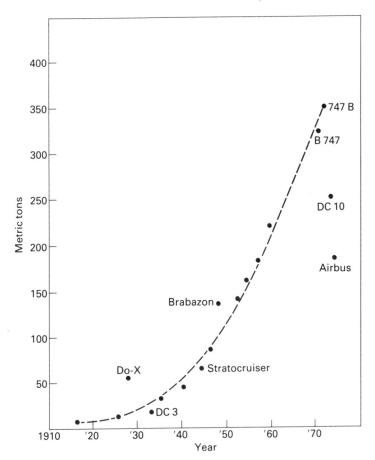

FIG. 4.6 Gross take-off weight of largest aircraft.
Source: Dathe, J. M., "Problems of Scale in International Air Transportation,"
paper prepared for a workshop on scale, International Institute for Applied Systems
Analysis, Laxenburg, Austria; June 1979.

The history of efforts to build larger and larger commercial aircraft provides
a good illustration [Fig. 4.6]. The gross take-off weight of planes is only one of
several indicators of scale, but it serves our purpose. As long as the piston
engine was the only available means of propulsion, designers faced a serious
problem: raising the capacity of planes required an increase in the number of
engines. But the weight of the engines and of the additional fuel they required
quickly led to a situation in which the capability of bigger planes to carry higher
payloads rose only marginally. In 1928, the German Dornier-X, a flying boat
sporting 12 engines, established a size record with a take-off weight of 52 tons.
Although several units were reportedly built, the aircraft remained strictly a
technical curiosity, as did a similar British effort, the Bristol Brabazon, in the
years after World War II. The development and rapid diffusion of the jet

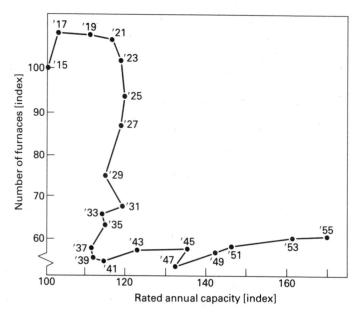

Fig. 4.7 Number of U.S. blast furnaces vs rated capacity, 1915-55 (Index, 1915 = 100).
Source: Gold, B., et al., *Technological Progress and Industrial Leadership* (Lexington, MA: Lexington Books, D. C. Heath, 1984), p. 474.

engine enabled aircraft builders to break through the weight-power barrier posed by the old technology. In less than 20 years, commercial aircraft with a capacity of up to 400 passengers had become the standard equipment of long-distance carriers, and costs per ton of payload had declined rapidly. While these developments took place at the scale frontier, technological innovations also improved the performance of aircraft whose sizes were well inside the frontier.[10]

Changes in the scale of operations may be motivated by efforts to rationalize production even if there is no great pressure to raise total capacity, or they may occur in response to increased demand for an industry's output. This point is illustrated by the history of American blast furnaces. In Fig. 4.7 we show how the number of production units and the industry's total capacity changed between 1915 and 1955; index numbers are used in order to focus on relative adjustments. We can distinguish two phases of development. From 1915 until the outbreak of World War II, firms were engaged mainly in replacing small furnaces with new, scaled-up units. During this period, total capacity increased by roughly 15 per cent, but the number of furnaces declined by almost 50 per cent. Thereafter, a very rapid expansion of industry capacity was achieved via a small increase in the number of units, as a variety of technological innovations enabled firms to build more efficient furnaces.[11]

An example of successful scaling-down occurred during the past two decades in the iron and steel industry. While Japanese firms pushed the annual capacity of large, integrated steel mills well beyond previously tried levels, to over 9 million tons, the rapid development of electric-furnace steelmaking technology made stand-alone plants of 400,000 to 1 million tons an economically attractive proposition. As a consequence, approximately 40 new "minimill" firms entered the United States steel industry since 1960. Most of them are operating profitably at a time when the large traditional producers face serious economic difficulties.

Pioneering forays beyond the known scale frontier involve technical and economic risks. Therefore, construction of such large plants is frequently marked by cost over-runs beyond original estimates. And their operation initially may result in unit costs that are higher than for plants inside the frontier. In such cases, managements obviously have every incentive to bring about changes and adaptations that will reduce these costs. The *learning curve* is meant to reflect the effects of accumulated experience on unit costs, but it is important to realize that such experience typically is not the only source of improvements. Modifications of equipment and additional investments are frequently required to validate expectations about the benefits of previously untried scales of operation. It is not uncommon to find that, after some time, operating results are better than anticipated. In such cases, the rated capacity of new, large plants is upgraded.

All these observations suggest that efforts to separate scale changes from technological changes can be justified only by analytical convenience. In practice, they are closely interconnected. Virtually every expansion of an industrial operation beyond previously tried limits involves the solution of technical problems. And it is rare to find product or process innovations that do not affect the capacities of individual production units or of whole plants, and therefore the scale of operations.

4.6   Scale Economies in Multi-Plant Firms

Our discussion so far has focussed on scale effects at the level of production units and single-plant firms. There remains the question whether the existence of large multi-plant firms can be explained at least partly in terms of scale economies that differ from those observed at the plant level. This issue is important mainly because it lies at the core of public, governmental, and judicial attitudes toward the large corporations that typify modern industry. The resolution of many antitrust problems as well as evaluations of the effectiveness of various types of regulation hinge on the answers. Interest has been heightened in recent years by the rapid growth of multinational firms with their worldwide networks of production and distribution facilities.

Even if the empirical evidence on scale economies in large firms were clear-cut (which it is not), there would still be room for controversy. This is so because evaluations must be concerned not only with the *static efficiency* of such firms, but also with their *dynamic efficiency*, i.e., their ability to initiate or respond to changes in technology or in input and output markets. Since we have no straightforward quantitative indicators of dynamic efficiency, arguments about it remain contentious. Here we want to do no more than to list some of the pros and cons in these arguments:

(1) Large, multi-plant firms can use superior techniques of production and more effective means for coordinating activities than small ones.

But: large firms may turn into bureaucratic structures whose *potential* efficiency may be high, but whose actual performance is characterized by inflexibility, sluggishness, and conservatism. They may possess all the trappings of modern technology, but they do not use it in optimal fashion.

(2) Large firms are able to centralize many managerial and staff functions, thus reaping the benefits of fully utilizing indivisible inputs.

But: such centralization may itself contribute to rigidities by reducing initiative and responsibility at the level of individual plants.

(3) Large firms are better able to diversify the risks of business, by not having "all their eggs in one basket."

But: it is precisely this kind of diversification that makes them less sensitive to the signals of the marketplace.

(4) Large firms can invest in large, well-equipped R&D facilities, and they can work on many projects simultaneously; small firms are typically unable to do so.

But: there is no evidence that simply spending more will bring better results. Besides, we do not know whether there are any scale economies in research.

(5) Large firms enjoy economies in marketing and distribution that give them great advantages over smaller businesses.

But: they may use these advantages for no better purposes than to shift market shares among themselves, thus wasting resources.

(6) Because of their ability to purchase inputs in bulk quantities, large firms benefit from lower prices, which ultimately translate themselves into lower unit costs.

But: if such firms sell their products in oligopolistic markets, there is no reason to assume that lower unit costs will also mean lower prices for customers.

No doubt we could extend this list of arguments and counter-arguments, but the point is made: none of them can be resolved on purely theoretical grounds, and many of them are not subject to empirical verification. Their detailed examination and evaluation must be left to economists working in the field of industrial organization.[12]

From our perspective, the most important question is whether the existence of large, dominant firms has an effect on the chances of newcomers to enter an industry. If new firms with new products or new techniques are able to challenge the market position of even the most entrenched giants, then we would regard this as the most important single assurance of an economy's long-run efficiency. If, on the other hand, we observe that existing businesses, whether singly or in concert, attempt to prevent the entry of new competitors into their markets, we would not expect the economy to function anywhere near an optimal level. Most disturbing in this respect has been the tendency of large, politically influential corporations to engage in what has become known as "rent-seeking," i.e., efforts to obtain governmental protection for their industries and markets. The variety of protective measures has been limited only by the ingenuity of business executives, union leaders of the industries in question, legislators, and regulators. In recent years, there has been growing concern about the effects of government policies, many of which are aimed at sheltering existing interests, on the innovativeness and therefore the international competitiveness of American industry. These are matters to which we shall have to return on several occasions in our discussions of the political and economic climate for technological change.

Notes

1. A comprehensive review of the theory can be found in Gold, B., "Changing Perspectives on Size, Scale, and Returns: An Interpretive Survey," *Journal of Economic Literature*, March 1981.
2. Robinson, J., *The Economics of Imperfect Competition* (London: Macmillan, 1933), p. 334.
3. A set of short essays on this issue is collected in Mansfield, E., ed., *Monopoly Power and Economic Performance* (New York: Norton, 1968). A more comprehensive treatment can be found in Machlup, F., *The Political Economy of Monopoly* (Baltimore, MD: Johns Hopkins Press, 1952).
4. The classic work in this vein is Clark, J. M., *Studies in the Economics of Overhead Costs* (Chicago: University of Chicago Press, 1923), especially Chapter VI, "How and Why Large Plants Bring Economy."
5. Pratten, C. F., *Economies of Scale in Manufacturing Industry* (London: Cambridge University Press, 1971), pp. 8-9.
6. Here as in many other such situations, our empirical assessments are often captive to the official statistics, whose definition of an industry does not take these matters into consideration.
7. Moore, F. T., "Economies of Scale: Some Statistical Evidence," *Quarterly Journal of Economics*, May 1959.
8. See, for example, Gold, B., "Evaluating Scale Economies: The Case of Japanese Blast Furnaces," *Journal of Industrial Economics*, September 1974.
9. Gold, B., *Foundations of Productivity Analysis* (Pittsburgh, PA: University of Pittsburgh Press, 1955), p. 116.
10. Interactions between technological changes and scale increases in the aircraft industry are discussed in detail by Phillips, A., "Air Transportation in the United States," in Capron, W. M., ed., *Technological Change in Regulated Industries* (Washington, DC: The Brookings Institution, 1971). For an integration of the various factors determining the scale of commercial air transport, see Nicol, D. J., "Determining the Capacity of a Transportation System—Passenger Airlines," *Omega*, October 1980.
11. A comprehensive review of these developments is presented in Gold, B., Peirce, W. S., Rosegger, G., and Perlman, M., *Technological Progress and Industrial Leadership: The Growth of the U.S. Steel Industry, 1900–1970* (Lexington, MA: Lexington Books, D. C. Heath, 1984), Ch. 16-18. See also Boylan, M. G., *Economic Effects of Scale Increases in the Steel Industry: The Case of U.S. Blast Furnaces*, (New York: Praeger, 1975).
12. An excellent treatment of these issues can be found in Scherer, F. M., *Industrial Market Structure and Economic Performance*, 2nd ed. (Chicago, IL: Rand McNally, 1980).

Appendix: A Note on Learning

Pratten's *dimensions of scale* (pp. 75, above) include two sets of independent variables as determinants of scale effects—the size, capacity or structure of production facilities *and* the length of production runs or the cumulative volume of output. We pointed out that the latter are time-related variables and therefore do not fit into the traditional theory of scale. Nevertheless, improvements in productivity and reductions in units costs as a result of experience in production are often observed in industrial practice.

The concept of *learning curves* or *progress functions* was developed to evaluate these effects empirically. Different forms of these functions have been explored, but one of the most common is the following:

$$L/Q = A(\Sigma\, Q)^{-r},$$

where L/Q is the labor input per unit of output, and A and $r < 1.0$ are constants. The kind of effect described by this function was first studied in detail during World War II. It was found, for example, that every doubling of the output of specific types of airframes resulted in a 15 per cent reduction in labor requirements per airframe.

The notion that one becomes better at doing a job as one gains experience is an inherently plausible one. And since the resulting curves tend to look like planning curves, it is not surprising that the two concepts are often treated as though they were one and the same. Note, however, that the statistical results obtained from formulations like the one above do not tell us anything about *how* the observed improvements were achieved, nor may we conclude that these improvements automatically led to analogous reductions in unit costs. Empirical studies show that improved worker skills alone generally do not explain observed learning effects, but that many other experimental adjustments play a role as well. Thus, changes in work layout and work flow, in materials handling, and in the set-up of machines are frequently found to affect performance in production.

Furthermore, many of these adjustments involve additional outlays, so that one should not necessarily expect corresponding declines in unit costs. Especially in connection with entirely new technologies, such reductions most frequently come from other experience-based sources: reductions in the amount of down-time due to unexpected troubles with equipment and processes, as well as increases in the proportion of output that meets specifications. A perfect example of the latter is the manufacture of electronic chips; initially, an acceptance rate of 7 to 10 per cent of output (or conversely, a scrap rate of 90 per cent!) was considered standard performance. Substantial drops in unit costs accompanied the steady improvement in the acceptance rate as producers accumulated experience.

In a study of the effects of a new technique in steelmaking, continuous casting, on the performance of a plant,[1] the author found the effects shown in

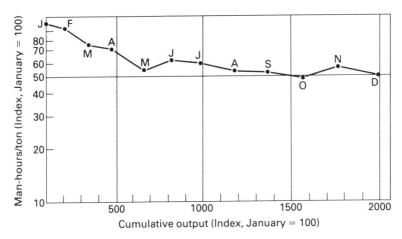

Fig. 4.A.1 Effects of cumulative experience in production on man-hour requirements per unit of output, first 12 months after introduction of a new process (Ratio scale; indices, January = 100).
Source: Adapted from Gold, B., Rosegger, G., and Boylan, M. G., *Evaluating Technological Innovations* (Lexington, MA: Lexington Press—D. C. Heath, 1980), pp. 197-201.

Fig. 4.A.1. Here man-hour requirements per ton of output are plotted against cumulative production for the first 12 months after commercial start-up. By the end of the period, these requirements were approximately half of what they had been at the outset. Detailed investigation showed that a whole host of factors contributed to this improvement. Especially noteworthy for our understanding of learning effects is the fact that progress did not occur along the smooth path suggested by the learning function. Rather, improvements came in fits and starts. Twice during the period production was pushed "too hard," with the result that previous reductions in man-hour requirements could not be sustained. Only by retrenching until further experience had been gained could management get the man-hour-per-ton curve back on its downward trend. Parallel cost studies found that the greatest benefits were derived from increases in the yield of the process, i.e., from a rise in the ratio of usable output to total output. Needless to say, the rate of improvement achieved in the first year after the introduction of a new technique typically cannot be kept up for very long.

The concept of the *experience curve* has been expanded well beyond its original frame of reference to include the more general, long-term effects of working with a given set of processes and products. Thus, for example, one notable investigation[2] traced the trend in the price of Ford's Model T from its introduction in 1909 to 1923. By that time, over 7 million units had been produced, and the (inflation-corrected) price had dropped from approximately $3,500 to around $1,000. The study also points out the limits and hazards of strategies aimed at achieving this kind of improvement: at some point, the production system has been honed to such a high level of efficiency in turning out a particular product that (a) the cost of achieving any further improvements becomes progressively higher, and (b) the system becomes very rigid and therefore unable to adapt to major changes in market demand or in the behaviour of competitors. This was, in essence, the fate of the Ford Motor Company, which took a long time recovering from its staunch commitment to the Model T.

More recently, similar improvements have been observed in the prices of integrated circuits and in the cost per bit of computer memory.[3] These findings show, however, that the notion of learning clearly has been taken beyond its original context, to include the effects of technological progress in general. These are matters we shall consider separately.

Notes

1. Gold, B., Rosegger, G., and Boylan, M. G., *Evaluating Technological Innovations: Methods, Expectations, and Findings* (Lexington, MA: Lexington Books—D. C. Heath, 1980), Ch. 10.
2. Abernathy, W. J., and Wayne, K., "Limits of the Learning Curve," *Harvard Business Review*, September-October 1974.
3. Ayres, R. U., *The Next Industrial Revolution* (Cambridge, MA: Ballinger, 1984), pp. 92 and 147.

CHAPTER 5

The Evaluation of Industrial Performance[1]

In the two preceding chapters we were concerned with what economists call *ex ante* models, i.e., with prescriptions of *how firms ought to act at a point in time*, under given assumptions, when confronted with certain information. But once a management has made and implemented decisions, it does not know whether the outcomes were optimal in the sense which theory postulates. *Ex post* (after the fact), all the firm has to go by is data about *what happened over a period of time*. It may regard these data as satisfactory or unsatisfactory, but since it does not know how much better or worse it could have done, there is no absolute standard against which to evaluate performance.

Therefore, the analysis of actual industrial operations has to content itself with assessments of *relative performance*—with the effects of managerial decisions and of events in the firm's environment in relation to some previous period, or in comparison to other plants and firms. Performance evaluation does not deal in scenarios of what might have been, it deals with the "facts" of the past.[2] What performance evaluation aims at is an understanding of the technological and economic factors, internal or external to the entity being evaluated, that caused observed changes in such variables as the productivity of inputs, costs, prices, and profits. The present chapter will outline the framework for such analysis.

5.1 The Firm—Structure and Environment

Words like *structure* and *environment* have been used in so many meanings that we must define what we have in mind when we use them. We do this by asking a seemingly trivial question: Why are there firms at all? Virtually every type of production could, hypothetically, be carried out by having one individual (call him or her the entrepreneur) negotiate contracts with other individuals to supply raw materials and component parts for a product, with yet other individuals to assemble each piece of output, and with yet another group to sell it. In each of these contracts, prices, quantities, qualities, delivery dates, payment terms, etc., would have to be arranged. Obviously, negotiating all these terms in each and every case would involve considerable *transaction costs*. Anyone who has ever tried to negotiate the best deal on a used car is aware of this fact. The alternative is for our entrepreneur to acquire physical capital and to hire people to perform the various jobs involved in production under his or her direction. This arrangement, too, involves costs, such as providing the proper incentives, gathering the necessary information about various tasks, and supervising performance.

Homespun as our example may look, it gets to the heart of the question: In a reasonably rational world, firms will *internalize* (undertake themselves) those activities which they think can be done more economically under one organizational setup, and they will rely upon arm's-length contracts with outsiders where that is more efficient. Therefore, we mean by a firm's *structure* the elements of production that are *integrated* under one set of ownership and management arrangements. An automobile manufacturer may find it economically attractive, for example, to own a steel mill but not to produce electricity or to manufacture tires. The firm's *environment* consists of all those economic agents with whom it has, or might have, contractual relationships, together with those institutions that influence relationships of this type. A firm might be tempted to collude with its competitors in order to fix prices, thus eliminating the uncertainty of the market, but if it did so it would have to face the consequences of rules imposed by an institution, the antitrust laws.

We have chosen these simple illustrations deliberately, in order to make an important point: The extent of the *vertical integration* (the combining of successive production steps under one ownership) or of the *horizontal integration* (the combining of activities at the same level of a vertical sequence of production) of a firm determines what we mean by its structure. A firm that owns and controls, for example, all steps in production from the mining of raw materials to the marketing of finished products is vertically integrated. A firm that owns and controls only the acquisition and retail sales of a line of products is horizontally integrated.

In our later discussions of firms' attitudes and strategies with respect to technological change, we shall use these concepts of structure and environment on several occasions. Here, however, we want to draw on them to provide a general description of the activities of a business unit and of the major strategic decisions confronting firms. One of our objectives will be to show that, important as they may be, decisions about technology are only part of a broader range of variables that managements must deal with in order to assure the long-run competitive survival of their business.

5.2   Managerial Decisions and Performance

What do we mean by the performance of a firm? The concept of profitability becomes ambiguous as soon as one moves out of the well-defined world of the short-run model. This is so because the model abstracts from chronological time: As we have seen, the distinction between the short run and the long run is made on the basis of constraints imposed on managerial decisions.

When we consider the passage of time, i.e., the flow of activities in a firm, we see that these involve two sets of data—a network of physical input–output relationships and a cost–price network. The accounting records generally do not distinguish between these two. Accounting is done strictly in value terms and is based on a simple identity: the dollar volume of sales plus the dollar value of inventory changes must be equal to dollar costs plus profits. In order to evaluate the performance of a firm, we must attempt to disentangle the effects of changes in either of the two sets of variables.

5.2.1 Physical and Financial Flows in the Firm

We may think of a business firm in a market economy as an entity that obtains financial resources from owners and lenders, converts these funds into physical inputs, and these latter into marketable outputs. When it sells these outputs, it receives financial inflows (its revenues). At each stage of these conversion processes, we can observe the interaction of three forces: (1) the physical characteristics of inputs and outputs; (2) their market prices; and (3) the ability of managements to organize, activate, and control the firm's operations.

We can visualize the operations of the firm in a simplified flow diagram like the one shown in Fig. 5.1. The firm's environment is indicated, in short-hand

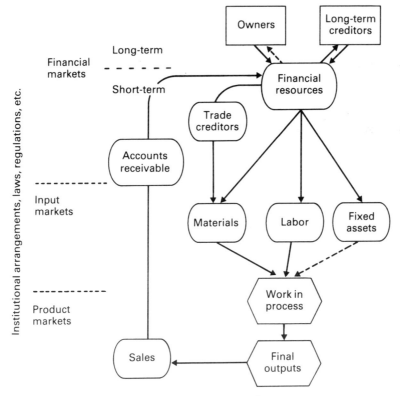

FIG. 5.1 Resource flows in the firm.

form, by the three markets it has to confront: the financial markets, where it bids for funds in competition with all other firms; the input (factor) markets, where it obtains capital goods, labor and materials; and the markets for its product. Financial-market conditions may intrude upon the latter two markets whenever materials are purchased, or final outputs sold, on credit.

The absolute magnitudes of these flows as well as their differential timing play a part in determining a firm's performance. Financial resources committed to fixed-capital investment are recovered only over extended periods of time, via the more or less arbitrary allocation of some proportion of acquisition costs to current operations.[3] But the speed with which physical inputs are converted into outputs, the size of inventories and the average time for which they are kept on hand, the rate of sales and the speed with which accounts receivable are collected, all will have an impact on the firm's performance. These and other influences enter into the picture in addition to the determinants of the physical efficiency of conversion, which in turn will depend on techniques of production, on the rate of capacity utilization, the coordination of flows among production stages, and all the other factors we discussed in the preceding two chapters.

5.2.2 The Task of Management

In this setting, the task of managers becomes more complex than is suggested by the two-stage decision process of microeconomic theory—the selection of techniques and plant size; and then, given these constraints, the determination of an optimal output rate in the face of given costs and prices. Now, managements also need to consider such matters as the sources of financing, the allocation of funds to various inputs, the trade-offs among substitutable inputs, the coordination and timing of purchases, production, and sales, and the negotiation of contracts in an environment no longer characterized by perfectly price-elastic supplies of inputs.

Decision-makers have to confront these tasks under conditions of uncertainty, with the outcomes depending not only on what happens inside the firm's structure but also on events in its environment. Therefore, the actual performance of a business is the result of both, management's decisions and events in the environment outside the firm's control. It is fundamental to performance evaluation that one must distinguish, as far as possible, between these two types of influences. At a minimum, this would involve the separation of changes in physical quantities from changes in prices, and of changes attributable to managerial action from those over which management had no control. In other words, when we no longer treat the firm as a black box, the notion that its actions are guided by the desire to optimize on a single short-run objective under known constraints loses explanatory power.

5.2.3 *The Bottom Line—Return on Investment*

Granted that the outcome of managerial decisions has to be evaluated along several dimensions, we may still ask: what is the purpose of the game? In a capitalist economy, i.e., one characterized by private ownership of the means of production, the percentage return achieved by the owners on their investment suggests itself as the final criterion of success or failure. This measure not only indicates how effectively managements have utilized financial inputs, but it also enables investors to make comparisons among the great variety of investment opportunities confronting them at any given time.

The general formula for the rate of return is

$$C_0 = \frac{B_1}{(1 + r)} + \frac{B_2}{(1 + r)^2} + \frac{B_3}{(1 + r)^3} + \ldots + \frac{B_n}{(1 + r)^n}$$

where C_0 is the original investment (cash outlay) required to initiate a project, $B_1 \ldots B_n$ are the expected annual net benefits (cash inflows), n is the expected life of the investment, and r the rate of return (yield). In solving the equation for r, one is finding the rate which makes the present value of a stream of future benefits equal to the initial outlay. The solution of such n-th degree polynomials is not a job one would expect business decision-makers to undertake. Rather, they can find the appropriate r from prepared tables, by trial, error, and interpolation; alternatively, many business calculators have built-in programs for computing the yield of an investment.

Owners (and, despite their different legal status, long-term lenders) will look at the prospects of a firm in terms of their assessment of future rates of return. In general they would welcome all projects (i.e., specific financial commitments undertaken by a firm) whose expected rate of return is higher than the current average rate of return. Note that this criterion places managerial decision-making squarely into the context of chronological time, away from the abstractions of the short and long run. To the extent that managers are committed to the goals of investors in the firm, they will be interested in achieving a sustainable level of costs and revenues, in the face of uncertainty.[4] They will make changes, including those involving products or techniques of production, only if there is a reasonable promise of a beneficial effect on future returns on investment—although this promise may, as we shall see in later chapters, frequently escape precise quantification and although the actual results of an individual decision may be submerged in the firm's overall performance.

The point deserves emphasis: unless decision-makers pursue the absurd objective of squandering a firm's financial resources, they *must* expect that investments in R&D and innovations will improve, or at least maintain, future performance. This is not the same as saying that the actual calculation of expected rates of return from such strategic investments is necessarily a meaningful exercise. The numbers for costs and benefits would be no more than guesses. In fact, if genuinely innovative projects have to compete with more conservative investment opportunities on a (strictly quantified) rate-of-return basis, they are bound to lose out in most instances.[5] One of the criticisms leveled at the managers of American corporations is that in recent decades too many of their decisions have been based on decision-making procedures that tended always to favor "sure things" over more venturesome types of investment, thus gradually undermining firms' international competitive positions.[6]

5.3   The Basic Determinants of Performance

Having looked at the task of management in real-life firms, we now turn to a general description of the key determinants of performance. Note that the relationships shown below are in the nature of definitions, i.e., identities, whose only purpose is to show up the relevant variables. In other words, changes in these relationships tell us nothing about underlying cause-and-effect sequences.

We start with the fundamental identity

$$\frac{\text{Profit}}{\text{Total Investment}} \equiv \frac{\text{Profit}}{\text{Output}} \times \frac{\text{Output}}{\text{Total Investment}}. \qquad (5.1)$$

It relates the return on total investment (for some time period) to two key factors, the profit obtained on each unit of output sold and the amount of output achieved per dollar of investment. Profit per unit of output also can be defined as

$$\frac{\text{Profit}}{\text{Output}} \equiv \frac{\text{Value of Products}}{\text{Output}} - \frac{\text{Total Costs}}{\text{Output}} \qquad (5.2)$$

which simply says that the average gross profit per unit produced and sold is the difference between average price and average total costs, for some mix of products. We refer to *gross profits* in order to indicate that here, and in all subsequent discussions, we ignore the effects of taxes.

The last component of identity (5.1), the ratio of output to total investment, is itself determined by three sets of factors: the rate of capacity utilization; the productivity of fixed assets, i.e., the amount of capacity that was obtained for a dollar of fixed investment; and the distribution of total investment between fixed assets (plant and equipment) and working capital (inventories, accounts receivable, etc.). Therefore, we can also write

$$\frac{\text{Output}}{\text{Total Invest.}} \equiv \frac{\text{Output}}{\text{Capacity}} \times \frac{\text{Capacity}}{\text{Fixed Invest.}} \times \frac{\text{Fixed Investment}}{\text{Total Investment}}. \qquad (5.3)$$

Thus, in order to trace the sources of changes in the return on investment, we have already identified five different areas of interest:

(1) product prices (Value of Products/Output);
(2) unit costs of production (Total Costs/Output);
(3) the utilization of facilities (Output/Capacity);
(4) the productivity of facilities (Capacity/Fixed Investment); and
(5) the allocation of financial resources between the physical capital stock and other investments required to sustain the flow of production and sales.

Each of these items can change independently, as a result of managerial decisions or because of environmental forces. Two simultaneous changes may be in the same direction, or in offsetting directions. Therefore, each has to be analyzed separately if one wishes to trace the reasons for a change in performance—or, for that matter, for the absence of such a change in the face of obvious variations in the underlying factors.

From the viewpoint of the firm's owners (stockholders), one further determinant of the rate of return on their investment is important—the relationship between financial resources belonging to them (i.e., their equity) and the resources obtained from long-term creditors. Thus

$$\frac{\text{Profit}}{\text{Equity Investment}} \equiv \frac{\text{Profit}}{\text{Total Investment}} \div \frac{\text{Equity Investment}}{\text{Total Investment}}. \quad (5.4)$$

Clearly, these various performance ratios represent a mixture of the effects of physical and financial stocks and flows. In order to take our analysis further, we have to disentangle these two, concentrating first on input–output (physical productivity) relationships and then on costs. Having examined the relevant variables, we can re-integrate them into our overall description of performance determinants.

5.4 Productivity Analysis

The term, productivity, refers to the relationship between physical inputs and physical outputs. The most frequently encountered productivity measure is the ratio of output to the single input, labor. As an overall indicator of changes in an economy's performance or for comparisons among economies, such a measure as output per man-hour, taken by itself, may be useful. Even in this context, however, the measure may give rise to misunderstandings or misinterpretations, chief among them the claim that improvements in output per man-hour are due, primarily or exclusively, to the characteristics and exertions of labor.[7]

At the level of a production unit, plant, or firm, we shall have to broaden our definition of productivity. A moment's reflection will show that it is not enough to look at the ratio of output to any *one* physical input as an indicator of changes in physical performance. Even our elementary theory of production told us that such changes occur either through substitutions among inputs (changes in

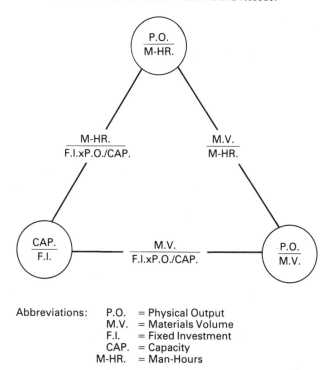

Abbreviations: P.O.   = Physical Output
                 M.V.   = Materials Volume
                 F.I.   = Fixed Investment
                 CAP.   = Capacity
                 M-HR. = Man-Hours

FIG. 5.2 Productivity Relationships among direct inputs.

technique) or through the development of new input-output relationships (changes in technology). Therefore, an analysis of productivity must recognize the interaction of all inputs. And it cannot do this within the framework of a predetermined production function, in which the respective contributions of the input factors are fixed by specification.

Such measurements will no longer consist of a single set of numbers but of a network of quantitative relationships that has to be considered in its entirety. Here we shall outline the conceptual basis for the analysis, without being concerned about the derivation of the relevant data. Some approaches to the latter task are discussed in a subsequent section. It should be clear, however, that meaningful results will be obtained only if the analyst is familiar with both, the technology in question and the structure of the entity (operation, plant, firm, industry) to be evaluated.

The concept of a productivity network can be illustrated with a simple diagram of Gold's model (Fig. 5.2). In the diagram, the circled items show the ratios between output (or capacity) and inputs. The ratios along the interconnecting lines indicate interactions between the respective inputs. Note that, given the necessary data, this network enables us to appraise the physical performance of the entire production system in terms of the following:

(1) Changes in each of the basic inputs relative to output. The categories could of course be disaggregated further, depending on the requirements of the analysis. In the network, the ratio of Capacity to Fixed Investment indicates how much the existing facilities *could* produce if they were fully utilized. Labor and materials inputs are then related to the capital input by recognizing that, at any given time, what matters is the *actively utilized fixed investment*. Therefore, the denominator in the two relevant ratios is Fixed Investment × Output/Capacity.

(2) Changes in the proportions in which inputs are combined. These may reflect substitutions, such as the replacement of labor by machinery, or the purchase of more highly processed materials inputs (which reduces labor requirements within the production system).

(3) Differences between the productivity of the system when it is operating at full capacity and its performance under conditions of underutilization of plant and equipment.

(4) Possible variations in all components of the network whenever one of the components has been changed, as a result of decisions or of outside influences.

5.5   Linking Physical Performance with Costs

Whatever the changes in physical input–output relationships, performance ultimately is determined by their effects on costs. Such effects may occur on account of changes in productivity, with input prices constant, or they may result from price changes, or from some combination of the two. The lower portion of Fig. 5.3 shows the connections between the productivity network and the cost network.

Factor productivities are linked to input costs per unit of output via the relevant prices. The sum of unit input costs constitutes total costs per unit of output. Note that this extended network reveals the interaction of several factors in the determination of unit costs. Let us illustrate these by using the labor input as an example:

(1) Costs will be affected by changes in output per man-hour.

(2) Even without a change in physical productivity, however, costs might also change because wage rates (the prices for labor) have changed.

(3) When both the above changes occur simultaneously, they can be reinforcing or offsetting. For example, an improvement in output per man-hour will bring no cost savings if it is accompanied by a proportional increase in hourly wages. When workers are paid on a piece-work basis or by some other incentive scheme, such an offset may be built into the system.

(4) Changes in the composition of the labor force, such as the replacement of lower skill levels with higher ones or *vice versa*, will affect unit wage costs. Substitutions of this type frequently occur as a consequence of changes in technique and must be taken into account in the evaluation of apparent productivity improvements.

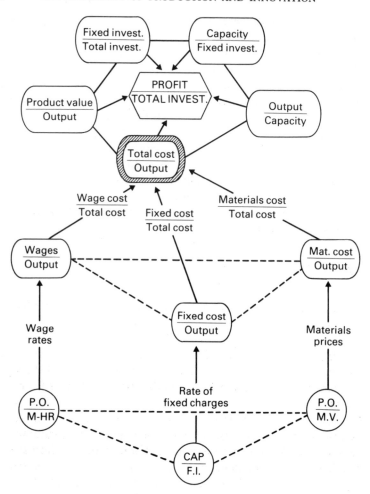

Fig. 5.3 Determinants of return on investment.

(5) The effects of a change in unit wage costs on total costs per unit of output depends on the share of wage costs in total costs. The linkage is shown as a ratio in the diagram. If, for example, wages amount to 20 per cent of all costs, then a 5 per cent reduction in the wage bill will tend to reduce total unit costs by only 1 per cent.

But these five items encompass only the possible direct effects in the network's labor segment. We must ask next, how a reduction in wage costs per unit of output was accomplished. One possibility is that labor was in fact putting forth more effort, all other things remaining equal. More likely, the improvement was due to the purchase of more highly processed input materials, to the replacement of human inputs by capital, or to a change in product mix requiring relatively less labor input. In all of these cases, other costs obviously will be affected as well.

A special comment must be made concerning the *price of capacity*, i.e., the rate at which fixed charges are allocated to current costs of production. We hinted at this problem in our earlier discussion of microeconomic production theory (see Chapter 3, p.52). There we extricated ourselves initially by assuming that the firm can hire (rent) capital equipment on an as-needed basis, although we quickly had to modify this assumption. Now we have to recognize that the allocation of the initial costs of equipment, though not of its time-dependent costs (e.g., insurance), involves an element of arbitrariness. Estimates of an asset's operational life and the method of depreciation chosen will influence the costs incurred per time period. We may view these changes as resulting from managerial decisions about the "price" of capital services, to be accounted for internally.

5.6   Integrating Unit Costs with Other Performance Determinants

So far, we have developed a network that enables us to trace the effects of changes in physical productivity and costs. But no firm has as its ultimate objective the maximization of productivity or the minimization of unit costs. Therefore, we must link the network with the determinants of overall performance outlined in Section 5.3, above. The top portion of Fig. 5.3 shows the interconnections among all these factors in producing our final measure, return on investment.

Strategic and tactical managerial decisions have to deal with all of the factors. This view places process and product innovations in proper relationship to other means of advancing the firm's objectives. For example, an alternative to reducing unit costs via technological advances might be the allocation of resources to advertising, in order to achieve higher rates of capacity utilization or to gain a price advantage through product differentiation. Or, improved inventory control and more effective procedures for billing and collection from customers may yield higher expected gains in return on investment than would process innovations. We could cite other examples, but the point is made: from management's perspective, the pursuit of technological change constitutes only one of many, equally defensible, strategies. And given the risks of innovation, it is not surprising that decision-makers often explore other paths to improved performance.

In large business organizations, with their many divisions and decentralized decision-making apparatus, conflicts among operational goals and strategies may arise. The task of reconciling these in the face of numerous, apparently deserving, claims to the firm's scarce resources can be accomplished only in a framework that considers their separate as well as their combined impact on the return on investment. At a minimum, the evaluation network we have outlined provides a basis for these difficult decisions. Even if some of the variables involved are highly uncertain or cannot be quantified directly, the network might at least allow some qualitative judgments about the directions of their impact.

At the same time, recognition of these factors suggests that the kind of analysis we have described must be performed at different levels of aggregation and in terms of different criteria. Thus, for example, evaluation of a division inside a plant may focus primarily on physical input-output relationships, because decisions affecting costs are not made at that level. For a whole plant, cost measures may constitute the most relevant bases for evaluation. At the level of the firm, all of the determinants we have outlined above will come into play.

For our purposes, the analytical concepts developed here have a twofold value. First, they provide us with a structure for our later discussion of the economic effects of technological changes. And second, they serve as a useful reminder that such changes may not be the uppermost concern of managements. For a firm, there is nothing inherently more desirable about performance improvements achieved via innovation as against other possible sources of economic advantage. Having said this, we must confront a basic dilemma: the competitive survival of firms requires a careful weighing of alternative strategies, of which technological innovation is but one; yet historical evidence also confirms the Schumpeterian concept of the innovator-entrepreneur as the prime driving force of fundamental economic progress. As the following critical observations suggest, it may well be that decision-makers in large firms think that there are good reasons to avoid radical innovation in favor of incremental improvements:

> "Management often has a tendency to avoid dynamic change and development and concentrate instead on efficiency in already established methods of operation through steady growth, rationalised manufacturing and distribution and more intensive marketing, that is to say on developments which do *not* involve large investments in novelties. It is easier for a manager to strengthen his power by refraining from taking any new initiative himself which might lead to significant innovations."[8]

Against this type of judgement we must set the recognition that only the success stories of major innovation are widely acclaimed, while even massive failures may go unreported . . . just like the steady performance improvements that firms may achieve by less spectacular means. In a later chapter we shall examine the question whether different stages in the evolution of basic technologies may not call for different types of competitive strategy, with a high premium on innovativeness during certain phases and on different targets during other phases.

5.7   Some Problems of Measurement

In translating general concepts and models into detailed frameworks for empirical analysis we always confront problems that necessitate adaptation and compromise. Some of these problems are rooted in the nature of the data available in a given case; some have to do with choosing the proper level of aggregation and the relevant categories of variables; and yet others occur in the process of making the variables fit the purpose of the analysis. It is a fact of life that businesses collect quantitative information for many purposes, but that most of this information is not tailored to the requirements of the kind of performance evaluation we have outlined above. Here we do not wish to deal with all the methodological problems that might arise in actual applications.[9] Instead, we shall present just a few illustrations of how the necessary measurements might be approached.

Certain general rules apply in all instances:

(1) The purpose of an evaluation determines the *level of analysis*. This may sound obvious, but it is often overlooked. One gains little insight into the effects of a specific innovation in one plant of a multi-plant firm unless one focusses the analysis on the units directly affected. Data at higher levels of aggregation are likely to contain so much "noise" that one cannot learn much from them. In other words, it is not sensible to try to answer questions like, "What was the effect of the introduction of automatic spot-welding on General Motors' return on investment?" or "How has the introduction of continuous casting in some plants affected the international competitiveness of the American steel industry?" The effects are no doubt there, but they cannot be traced at such high levels of aggregation.

(2) Once the level of analysis has been chosen, all *relevant* inputs, costs, outputs, and revenues must be captured, and all irrelevant ones left out. For example, the overhead costs of headquarters operation are relevant to an analysis of a firm, but they are irrelevant in the evaluation of an individual operation or plant. From the managerial viewpoint, this rule also means that persons in charge of an operation or plant should be held accountable only for those performance variables over which they have control. Nothing is more demoralizing to an employee than to be judged in terms of criteria that have nothing to do with his or her scope of responsibility.

(3) Inputs and outputs must be identified and kept separate. Input costs are not measures of output; $3 million spent on R&D or on advertising is a cost—it does not tell anything about the benefits produced. We cannot evaluate the expenditure by simply assuming that it brought 3 million dollars worth of results. This observation reinforces our earlier discussion of the difficulties of evaluating the performance of all those activities for which there exist no unequivocal measures of output (see Chapter 2, pp. 42–3).

(4) Since, as we pointed out at the beginning of this chapter, we have no standard of optimality against which to judge performance, our measurements must deal with changes over time, rather than with absolute values. This point will be illustrated in the following examples. Observed changes can then be assessed in terms of how close they come to expectations, of how they compare with the performance of other units, or by some other, externally set criteria.

In this context, the notion of *satisfactory performance* (Chapter 3, p.61) would seem to be more useful than the assumption that firms always maximize on some objective.

5.7.1 Output and Capacity

Most real-life plants and firms do not turn out a single, homogeneous product. How, then, can one arrive at an acceptable measure of *physical* output? The statistical device of a *value-weighted quantity index* provides an answer. It is based on the following reasoning: The *total value* of a plant's output and sales is determined by the *prices* and the *quantities* of the various products manufactured. A change in this value from one period to the next therefore can be due to either changes in prices or changes in the respective quantities of products sold. The *change in physical quantity* can be captured only if one eliminates price effects. Several methods, none of them *the* perfect one, exist for accomplishing this. Here we show how one can weight (multiply) the quantity of each product in the mix, in each period, by its average price for the base period and the observation period. The formula can be written as

$$I_n = \frac{Q_n(a) \cdot P(a) + Q_n(b) \cdot P(b) + Q_n(c) \cdot P(c) + \ldots}{Q_0(a) \cdot P(a) + Q_0(b) \cdot P(b) + Q_0(c) \cdot P(c) + \ldots} \cdot 100$$

where I_n = value-weighted index of output for period n,
Q_n = physical quantities of products a, b, c, etc. in period n,
Q_0 = physical quantities of products a, b, c, etc. in base period 0,
P = average price for products a, b, c, etc. in the two periods,
i.e., $(P_0 + P_n)/2$, for each product.

A simple numerical example will illustrate the calculation of such an index and will help us to explore its meaning. Table 5.1 shows the products of a plant, for two periods.

TABLE 5.1   *Quantities and prices for a multi-product plant, two time periods*

| Product | Period o | | Period n | |
	Quantity (lbs)	Price	Quantity (lbs)	Price
A	1,000	$13.00	1,200	$13.60
B	1,500	13.50	1,800	14.00
C	800	7.00	600	6.80

From these data, we can calculate the index as follows:

$$I = \frac{\begin{array}{l} 1,200 \cdot [13.00 + 13.60)/2] + 1,800 \cdot [(13.50 + 14.00)/2] \\ + 600 \cdot [7.00 + 6.80)/2] \end{array}}{\begin{array}{l} 1,000 \cdot [13.00 + 13.60)/2] + 1,500 \cdot [(13.50 + 14.00)/1] \\ + 800 \cdot [7.00 + 6.80)/2] \end{array}} \cdot 100$$

$$= 114.8.$$

In relation to the base period (= 100), value-weighted output in period n had increased by 14.8 per cent. Note that the index takes into account shifts in quantities as well as in relative prices, thus focussing on the economic effects of changes in the product mix. Had we simply added up quantities and compared them, we would have observed a 9.1 per cent increase, but this would have ignored a shift in the mix to higher-priced products. Had we considered the change in total revenue only, we would have observed an increase of 17.4 per cent, though not recognizing changes in the respective quantities of products.

A number of technical problems may arise when one works with such an index. For example, how should one handle products that are dropped altogether, or new products added at some later time? These need not concern us here. Our example also shows that what we consider the rate of capacity utilization of a plant will depend on the product mix turned out in a given period.

5.7.2   Input Measurement

Even when the operations of a plant are relatively simple, it will still be necessary to aggregate different types of inputs into manageable and meaningful groupings. Figure 5.4 shows an example of the kinds of evaluation units that might be appropriate for a plant producing metal castings. Each of the major labor and materials inputs at the various stages of production consists of several types, having different wage rates and prices. Therefore, the use of a value-weighted index of inputs, analogous to the output index illustrated in Section 5.7.1 is appropriate.

In order to test his or her understanding of the method, the reader may wish to calculate a labor input index for the three categories of labor shown in Table 5.2.

TABLE 5.2   *Hours worked and hourly costs in a plant, two periods*

Type of labor	Year 1		Year 2	
	Hours	Cost/hour	Hours	Cost/hour
General operating	12,570	$7.28	8,922	$7.58
Stockyard	38,201	6.76	36,691	8.34
Melt shop	38,424	8.32	41,038	10.37

If we assume that the product did not change in the two years, and that total output in Year 1 was 213,884 pounds and in Year 2 it was 220,018 pounds, then we can also calculate an index of output per man hour which reflects the above changes in the composition of labor input. Obviously, a simple adding up of hours for each year would ignore the economic implications of these changes for the plant.

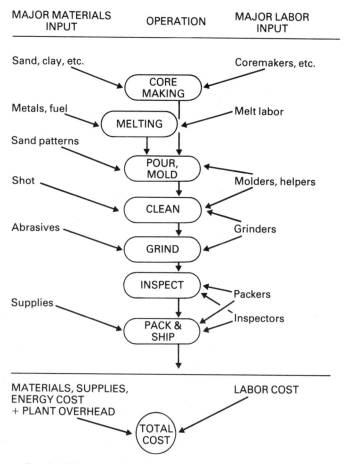

FIG. 5.4 Disaggregated performance evaluation, metal casting plant.

5.7.3 Current vs "Real" Costs and Prices

One of the bothersome problems in performance evaluation over longer periods of time arises in connection with changes in the general price level, i.e., inflation. If all input costs and output prices of a firm moved in proportion with these changes, we could ignore them. But this is not likely to be the case. Therefore, we confront the question whether an observed shift in the price of an input or output was due to some change in its qualitative characteristics or to a change in general prices, as measured by some index. The same problem arises even in connection with consumer goods; thus one has to decide, for example, what portion of the increase in the price of the "representative" automobile model of the consumer price index is the result of quality improvements (e.g., the installation of impact bars in the doors) and what portion is the result of general inflation.

In long-term evaluations nominal (current) costs and prices for each period are often deflated with the help of an index of general price behavior, such as the producer price index of the Bureau of Labor Statistics (U.S. Department of Labor). The "real" costs and prices thus arrived at are real only in the sense that they permit retrospective comparisons. At any given point in time, current and prospective inflation is one of the variables that influence managerial decisions about substitutions among inputs, investment in new techniques, changes in the product mix, etc. Decision-makers have to deal with current data, not with deflated ones.

The Bureau of Labor Statistics (BLS) also prepares and publishes separate price indices for close to 2,000 commodities and commodity groups. By using these, one can take a more accurate account of the impact of price changes in the sector of industry relevant to the evaluation of a particular plant or firm. For example, by deflating the prices obtained by a firm in the plate glass industry with the BLS index for "flat glass," one obtains data indicating how far the firm's performance has deviated from the average for the whole industry.

The interpretation of deflated costs and prices requires some care. If, for example, deflated labor costs per unit of output in a firm have followed an essentially horizontal trend over some longer period, this does not mean that "nothing happened." In the face of a rising general wage level, such a trend might well reflect considerable technological and other efforts to keep labor costs under control. Similarly, a firm that managed to maintain constant real energy cost per unit of output during the past fifteen years, was "running very fast, just to stay in place." Under conditions like the ones in the energy markets, this would have been no mean accomplishment.

From a broader perspective, the long-term stability of deflated unit labor costs in established industries reflects the working of a market economy: despite cyclical fluctuations and despite the actions of labor unions, the trend of increases in *real* wage rates is tied to improvements in labor productivity. In a later chapter, we shall explore the processes whereby owners, workers, suppliers of materials inputs, and an industry's customers successively participate in the economic absorption of the effects of technological advances.

5.8   Concluding Observations

The main purpose of our discussion of performance evaluation was to establish a conceptual framework. We did no more than to hint at some of the methods for translating concepts into empirical observations and at the problems one confronts in doing so.

Three general conclusions will be of importance to our later explorations of the motives for, and the effects of, technological innovation:

(1) Our distinction between the structure and the environment of a firm enables us to differentiate changes in performance brought about by mana-

gerial decisions from those triggered by external events. It should also alert us to the possibility that a firm may wish to expand its structure, i.e., to internalize relationships with its environment or to cast off operations no longer offering advantages of internalization. As we shall see, efforts to appropriate the benefits of technological information are a major motivating force in such structural changes.

(2) We showed that, despite frequent assertions to the contrary, there is nothing in productivity improvement that would make it inherently preferable to managements as a means of achieving higher returns on investment, just as cost reduction as such may not be an operationally valid objective. Our productivity-cost-performance network demonstrated the variety of strategic options that are open to decision-makers. Not all of these options are equally attractive at all times, nor may some of them assure the long-term competitive success of businesses, but judgments on these issues have to be made on empirical grounds. There are no theoretical reasons why technology-oriented strategies should have priority over other policies for advancing the objectives of the firm.

(3) The empirical task of tracing actual changes in performance must be focussed on the relevant level of analysis. Only truly gigantic changes in technology, or in any of the other factors affecting a firm's or an industry's performance, can be observed at high levels of aggregation. Most product and process innovations affect only individual components of a production system, and one has to look at these components in order to assess their impact. Furthermore, our survey also added further to our understanding why not all technological changes are equally attractive to all of an industry's member firms, at some given point in time.

Even with these quite modest forays into the complexities of real-life industrial operations, we have moved a substantial distance from the framework of basic microeconomic theory.

Notes

1. The concepts and analytical models of this chapter are derived virtually in their entirety from the work of my former colleague, Professor Bela Gold, now of the Claremont Graduate School. He first presented his approach in *Foundations of Productivity Analysis* (Pittsburgh, PA: University of Pittsburgh Press, 1955). Since then, it has been developed in a variety of directions, to facilitate empirical application. Its latest development can be found in his *Productivity, Technology, and Capital* (Lexington, MA: Lexington Books—D. C. Heath, 1979), as well as in numerous articles. As his collaborator in research for many years, I absorbed Professor Gold's way of looking at industrial operations, as it were, by osmosis.

2. The word, facts, is placed in quotation marks, because accounting and statistical records may be biased in the interest of individuals, incomplete, or wrong. No amount of clever manipulation can make evaluations any better than the underlying data permit.

3. Saying that these allocations are more or less arbitrary means only that managements must decide on one of several methods of depreciation. Once a method has been selected, there is nothing arbitary about its application.

4. In making this statement, we avoid a much-discussed issue: does the separation of ownership

and control in large corporations mean that managers pursue objectives that are different from, and perhaps inimical to, the interests of the shareholders?

5. On this subject, see Gold, B., "The Shaky Foundations of Capital Budgeting," *California Management Review*, Winter 1976.

6. This argument is made in Hayes, R. and Abernathy, W., "Managing Ourselves into an Economic Decline," *Harvard Business Review*, August 1980.

7. Such a claim may strike one as naive unless one considers a flat assertion like the following: "The biggest cause of productivity gains over the years is the improvement in the quality of American labor," This statement is made in an article, "Sharing the Benefits of Productivity," *AFL-CIO American Federationist*, October 1972. Since the article also refers to the benefits of high rates of investment in human capital, the argument is unexceptional in its broader implications; however, human-capital considerations are not likely to enter into collective bargaining.

8. Ljungberg, G., "Industry and Innovation," *Skandinaviska Banken Quarterly Review*, 1968:1.

9. These problems are discussed at length in Eilon, S., Gold, B., and Soesan, J., *Applied Productivity Analysis for Industry* (Oxford: Pergamon Press, 1976). For another application of the general analytical framework, see Gold, B., Rosegger, G., and Boylan, M. G., *Evaluating Technological Innovations: Methods, Expectations, and Findings* (Lexington, MA: Lexington Books—D. C. Heath, 1980).

CHAPTER 6

Inventing as an Economic Activity

In this chapter, we shall examine the production of inventions from an economic point of view. Let us remind ourselves of our earlier definition: Inventing involves the *generation of new ideas* concerning previously unthought of applications of scientific and technical principles. We may speak of the production of inventions as an economic activity, because it requires the commitment of resources to the *purposeful search for new knowledge*. At the same time we must recognize, however, that successful inventing involves acts of insight; it is a *mental activity* whose psychological roots, despite some recent progress, are not very well understood. Even in an economic analysis we cannot ignore this feature of inventive activity. It probably has a lot to do with answers to such questions as whether there are certain types of new ideas most likely generated by persons working independently, whether there are other types of invention depending on the fortunate merging of several individuals' contributions (synergism), and whether economies of scale are likely to be achieved in applied research.

6.1 Basic Concepts

In our earlier discussion of the stage model of technological change (Chapter 1), we emphasized the fact that, once they have been made, inventions constitute a *pool of potentially useful information*. In order to have any further economic effects, an invention must be developed and turned into an innovation. In other words, the new idea must pass the tests of technical and economic feasibility, and—ultimately—of market acceptance. Although the route from invention to innovation is often reasonably direct, especially when laid out within the framework of an individual organization's strategy, it is nevertheless true that the number of inventions that never get beyond the idea stage is much larger than the number of utilized ones. Even in the case of patents, which cover only a fraction of all inventions, we find that many more lie idle than are turned into innovations.

If we accept the assumption that most inventors are motivated by the prospect of an economic return from their effort, the concept of inventions as

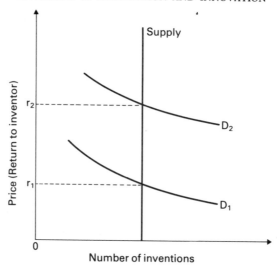

FIG. 6.1 Short-run supply and demand in the market for inventions.

a pool of ideas gives rise to an interesting economic problem. Each inventor will think of the prospective return as the price he obtains for his idea, but since the short-run supply of inventions is perfectly price-inelastic, this return depends entirely on the demand for inventions. The situation is illustrated in Fig. 6.1, where two different demand curves are shown in order to make the case. Clearly, returns to inventors would be greater under the demand conditions described by D_2 than under those of D_1. (The various forms in which an inventor may receive the "price" for his idea will be discussed in Chapter 7.) From a *static* viewpoint, therefore, returns to inventors are in the nature of what economists call a *quasi-rent*. The term is derived from the theory of returns to the factor of production land, which—like the pool of inventions—is characterized by the same perfectly price-inelastic, short-run supply, with the owners' rent deriving entirely from the demand for his or her piece of land.

Whether the returns to inventors are high, low, or nonexistent, there is nothing that will change the static picture. From a *dynamic* perspective, however, we must ask what the effect of actual returns achieved will be on the long-run supply of inventions. Will inventors continue to devote resources to the purposeful search for new ideas if none of these ideas are ever turned into innovations that provide a pay-off? What would be the motives for further inventing? Furthermore, if all existing inventions were there for the taking, who would have an incentive to invest in development and innovation? After all, imitators could quickly wipe out any potential gains from such an investment. In other words, under these conditions it would be difficult for inventor and innovator to *appropriate* the benefits of their efforts.

It is for this reason that societies have created the institution of *intellectual property rights*, such as those bestowed by a patent or a copyright. These rights are based on the notion that the generation of new ideas must be rewarded in order to be encouraged. In the next chapter, we shall undertake a more detailed exploration of the patent system. Here we want to make just two additional observations: (1) The economist's rationale for rewarding an inventor has little to do with issues of fairness or equity, important as these may be in the broader context of the theory of property rights; rather, it is concerned with incentive effects, i.e., with the dynamic efficiency of the economic system. And (2) inventors, developers, and innovators do not *have* to rely on legal institutions in order to appropriate the results of their investments; they may achieve the same goal by maintaining secrecy about certain aspects of their ideas, by retaining the know-how required to utilize these ideas effectively, or by developing and implementing new ideas so rapidly that they always stay ahead of their competitors.

Appropriability is, of course, only a necessary but not a sufficient condition for the continuing generation of inventions and for the translation of these into innovations. Many social and economic factors will influence the actual rate of innovation in an economy. Historians have long been fascinated by differences in this rate among countries, as well as by spurts and slow-downs within a given country. Consider the following illustrative observation:

> "The most striking contrast between Britain and France at this period [the first half of the nineteenth century] is the higher rate at which, in Britain, inventions were adopted, developed and passed into application. No nation in the world showed more vivid inventive genius than the French, but a high proportion of their inventive talent proved abortive or was put to profitable use elsewhere—notably in England and Scotland."[1]

Britain herself appears to have experienced a similar slow-down in innovation later in the nineteenth century, even though inventive activity continued at a fast pace. Thus, for example, a British chemist, W. H. Perkin invented the first synthetic dye in 1856, while trying to synthesize the drug quinin from coal tar.[2] He saw the potential for the development of a whole industry based on coal tar chemistry, but no one in Britain seemed interested. Instead, Germany was the first country to build up a powerful organic-chemical industry. One writer has attributed the British lack of interest to the fact that the country had large natural dyestuff plantations in India, while the Germans had no such sources of supply.[3]

A whole host of questions about the determinants of the *demand for new ideas* is raised by such observations, and attempts to find at least some answers will occupy much of the rest of this book. Here we want to concentrate mainly on matters of supply. The only conclusion that should be obvious even at this point in our exploration is that an economy's technological progressiveness is influenced by a complex network of institutions, mechanisms, and incentives. Inventions are merely a starting point, and they do not even have to originate within a given country in order to provide it with the basis for industrial growth.

6.2   The Supply of Inventions

What determines the number of new technological ideas produced by an economy in a given period? We may try to answer this question from two different points of view: one would look toward the cultural, social, and political setting for explanations in terms of broadly conceived sets of forces that influence the rate of inventive activity; the other would examine the specific incentives for inventors (whether individual or corporate), the relationship between inputs and outputs in the production of inventions, and the role of firms' strategies in giving direction to the search for new ideas. Let us briefly discuss some implications of the first point of view and then deal somewhat more intensively with the second.

6.2.1   Social Forces and Inventive Activity

A number of theories attempt to explain why and when inventions occur in a society. A complete survey of these would go well beyond the scope of our efforts, but a few illustrative examples will give the reader a flavor.

(1) We can quickly dispose of the notion that *inventions are the result of random genius*—unpredictable, sporadic, inexplicable. According to this view, major inventions can be no more traced to social and economic forces than, say, the creation of the great works of music by geniuses like Bach, Haydn, or Mozart. No doubt there are some inventions that mark genuine discontinuities in the flow of technical ideas and therefore may have to be ascribed to the unique intuitive powers of their generators. But these are rare exceptions. The stories of even the most successful inventors show that sudden flashes of major insight were generally preceded by long and hard work. Furthermore, most of technological and economic progress is not the result of major breakthroughs to radically new conceptions but rather of the journeyman efforts of thousands of anonymous invention workers.

(2) Another interpretation sees *inventions as the result of social evolution*, i.e., as major or minor mutations in a developmental process which occur "when the time is ripe." As an approach to historical analysis this interpretation is unexceptional. By focussing on the technical characteristics of inventions, one can explain virtually all of them as reflections of all preceding knowledge, and one can then investigate the social and economic conditions that stimulated the inventions that occurred. Yet the focus is probably too narrow. It may well be that someone was bound to invent a steam engine in the eighteenth century, given the state of knowledge at the time. But would we also be prepared to make statements like, "If the Biro brothers had not invented the ball-point pen in 1938, someone else surely would have, in short order?"

(3) Another school would see *the pressure of demand or social need* as the prime mover in invention. No doubt the old proverb, "Necessity is the mother of invention," contains a good deal of truth. As many students of the subject have

shown, actual or potential demand is probably the most important determinant of the ultimate technical and economic success of inventions.[4] More generally, perceptions of market opportunities motivate much of inventive effort. But such a statement tells us little about the *kinds* of inventions that will ultimately meet the perceived demand.

An example will illustrate the point. At the conclusion of World War I, the technology of aviation had progressed to the point where the development of commercial air transport was a distinct possibility. Most experts realized that weather conditions, especially low clouds and fog, were a major obstacle to regular air service. The economic rewards for overcoming the problem of adverse weather would be huge. At the same time, there were no technological antecedents to provide guidance. As the first invention, proposed by a consultant in 1919, shows, analogies with the requirements of ocean navigation proved inadequate. He suggested "sending up a series of kite balloons along an aerial route, which will fly conspicuously above the fog-belt . . ." as well as strong light beams "to indicate the contour of the aerodrome . . .".[5] The invention came to nought, and the problem persisted well into the 1930s. Delays, re-routings, and frequent crashes on take-off and landing in bad weather continued to plague the budding airline industry. A comprehensive study undertaken in 1937[6] listed twenty-five possible approaches to solving the bad-weather problems, ranging from "training the pilot to fly by the feel of his sitting" to "dispelling fog by calcium chloride droplets . . . or by spraying electrified sand." Radio beams were mentioned as one of the possibilities but were not accorded greater significance than others. A few years later, radar proved to solve most, if not all, navigational problems.

(4) Probably most congenial to the economist's viewpoint is the hypothesis that *inventions are the result of purposeful search*, with the general directions of exploration determined by what one student of the subject has called "social forces driving research."[7] For the individual inventor, these forces—which change over time and are themselves influenced by past technological developments—may be seen as signals that suggest areas of technology which promise high potential rewards.

If this interpretation is approximately correct, we would expect the historical evidence to show that inventions in a particular field of technology do occur in bunches, and that shifts in the bunching reflect changes in the underlying social and economic conditions. Unfortunately, the actual evidence is mixed and permits several interpretations. As we shall see later on, the main difficulty with historical data arises because certain major inventions almost inevitably trigger a search for alternatives and improvements, thus producing the observed bunching . . . but we know that inventions were "major" only *after* they have been turned into successful innovations. Thus, the feedback between inventions and social forces runs in both directions and makes the attribution of cause and effect difficult. A good example of these difficulties is provided by the story of Edison's invention of a practical electric bulb and with it, of economical lighting systems. His dogged search has been explained by the enthusiasm and the "unalloyed hope" with which his work was regarded by the public, but at the same time the success of large-scale electric lighting hinged on the contributions of a host of other inventors, most of whose efforts were no doubt stimulated by the original ideas of Edison.[8]

6.2.2   The Motivation of Inventors

When we retreat from efforts to interpret the broad sweep of social forces to an examination of the individual inventor's motivation, we find ourselves on somewhat firmer ground. One economist has proposed the following list of motives: (1) inventing for fun, (2) inventing for fame, (3) inventing for the service of mankind, (4) inventing for money, and (5) inventing as an expression of the "instinct of workmanship."[9]. These are not, of course, mutually exclusive categories. He points out, however, that pecuniary motives surely play the most important role, if only because most individuals [and all business firms] would not allocate scarce resources to inventive work if it did not hold the promise of a pay-off.

This permits us to state two propositions about inventing as an economic activity:

(1) The prospect of an, at least temporary, monopoly position of some sort is an important driving force for inventors. This may be only a monopoly on public acclaim or on recognition by peers, but it is more likely a monopoly with direct economic implications. Whenever we find evidence of efforts at appropriating the ideas contained in an invention, we may suspect the existence of pecuniary motives. We must recognize, however, that the actual rewards may be indirect, e.g., in the form of greater job security or in new opportunities for monetary gain resulting from recognition (e.g., consultancies or commissions for further work).

(2) Net monetary gains (quasi-rents) from an invention will be the greater, the lower the cost of making an invention, other things equal. This means that the production of inventions benefits from the application of efficiency criteria, difficult as that may be in practice. Nowhere is this point more obvious than in the management of organized applied research, where decision-makers have to cope with both, the problem of determining the directions of investigation most promising from a given organization's point of view *and* the question of how best to organize such work.

For the performance of the economy as a whole, however, yet a third problem may be even more significant—how to motivate inventors working in corporations. In recent decades, most patented American inventions have been made by employee-inventors. Normally, they do not share in the economic benefits gained by their employers from these inventions, although they may receive "nominal rewards ranging from a bonus of a few hundred dollars to pen sets and plaques."[10] Some critics have argued that technical progress in industry might have been more rapid if invention workers were more adequately compensated for successful ideas. This contention is difficult to prove or disprove. It is worth noting, however, that in a number of recent lawsuits inventors have won substantial awards from their employers for especially profitable inventions.

6.2.3   Characteristics of the Invention Sought

We have already raised the possibility of some fundamental distinctions between the supply of major, key inventions and the flow of derived, incremental inventions. If such distinctions exist, they might well influence what types of problems are addressed most successfully by independent inventors and what types require the kind of research that can be mounted only by a major organization. Furthermore, they may help to shed some light on the question whether a massing of resources in pursuit of a particular objective will in fact increase the probability of success or whether it will lead only to a lot of wheel-spinning.

There are no easy answers to these questions. In his book, *Chase, Chance and Creativity: The Lucky Art of Novelty*[11] a neurological scientist, Professor James H. Austin, proposes the interesting hypothesis that the outcome of intellectual activity in discovery and invention is in fact influenced by what he calls the *type of chance* encountered. According to Austin, "chance comes in four forms and for four different reasons."[12]

Chance I involves pure accident . . . blind luck that comes through no effort on the inventor's part. Little can be said about how to encourage it. *Chance II* results from action, even if there are no clearly defined goals for the search. Professor Austin also calls this the Kettering Principle, after the famous automotive inventor, who said, "Keep going and the chances are you will stumble on something, perhaps when you are least expecting it. I have never heard of anyone stumbling on something sitting down."[13] It would seem that in the grasping of both of these types of chance the individual plays a minor role . . . in the first case because blind luck can favor anyone, and in the second, because action is more important than some particular characteristics of the searcher. The purely empirical, trial-and-error kind of applied research would probably face improved probabilities of success if as many people as possible were involved in the action.

Chance III is of a different nature. It requires a unique ability to recognize some constellation of observations for what they really mean. Austin quotes Louis Pasteur's famous saying, "Chance favors only the prepared mind," and he cites the story of Alexander Fleming's recognition of the therapeutic significance of penicillin, which resulted from a series of laboratory accidents. *Chance IV*, finally, involves the kind of luck that comes from well-directed, probing behavior. Unlike Chance II, it "connotes no generalized activity, as bees might have in the anonymity of a hive."[14] Whether such probing behavior is the province of the expert in a field, who already knows in which directions to search, or whether a completely open mind is more likely to produce results, must remain an open question.

To an economist, who is interested primarily in the efficiency and productivity of inventive activity, Professor Austin's hypothesis suggests that purposeful search may require different forms of organization and different types of people, depending on its objectives. Therefore, the supply of inventions would hinge in an important way on the nature of the technical problems to be solved or opportunities to be capitalized on.

6.2.4   Other Factors in the Supply of Inventions

While the factors we have discussed above probably play a major role in an economy's capacity to produce inventions, others appear influential as well. Among these, the existing states of scientific knowledge and of technology, as well as the pool of unutilized inventions, no doubt weigh heavily.

This is so because, despite the private-goods characteristics of inventions, they also generate a host of externalities, i.e., information which is in the nature of a public good. In other words, the development of any particular technology is accompanied by a large amount of social learning that creates the potential for further new ideas. The importance of such generalized knowledge about a technology can be illustrated by counter-examples, i.e., by situations in which there has been massive "forgetting" of a technological base, because development had stopped. When the "energy crisis" of 1973–74 led to a sudden revival of interest in wind power, inventors (encouraged by government subsidies) had to start virtually from scratch. In the 1920s, some 130 manufacturers made and sold windmills in the United States. Rural electrification led to the decline of interest in wind power. Nevertheless, an estimated 240,000 windmills were scattered across the country in the middle 1970s, many of them ready to be put back into operation with but minor refurbishing. Yet only one university in the country offered a course in windmill technology, and there were just three small windmill manufacturers left.[15]

But the current state of technologies influences the supply of inventions in a way that goes beyond their information content. In the case of many of these technologies, the physical capital (laboratory equipment) required for applied research has become an increasingly specialized, and costly, input. Where such facilities are in place, we would expect the probability of further inventions to be higher than in situations where an organization has to acquire them before work can begin. The success of the famous Bell Laboratories, for example, has been attributed not only to their ability to attract outstanding scientists and engineers, but also to the fact that they provided highly developed plant and equipment.

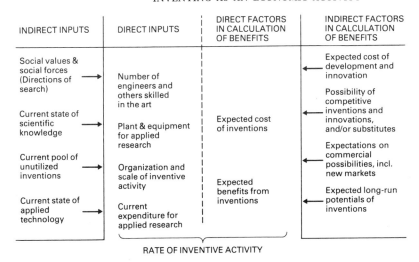

INDIRECT INPUTS	DIRECT INPUTS	DIRECT FACTORS IN CALCULATION OF BENEFITS	INDIRECT FACTORS IN CALCULATION OF BENEFITS
Social values & social forces (Directions of search)	Number of engineers and others skilled in the art		Expected cost of development and innovation
Current state of scientific knowledge	Plant & equipment for applied research	Expected cost of inventions	Possibility of competitive inventions and innovations, and/or substitutes
Current pool of unutilized inventions	Organization and scale of inventive activity		Expectations on commercial possibilities, incl. new markets
Current state of applied technology	Current expenditure for applied research	Expected benefits from inventions	Expected long-run potentials of inventions

RATE OF INVENTIVE ACTIVITY

FIG. 6.2 Factors influencing the supply of inventions.

Finally, we must recognize that the social status accorded to invention workers may play an important role in the long-run supply of new ideas. If inventors are regarded as the destroyers of hallowed traditions in the art of manufacturing, as they were by the medieval guilds, we would expect the supply of inventions to be slowed significantly, especially when the introduction of new ideas is actually a punishable offense. Conversely, when engineers and technologists receive the kind of unquestioning public adulation that they seem to have enjoyed during the Victorian age, inventive activity will flourish.

In Fig. 6.2 we have summarized these and other, self-explanatory, factors that influence the supply of inventions. At the same time, however, our preceding observations should have made clear that it would be presumptuous to speak of something like a production function for inventions: chance, luck, serendipity, accident, genius—call it what we may—play too important a role in determining the rate of inventive activity. While looking at the inventive process from the economist's point of view, we ought to remain mindful of what Professor Elting E. Morison, a historian of technology, had to say about this process:

> "The production of ideas, contrary to the mere selection of appropriate ideas from an available pool, cannot be achieved with great economy of energy and elegance, because it requires investigation and thought, and thinking is a wasteful process."[16]

6.3   Independent Inventors and Organized Inventive Activity

Although most great inventions of the past are due to the work of individuals working independently, it is often said that the day of the free-lance inventor is over, and that modern inventions are "almost made to order"[17] in the R&D

laboratories of corporations. A number of reasons are given for what is seen as the demise of individual enterprise in invention:

(1) the increasing importance of scientific work as a base for inventions, which necessitates the combining of scientists and engineers in one setting;

(2) the replacement of the inventor's traditional empiricism with approaches to inventing that resemble what is taken to be "the scientific method";

(3) the high capital requirements of modern applied research;

(4) the economies of scale inherent in large-group inventive activity;

(5) the growing power of corporations over resources and markets; and

(6) the increasing reluctance of financiers to stake inventor-entrepreneurs to the capital necessary for the development of their ideas.

These are explanations which, at least conceptually, could be submitted to empirical tests; most of the data for doing so are missing. We may speculate, however, that this view probably contains some exaggerations. Since there is no *ex ante* measure of the importance of particular inventions, we cannot even be sure that the independent inventor's role has actually diminished. We have also referred to the possibility that different types of search may require different approaches, some having the greatest chance of success if undertaken in a massive, organized way, others being best pursued by small-scale methods. And we must finally remind ourselves that, despite the distinction between independents and organizations, inventions are always made by individuals, even in the largest R&D laboratories. Perhaps it is more productive to look at the distribution of effort between the two types of inventing in terms of a useful division of labor . . . without pre-judging the advantages of either.

6.3.1   *The Empirical Evidence*

If we want to examine the question whether independent inventors are progressively yielding the field to organizations, we must first establish precisely what we mean by this dichotomy. Presumably, it has to do with the economic status of the invention worker. If he or she is an entrepreneur who expects either to raise the capital for development and innovation or to sell new ideas to established firms, we can classify such an individual as an independent. If the inventor is a salaried employee who works together with others of the same status, he or she becomes part of what we have called organized R&D. Other distinctions, such as the one that portrays the independent as an untrained basement tinkerer and the employee-inventor as a well-educated scientist or engineer do not stand up to the facts. Nor is it necessarily true that the methods employed by the two groups differ in any fundamental way.

Having made these points, we can ask whether the independent inventor's role has actually declined as much as claimed. The best-known empirical study dealing with this question[18] shows that increasing numbers of inventors have indeed done their work in organized establishments, either because they required facilities whose cost lay well beyond their own resources or because these establishments offered them greater economic security. But set against this undeniable trend is a list of over sixty key inventions of the twentieth century, a surprisingly large number of which continued to be made by independents.

Such evidence is inconclusive to the extent that, of necessity, it has to be restricted to inventions that were developed into commercially successful innovations. That even such success may be fleeting is suggested by the study's listing of the Wankel (rotary) engine, which has since declined to virtual insignificance. We may be able to cull from the evidence just one tentative speculation: perhaps the balance between independents and organized inventive activity has to do with the evolution of a given technology, the former playing a major role during the early stages and the latter becoming more and more important in a technology's mature phase. This is a matter to which we shall return in a later chapter.

The only indicator we have of the production of new ideas as such is the patent record. But we have already referred to the limitations of patent-counting in order to measure inventive activity. With this caveat in mind, we offer the following observations: the percentage of all patents held by American corporations rose from approximately 18 per cent at the turn of the century to around 60 per cent in the 1950s. But since the total number of patents issued grew by over 50 per cent during this period, the decline of the independents in absolute terms was not as great as might appear at first glance.[19] In the 1960s and 1970s, the share of corporation-held patents rose to around 70 per cent, with the percentage of individual patents ranging from 22 to 28 per cent (the residual percentages reflecting assignment of patents to the U.S. government and to foreigners). In 1982, individuals accounted for 25 per cent of all patents granted[20]. In other words, in the last quarter century there has been great stability in the contribution of independents to the patent record. To speak of their demise is obviously an exaggeration.

6.3.2 Strengths of the Independent Inventor

The single greatest advantage the individual inventor may enjoy over a corporate employee is the freedom and flexibility to pursue whatever interests him or her. The independent does not have to submit proposals, does not have to compete for budgetary allocations, and is unencumbered by the need to submit progress reports, attend committee meetings, and fend off attacks on a project.

The second advantage of independents is that they can work in fields for which they are not professionally qualified, thus often bringing fresh ideas and approaches to the solution of problems. The importance of "outsiders" to the production of inventions was recognized during World War II, when both the

United States and Britain assembled persons of greatly varied training and experience in what were called "operational research groups." These groups were charged with the solution of a host of tactical and strategic problems as well as with inventing new devices and production methods. It is instructive to note that in the postwar era Operations Research became a professional discipline in its own right, with all the attendant requirements for specialized academic preparation, for a distinctive methodology, and for a well-defined status of practitioners. Somewhere along the way, the free-wheeling approach to problem-solving and inventing was subordinated to the rules and the methodology developed by the new discipline. May we suspect that similar developments have created similar conditions in other areas of technology, assuring the independent a continuing place in the production of fresh new ideas?

A third reason for the survival of individual inventors is their ability to stick with an idea long after they would have been told to abandon a project by a responsible manager of research. The history of major inventions is replete with cases of inventors who stubbornly, single-mindedly, and with great economic sacrifices, persisted in their search. Some succeeded and some failed, but they probably would have been stopped in any R&D organization conscious of the need to produce results within a defensible period of time.

A final explanation for the independent inventor's continuing importance is psychological: just as some individuals may be attracted to the relative security and the elaborate facilities of a corporate research establishment, so will others place a very high value on the opportunity to work in an environment unencumbered by organizational constraints. Indeed, it is not uncommon to encounter persons who, finding themselves balked in the pursuit of an idea within an organization, quit their jobs and take up as independents. Many new firms in the electronics industry have been founded by employees who turned inventor-entrepreneurs.

6.3.3   The Growth of Organized Inventive Activity

In the twentieth century, industrial production has come increasingly to be dominated, in style and economic weight, by the large, multi-product firm. A corollary of this development has been a growing reliance by these firms on their own, purposeful search for new technological ideas, accompanied also by an increasing cooperation with universities and other institutions. The basic pattern is said to have been set during the second half of the nineteenth century by the German chemical industry, which owed its rapid growth to world dominance to this new approach. Be that as it may, one would not expect to find many modern corporations without their own R&D establishments.

As operating parts of profit-seeking firms, research divisions are pragmatic organizations. The firm supports the production of inventions not as a wealthy patron of the industrial arts but in pursuit of specific objectives, which are expected ultimately to provide more or less predictable economic benefits through:

(1) improvements in the marketability of products;
(2) the development of new materials, processes, or devices for existing or new markets;
(3) the development of new uses for existing materials, processes, or devices;
(4) the achievement of cost savings;
(5) the abatement of dangers or nuisances;
(6) the solution of problems in production or use;
(7) the standardization of processes and products.[21]

If the purposeful, managed pursuit of these objectives within a business is regarded as more likely to produce results than would reliance on an essentially random supply of ideas, then we would expect R&D activities to be internalized in the firm. At the same time we must recognize, however, that this constrains the search process to certain directions, which are going to be defined at least in a general way by managements' perceptions of their firms' line of business. In his Nobel Lecture of 1971, Dennis Gabor provided a perfect illustration of the point:

"In 1947 I was working in the research laboratory of the British Thomson-Houston Company in Rugby, England. It was a lucky thing that the idea of holography came to me via electron microscopy, because if I had thought of optical holography only, the Director of Research, L. J. Davies, could have objected that the Company was an electrical engineering firm, and not in the optical field. But as our sister company, Metropolitan Vickers, were makers of electron microscopes, I obtained permission to carry out some optical experiments."[22]

Although economists like John Kenneth Galbraith have hailed large modern corporations as perfect instruments for producing, developing, and marketing inventions almost at will,[23] there always exists the possibility of a tension between the pursuit of corporate goals on the one hand, and the directions of inventive activity on the other. Therefore, some have argued that this activity, in the aggregate, is not as productive as it might be. Consider the following acerbic opinion of an experienced researcher:

"The best person to decide what research work shall be done is the man who is doing the research. The next best is the head of the department. After that you leave the field of best persons and meet increasingly worse groups. The first of these is the research director, who is probably wrong more than half the time. Then comes a committee, which is wrong most of the the time. Finally there is a committee of company vice-presidents, which is wrong all the time."[24]

Case studies of the accomplishments, and even of some failures, of industrial research abound. These are not adequate, however, to prove or disprove the contention that corporate R&D laboratories are the best kinds of organization for producing inventions. Nor can they justify the criticism frequently levelled at industrial inventive activity: that it tends to operate within too-narrow planning horizons and therefore is not free-roaming enough. Examples supporting such judgments can always be found, as can be cases supporting the opposite point of view.

When we look at organized, corporate R&D in the aggregate, the following observations about its growth can certainly be defended:

(1) It has produced large numbers of inventions and has translated many of these into significant new processes and products. We cannot say whether it has done so in anything like an "optimal" fashion, any more than we can make such *ex post* statements about other kinds of productive activity.

(2) Industrial research is not concerned with the discovery of ultimate scientific or technical potentials but with the purposeful search for broadly preconceived results. If the available knowledge is inadequate, firms may undertake basic research. But the production of scientific information and the creation of other positive externalities are incidental to the pursuit of the firm's economic goals. Although the search is purposeful, i.e., goal-directed, it may of course produce unexpected side results, often called spin-offs. Thus, for example, it was reported that a small company had invented a waterproof but air-permeable fabric coating while working on applied research aimed at developing an artificial heart. The invention turned out to have a number of applications, such as in wound dressings and in sports clothing.[25]

(3) Once industrial research departments have become integral parts of large corporate structures, there is no reason why we should expect them to be exempt from the organizational pressures and constraints that characterize all such structures. How best to set up and manage R&D establishments so as to assure a continuing stream of contributions to a firm's objectives, must remain an open question. But it is well recognized that the management of technological change in general, and of inventive activity in particular, has become part and parcel of the ongoing tasks of corporate leadership, requiring continuous attention. It is not, in other words, a matter for occasional, episodic decisions, as might be suggested by our stage model of change.

6.4   Corporate Strategies for Inventive Activity

We may think of the space for corporate inventive activity as being bounded by three sets of constraints: (1) the existing scientific knowledge, (2) the prevailing conditions in input and output markets, and (3) governmental rules and regulations. Within this space, however, decision-makers are free to pursue a variety of basic strategies, and these strategic lines may vary with the evolution of technologies as well as with the changing fortunes of an enterprise. An authoritative study[26] proposes the following hypotheses about managerial behavior:

(1) If the objective is to generate a succession of relatively small improvements in products or processes, managements may perceive chances for technological gains as

a. uniformly distributed around currently known *nodes* of information, so that modest returns can be obtained from search in virtually any direction, as long as one does not go too far (as though one were mining an ore bed from its rich center, outward toward leaner material);

b. distributed only along certain *paths* which are not fully known and understood, but the pursuit of which promises, on balance, more successes than failures;

c. appearing in *clusters* randomly distributed around the known nodes, so that a broad sweep in many directions improves the chances of a satisfactory average yield from searching (as in drilling for oil in a promising geological structure, where one knows that some holes will be dry and some will bring in oil).

(2) If, in the process of seeking modest gains, decision-makers also expect major inventions to occur every now and then, such a belief may be based on the view that

a. major advances are triggered periodically by the cumulation of smaller, incremental ideas;

b. major new inventions can result only after a series of small improvements to existing technology has established a "mature equilibrium";

c. chances for a high pay-off are distributed randomly among minor inventions, and thus cannot be hunted out directly, but are welcome byproducts of small-step searches.

(3) Strategies aimed directly at generating major advances may rest on the assumption that

a. these represent "giant steps" along established lines of development and therefore can be identified by experts as likely targets for search;

b. major breakthroughs require new expertise and new modes of thought, and therefore can be best achieved by bringing together entirely new groupings of scientists, engineers, and technicians;

c. economically rewarding breakthroughs are most likely to suggest themselves in the process of conducting scientific and exploratory research; therefore, the commitment of resources to target-oriented projects should be restricted to minor, well-defined advances.

These hypotheses help us not only in understanding actual patterns of inventive activity, but they are useful also in interpreting differences in behavior among industries. Nevertheless, many questions remain: (1) What is the influence of an industry's existing technology and product mix on applied-research decisions? (2) Can we conclude anything about differences in strategy from the relative amounts firms spend on applied research? (3) Does the authoritative announcement of lines of strategy improve or impair the acceptance of new ideas in an organization? (4) Do old and new firms pursue notably different strategies? (5) Why do some inventive firms continue to succeed, even when the industry to which they belong appears to be stagnant or declining?

On the basis of the evidence accumulated so far, the answers to these and other questions are inconclusive. Much work remains to be done if we want to get a better understanding of how organized inventive activity works. Such an understanding is not just of academic interest. For better or for worse, public policies aimed at stimulating or directing the production of inventions are based on what we think we know about the inside of that black box, the firm, which turns out new ideas. To a great extent, these policies to date have rested on the simple assumption that spending more money for certain types of search will somehow result in the eventual solution of problems. This assumption has no doubt been strengthened by some spectacular successes, such as the development of nuclear power or the space program. But on balance, the record has been far from encouraging.[27]

6.5 Industry Structure and Inventive Performance

The question that has preoccupied economists for a long time is whether there exists any relationship between the firm structure of an industry on the one hand, and the production of inventions on the other. Although the development of large-scale, organized applied research has been intimately connected with the growth of giant corporations, it is far from clear that the domination of an industry by a few large firms is conducive to high rates of invention and innovation. Such structures seem to have inhibited technological progress in some instances, whereas in others even monopolies proved themselves highly inventive.

On purely theoretical grounds, the issue should not be subject to a lot of dispute. As we have pointed out, inventors are motivated by the prospect of at least a temporary monopoly position. Firms that have turned inventions into innovations will attempt to protect this position with all means at their disposal. This observation is so obvious that Joseph Schumpeter called it "nothing but the tritest common sense."[28] Whether businesses succeed in gaining and retaining such positions does not, of course, depend on their inventive and innovative strategies alone.

The contentious issue is how firms behave once they have attained dominance in their industry . . . in other words, what is the effect of (absolute or relative) firm size on their production of inventions? Theoretical arguments can be adduced for almost any answer to this question, mainly because in this context we once again encounter differences between a static and a dynamic view of efficiency. In a static sense, a firm with a strong quasi-monopolistic position would seem to have little incentive to continue being innovative. But as soon as we consider a dynamic setting for decisions, the rationale underlying short-run profit maximization rules for monopolies (or, for that matter, firms in monopolistic competition or in oligopolies) is far from unequivocal. In this setting, the firm would have to formulate its strategies not only with regard to competitors in its own industry, but it would also have to consider the threat of entry into its markets by inventive firms from other industries. This threat would surely be intensified if the firm behaved like a perfect short-run profit maximizer, thus signalling the attractiveness of its markets to potential entrants.

No wonder, then, that theoretical arguments are inconclusive and that the empirical evidence is mixed. The only statements we can make with some degree of confidence concern the *input side* of the inventive enterprise: large firms are more likely to have separate R&D departments than small ones; large firms spend bigger absolute amounts on applied research than small ones; and large firms are more likely to maintain a diversified portfolio of projects at any given time. Whether the *output* of inventions and innovations is proportionately larger is not so certain.

If it could be shown that the inventive output is a function of total investment in applied research, the case for bigness (in the sense advocated by Galbraith and others, for example) would be easy to establish. As it stands, however, there is some suspicion, supported by not very strong statistical evidence, that the output of inventions per dollar invested may be higher in medium to medium-large corporations than in super-large ones.[29] When one considers market position rather than absolute size, the evidence becomes even more elusive. And evaluations are further confounded in all those situations where the absolute or relative size of a firm in a particular economy is more or less irrelevant in the face of global competition.

In the face of these uncertainties, it would seem more important for public policy to assure conditions for the free entry into an industry of new firms with new technological ideas than to worry about the progressiveness of existing firms, large or small. In other words, to the extent that we have governmental rules and regulations that shelter businesses against competition and (potential) entry, we should not be surprised to encounter something less than a dynamic openness to inventions. Although it was made some years ago, the conclusion reached by an econometrician, Professor Zvi Griliches, still seems valid:

> "Given the paucity of our knowledge about so many aspects of this problem, probably too much attention has been paid by economists to the relation between market structure and inventive activity . . . Whatever evidence we have points to no particular relationship between monopoly, oligopoly or competition and inventive activity. Even if there were some relationship between the two (positive or negative), it could at best have only a second order effect. It would be quite inefficient, I believe, to try to affect the rate of inventive activity in the United States by manipulating antitrust laws."[30]

It is an interesting reflection on the changes in attitude that have occurred on account of both, developments in technology and in international competition, that in recent years there has been increasing doubt whether antitrust laws, conceived essentially on the assumption of a closed economy (i.e., one isolated from international competition), have not stood in the way of applied-research projects so large that they require the pooling of several firms' resources. Thus, for example, antitrust had to be set aside deliberately in order to permit the cooperative efforts aimed at building new, super-large computers.

The economist's task would be a lot simpler if traditional theoretical concepts about the effects of (static) competitiveness on inventive activity were more closely matched by the empirical evidence. Unfortunately, the real world refuses to behave in such a neat fashion. Therefore, we can sympathize with the author who summarized theoretical work on the subject and concluded his discussion of inventive and innovative activity as follows:

> "The outcome of all this is to argue that there are strong theoretical reasons to believe that from economic analysis we can make predictions as to the determinants of the rate of technological advance and the nature of technological advance in different industries . . . However, the empirical support for many of these theories is not really as encouraging as one might hope."[31]

In part, this state of affairs is no doubt attributable to the fact that most empirical work by economists is of relatively recent vintage and that revisions of theories must await the accumulation of more comprehensive data. Given the intellectual and organizational complexities of the inventive process, however, it may well be that the scope of these theories has to be enlarged so as to include variables which economists have traditionally regarded as outside their sphere of interest.

Notes

1. de Jouvenel, B., "Technology as a Means," in Baier, K., and Rescher, N., eds., *Values and the Future* (New York: The Free Press, 1969), p. 221.
2. Friedel, R., "The Plastics Man," *Science 84*, November 1984.
3. Ayres, R. U., *The Next Industrial Revolution* (Cambridge, MA: Ballinger, 1984), p. 122.
4. The role of demand, at least for the case of patented inventions, is discussed at length in Schmookler, J., *Invention and Economic Growth* (Cambridge, MA: Harvard University Press, 1966).
5. Graham-White, C., and Harper, H., *Our First Airways: Their Organization, Equipment, and Finance* (London: John Lane, The Bodley Head, 1919), pp. 76-77.
6. National Resources Committee, *Technological Trends and National Policy* (Washington, DC: U.S. Government Printing Office, 1937), p. 22.
7. Gordon, T. J., "The Feedback between Technology and Values," in Baier, K., and Rescher, N., *op.cit.*
8. Friedel, R., "New Light on Edison's Light," American Heritage of Invention and Technology, Summer 1985.
9. Machlup, F., "The Supply of Inventors and Inventions," in National Bureau of Economic Research, *The Rate and Direction of Inventive Activity: Economic and Social Factors* (Princeton, NJ: Princeton University Press, 1962).
10. Stipp, D., "Inventors Are Seeking Bigger Share of Gains from Their Successes," *The Wall Street Journal*, September 9, 1982.
11. Austin, J. H., *Chase, Chance, and Creativity: The Lucky Art of Novelty* (New York: Columbia University Press, 1978).
12. *Ibid.*, p. 72.
13. *Ibid.*, p. 72.
14. *Ibid.*, p. 77.
15. Hillinger, C., "'Windy' Prof One of a Kind," *The Plain Dealer*, August 14, 1977.

16. Morison, E. E., *Men, Machines, and Modern Times* (Cambridge, MA: M.I.T. Press, 1966), p. 198.

17. MacLaurin, W. R., "The Sequence from Invention to Innovation," *Quarterly Journal of Economics*, February 1953.

18. Jewkes, J., Sawers, D., and Stillerman, R., *The Sources of Invention*, 2nd edn. (New York: Norton, 1969).

19. U.S. Department of Commerce, *Historical Statistics of the United States, 1789-1945* (Washington, DC: U.S. Government Printing Office, 1949), and *Statistical Abstract of the United States*, various annual volumes.

20. National Science Board, *Science Indicators 1982* (Washington, DC: U.S. Government Printing Office, 1983), p. 288.

21. Furnas, C. C., ed., *Research in Industry* (New York: Van Nostrand, 1948), p. 2.

22. Quoted in Kaminov, I. P., and Siegman, A. E., eds., *Laser Devices and Applications* (New York: I.E.E.E. Press, 1973), p. 451.

23. Professor Galbraith first proposed this thesis in his *American Capitalism* (Cambridge, MA: Houghton Mifflin, 1952) and pursued it further with the concept of a dominant corporate "technostructure" in *The New Industrial State* (New York: New American Library, 1967).

24. Jewkes *et al.*, *op. cit.*, p. 111.

25. Bishop, J. E., "Research on an Artificial Heart Leads to a 'Breathable' Fabric," *The Wall Street Journal*, October 19, 1984.

26. Gold, B., "The Framework of Decision for Major Technological Innovation," in Baier, K., and Rescher, N., *op. cit.*

27. See, for example, Ebinger, C. K., "Eclipse of Solar Power Leaves a Burning Need," *The Wall Street Journal*, October 29, 1984, and Peirce, W. S., "Naive Forecasting: The Fiasco of Coal Gasification," *Omega*, September 1985.

28. Schumpeter, J. A., "Capitalism and the Process of Creative Destruction," in Mansfield, E., ed., *Monopoly Power and Economic Performance*, rev. ed. (New York: Norton, 1968), p. 34.

29. Of a vast literature on the subject, the following are especially instructive: Nelson, R., Peck, M. J., and Kalacheck, E. D., *Technology, Economic Growth, and Public Policy* (Washington, DC: Brookings, 1967); and Scherer, F. M., *Industrial Market Structure and Economic Performance*, 2nd ed. (Chicago, IL: Rand McNally, 1980).

30. Griliches, Z., "Comment," in National Bureau of Economic Research, *op. cit.*, p. 353.

31. Stoneman, P., *The Economic Analysis of Technological Change* (Oxford: Oxford University Press, 1963), p. 62.

CHAPTER 7

The Patent System

In the preceding chapter we adopted the view that inventing is a productive activity, involving the commitment of resources to the generation of new ideas. We emphasized the fact that the ability to appropriate the (potential) economic benefits of an invention acts as an important incentive for inventors, and we finally pointed out that nevertheless the production of inventions also creates substantial externalities, i.e., increases in generally accessible new information.

One institution whereby most countries assure inventors a monopoly on their ideas is the granting of patents—property rights of limited duration. Although we have seen that there exist considerable differences in the extent to which various industries rely on patent protection (Table 1.1, above) and although there are many situations in which individual firms resort to other means of appropriating new ideas,[1] the patent system has remained an important, albeit frequently controversial, feature of the U.S. economy. In the present chapter we shall explore the nature of this system, describe briefly the main legal features of a patent, examine the historical development of the institution, and consider the main economic arguments about the pros and cons of patent protection.

7.1 Patents and the Patent System

For the purpose of an economic analysis, it is useful to distinguish between the *patent as a right conferred upon an individual inventor* and the *patent system*, which consists of the sum total of all patents in existence and the information contained in them, as well as of the institutions, expectations, and modes of competitive behavior that have grown around them.

Whenever an arrangement of this type becomes an integral part of the social fabric, the question whether it represents the most efficient means of handling some part of human affairs becomes difficult to answer. In the case of the United States, the granting of patents was regarded as sufficiently important for the new country's development that Article I, Section 8 of the Constitution explicitly confers on Congress the power "to promote the progress of science and the useful arts, by securing for limited times to authors and inventors the exclusive right to their respective writings and discoveries." Although, as we shall see, the copyright and patent laws passed on this basis have undergone substantial changes over the past two centuries, the patent system has remained one of the more firmly entrenched components of the institutional environment in which technical and economic decisions are made.

The question that mainly concerns the economist is whether the social costs of creating monopolies are outweighed by the dynamic benefits that are meant to justify the granting of patents. Despite many efforts to investigate this issue, the results have been anything but conclusive. Attempts to ask people whether they would have made certain inventions, or whether they would go on inventing in the absence of patent protection, have predictably yielded mixed and unconvincing answers. And studies which compare the levels of inventiveness among countries with different types of patent protection run up against the fact that other institutional factors might be just as important in explaining differences in behavior as the patent systems themselves.[2] As with so many social institutions, our uncertainty about the system's net effects is outweighed only by our ignorance of the costs and benefits of eliminating the institution altogether.[3]

Despite repeated and vocal attacks, the patent system has persisted, though changing over time. But most of these changes have been gradual and incremental, reflecting legislative and judicial adaptations to changed conditions. Certainly the growth of patents held by corporations rather than by individual inventor-entrepreneurs has been one of the most significant developments of the current century. It raises the second fundamental economic question: have the original assumptions about the working of the economy, and with them the rationale for patent protection been invalidated by the transformation of modern, industrial economies into systems apparently dominated by the inventive activity of established, large firms?

Before we can try to evaluate some possible answers to these questions, we must get an understanding of what is involved in obtaining a patent and what rights are conferred by it, as well as of the historical evolution of the present-day patent system. We can do no more here than to sketch out some essentials.

7.2   Legal Features of Patents

The details and complexities of patent law are such that its interpretation requires the expertise of a specialized group of professionals, the members of the patent bar. Cynics may claim that many of the law's intricacies are the creation of the lawyers themselves, but the fact remains that both individuals and corporations have to rely on the services of these legal experts in all phases, from the application for a patent to fending off infringement.

When we read the language of the Constitution, as cited above, we realize that the framers of that document did not use the words "science" and "discovery" in the sense in which these terms are defined in Chapter 1.

Nevertheless, as we shall see below, the intent of patent law clearly is to protect inventions, as we use the word today.

7.2.1 Patentable Inventions

In order to be eligible for patent protection, an invention must be: (a) new and unobvious, (b) not previously achieved by someone else, (c) useful and important, and (d) not injurious to public morals and health. Patents may be obtained on "machines," "manufactures," and "compositions of matter," as well as on combinations of these. In addition, patents can also be obtained on certain designs and on new strains of "botanical plants," but design and plant patents play a relatively minor role in the economy at large (although they may be important to an individual or firm).

The provisions of the law are comprehensive and are backed up by a host of judicial decisions. Yet it should be obvious from the very words used in the preceding paragraph that there is considerable latitude for interpretation and consequently for controversy. This problem is intensified by the fact that the U.S. Patent Office has been chronically understaffed and that, as one critic points out, "standards of patentability suffer accordingly."[4] One particular result of this state of affairs has been a tendency for the Patent Office to interpret the "usefulness" criterion so loosely that patent applications are rarely turned down for failure to meet the requirement. In fact, it has been said that only the idea for a perpetual-motion machine is likely to be turned down.[5] Worse yet, patents may be awarded to different individuals for essentially the same invention because of inadequate checks and cross-checks. This increases the likelihood of later infringement suits. Needless to say, there are reasons other than lack of usefulness for which applications may be rejected.

Due mainly to a series of court decisions, the yardstick of "non-obviousness" has been interpreted more stringently. It should be clear, however, that neither criterion is adequate to the task of sorting technically significant inventions from trivial ones. As Professor Scherer points out in his survey, anything from a coin-holding pocket comb to an invention as significant as a method for removing radioactive contaminants from reactor coolants has been thought worthy of patent protection.[6] If we accept the notion that the ultimate test of any invention's worth is provided by the marketplace, this feature of the patent system should not trouble us too much. If the system is defensible as such, then we have to be willing to accept the ridiculous with the sublime. Besides, the distinction between the two often can be made only after the fact, i.e., when an idea has been put to use.

7.2.2 Patent Procedure

An inventor wishing to obtain a patent has to prepare a *petition*, a standardized legal document containing the *specifications* of the invention; these include the general nature of the invention and the purpose for which it is intended, appropriate descriptions and drawings, and a list of *claims* made for the idea. Payment of various fees is connected with successive steps in the proceedings.

Upon receipt of the petition, the Patent Office classifies it. An examiner then searches under this classification for claims in earlier patents that anticipate those made in the new application. If none is found, and other requirements are met, *notice of allowance* of the patent is sent to the petitioner. If anticipating claims are found, the application is rejected (or the inventor withdraws it voluntarily). Under certain conditions, amendments to the petition may be possible.

An inventor whose petition has been rejected may carry his or her case to the Board of Appeals of the Patent Office, and from there to the Court of Customs and Patent Appeals. Each of these steps, from preparation of the petition in proper form to any possible appeal, requires the counsel of a patent attorney.

Once a patent has been issued, it is out of the jurisdiction of the Patent Office. Infringement and other cases now fall within the jurisdiction of the regular courts. Under the U.S. system, there is no presumption of the validity of a patent. This means that the burden of proof rests equally on the patent holder to show that the patent is valid, and on the alleged infringer that it is not. Furthermore, such terms as "patent applied for" or "patent pending," when attached to new products, have no legal significance. In this respect, as well as in certain others, the laws of countries are anything but uniform, frequently giving rise to international misunderstandings and disagreements.

7.2.3 The Nature of Claims

The claims made by an inventor for his idea constitute the heart of a patent. The language in which such claims are described determines the extent of legal protection the patent holder can expect. If claims are too narrow, it becomes easy for others to "invent around" the original idea. If they are phrased too broadly, the Patent Office may find them to extend into the domain of an existing patent and therefore reject them.

The case of the famous Selden automobile patents illustrates the hazards of a too-narrow set of claims. Legal controversy over these patents raged for years, but in essence the matter revolved around Selden's specification of a particular engine type for his automobile. When Henry Ford refused to pay royalties for the alleged use of Selden's inventions, and the case went to court, Ford's attorneys pointed out that the Model T utilized a different form of propulsion than that claimed by Selden. Ford won the case.[7]

7.2.4 The Question of Priority

When two petitions covering essentially the same invention are received, the Patent Office declares *interference*. In such cases, priority of filing does not establish an unassailable position for the inventor. Rather, the *date of conception* ("reduction to practice") becomes the criterion for the award. This date, evidenced by the inventor's own work logs and descriptive documents which have been shown to witnesses help to establish the inventor's claim to having "got there first." In other words, priority of conception rests upon one's ability to write down and explain what the essence of the new idea is.

A classic fight took place between Alexander Graham Bell and a number of other inventors claiming prior conception of the telephone. One of these, Daniel Drawbaugh, alleged that he had conceived of an "electric telephone" as early as 1867-8, whereas Bell claimed conception in 1874, although he obtained his first patent in 1876. Drawbaugh fought the case all the way to the U.S. Supreme Court but lost, because none of the hundreds of witnesses he called to support his claimed date of conception could give an approximately intelligible description of the device.[8]

The problem of simultaneous invention is not an uncommon one. On the one hand, certain scientific or technological developments may increase the chances that several people will draw the same inferences and come up with a new idea. On the other hand, the apparent simultaneity may be no more than a case of imitation. As one writer put it at the turn of the century, when a number of such conflicts had attracted public attention: "When a troop of prattling boys hunt butterflies among the daisies, and some sharpeyed youngster has captured a prize, there are always others of his mates to cry, 'I saw it first'."[9]

Whatever the legal resolution of interference cases, their economic implications are far from clear. From one point of view, incentive effects would remain in force even if the decision on priority were made on arbitrary grounds. But from another, the fact that several individuals or organizations may have committed substantial resources to the production of an invention, with only one getting an exclusive monopoly, may raise the riskiness of inventive activity in a questionable way. Furthermore, when firms suspect or know that they are in a winner-take-all footrace for a major invention, applied research may well be carried out in a costly, crash-program fashion.

Yet, while at least one authority has judged that in such cases "the reward, a monopoly of the product, seems incommensurate with the patentee's actual achievement,"[10] it is also difficult to think of any method for allocating protected property rights among competing inventors in a way that has no adverse effects on incentives, not to mention questions of equity.

7.3   The Origins and Development of the Patent System

The evolution of the patent as a legal institution and the role of patents in advancing technical progress provide an illustration of how societies adapt to changing technological and economic conditions. At the same time they demonstrate how firmly entrenched an institution like the patent system can become.

7.3.1   Historical Background

In his review of patent history, Professor Fritz Machlup[11] points out that the granting of "letters patent," which goes back to fifteenth-century Europe, had its origins in two quite different sources. The first was the tendency of the guilds of craftsmen to operate under very restrictive rules, which included the exact specification of products and of production techniques. Since the guilds could take legal action against any person who violated these rules, the granting of royal patent privileges to an inventor implied a *de facto* permission to do what otherwise would have been prohibited—to introduce a new product or process. In this respect patents, rather than inhibiting competition through the granting of monopoly rights, probably helped to liberate inventor-entrepreneurs from the stranglehold of what had amounted to a tight producers' cartel.

The second source of letters patent was the desire, especially of the British monarchs, to grant special monopoly privileges not only to inventors but also to other favorites. Needless to say, those not so favored resented this practice, which seemed to give some persons an economic headstart through no technical or economic merit of their own. Therefore, in 1623-4 Parliament passed the *Statute of Monopolies*, forbidding the granting of exclusive rights to trade by the Crown, with one exception: letters patent could be awarded to "the first and true inventor" of a new manufacture, for a period of fourteen years. This time limit was based on the then-prevalent, seven-year apprenticeship term. Over the life of the patent, two generations of apprentices could be trained to acquire the know-how connected with an invention, then the idea fell into the public domain.

Although the British law served as a model for the development of similar statutes in many other countries, considerable differences existed in the legal philosophies underlying the institution of the patent. In some legal systems, patents came to be regarded as part of the "natural" property rights of persons; in others, the award of a patent was viewed as a privilege bestowed upon the citizen by state, not as a natural entitlement; and in yet others, the issue of right vs. privilege was side-stepped in favor of a simple, operational definition of the protection implied by a patent. This diversity in fundamental conceptions, as well as in the actual provisions of patent laws, has made for continuing problems in the international enforcement of patent rights. An International Union for the Protection of Industrial Property, to which all industrial and many developing countries belong, has been successful in reconciling some conflicts, but much remains to be done.

Throughout the nineteenth century, the patent systems of European countries had their ups and downs under frequent attacks from those who thought that patents were inhibitive of industrial development and free trade. Some countries even abolished their patent laws for a time, only to return to the institution once again. Aside from such fundamental objections to the granting of monopolies via intellectual property rights, virtually every country has also had reform movements of various types, whose aim it was and is to bring the patent system into closer conformity with the reformers' particular interpretation of the goals of equity and efficiency.

7.3.2   The Development of the American Patent System

In colonial America the British Statute of Monopolies was applied unevenly in the several colonies. In general, the absence of a strong manufacturing class meant that there was no great interest in the subject of patent protection. In a brief but comprehensive historical survey, Professor Sherwood[12] shows that the authors of the Constitution were by no means unanimous about the desirability of patents. According to him, the wording of Section 8, Article 1 (see p. 129, above) represented a compromise which simply followed the English model, because the framers of the document had more important problems to deal with in their debates.

That no one expected large numbers of patent applications is perhaps best indicated by the fact that the first American patent law, passed by Congress in 1790, provided that all such applications should be reviewed by a Patent Board consisting of the secretary of state, the secretary of war, and the attorney general. Although not many patents were in fact applied for, these three gentlemen really did not have time to do their jobs as evaluators of inventions. Therefore, the law was changed in 1793, requiring simply that the applicant swear that he had made a "new" invention upon registering his description and claims. The registration system obviously invited abuses, and so a new law of 1836 created the Patent Office, which was to examine inventions before a patent was issued. This law laid the foundation of the present-day patent system, although later amendments, new statutes, and a host of court decisions greatly modified many of its original conceptions. The most recent complete rewriting of the law occurred in the Patent Act of 1952, which however has since been amended on numerous occasions.

We cannot follow all of these developments in detail, but it is worth pointing out that, perhaps more than ever before, the evolution of new fields of technology in recent years has created the need to redefine the scope of intellectual property rights as well as the meaning of patent and copyright protection. Of necessity, the first steps are taken by the courts when they are confronted by entirely new types of cases. Thus, for example, the issue whether new computer software could be protected by either patents or copyright was settled differently in a number of judicial opinions, until Congress explicitly granted copyright protection to computer programs. In the meantime, however, the further development of hardware and software technology frequently required that users make working copies of programs, thus ostensibly violating copyright. Therefore, in December 1980 Congress once again had to pass an amendment dealing with this new contingency. We cite the relevant wording in order to give the reader some flavor of what is required to deal with a relatively simple new fact of technology:

> ". . . it is not an infringement for the new owner of a copy of a computer program to make or authorize the making of another copy or adaptation of that computer program provided:
>
> (1) that such a new copy or adaptation is created as an essential step in the utilization of the computer program in conjunction with a machine and that it is used in no other manner, or
> (2) that such new copy or adaptation is for archival purposes only and that all archival copies are destroyed in the event that continued possession of the computer program should cease to be rightful.
>
> Any exact copies prepared in accordance with the provisions of this section may be leased, sold, or otherwise transferred, along with the copy from which such copies were prepared, only as part of the lease, sale, or other transfer of all rights in the program. Adaptations so prepared may be transferred only with the authorization of the copyright owner."[13]

If the reader suspects that further law suits involving this provision will occur despite (or perhaps because of) its intricate formulation, he or she is probably correct. Another example of how technological advances can challenge established concepts of entitlement to protection is provided by genetic engineering. In June 1980, the U.S. Supreme Court ruled that man-made microorganisms, i.e. new forms of life, are subject to patent protection. The Court also stated that if Congress disagreed with this ruling, it should debate the matter and pass an appropriate statute.[14]

In addition to dealing with the implications of new technologies, patent law also must reflect changes in the nature of domestic and international competition, changing perceptions about the role of the federal government in supporting inventive activity, and other institutional developments. No wonder that in 1982 a U.S. senator claimed that "We have passed more positive patent legislation in the last two years than we did in the previous 20."[15] Whether all this legislation is needed or "positive" must remain an open question, but it certainly shows that the patent system itself is subject to change and adaptation, just like the technologies whose development it is meant to stimulate.

An interesting example of how institutional change can raise new issues of law is provided by the recent growth of joint ventures in applied research. These ventures are motivated either by a desire to reduce the inherent riskiness of inventive activity (or, for that matter, of development) through a pooling of investment by several companies, or by the persuasive economies of scale of R&D in certain fields of technology. The evaluation of their consequences for competition and for the efficient allocation of resources over the long run must consider both, antitrust implications and questions of patent law. The original intent of the law clearly was to stimulate competition in invention and innovation. What happens to this rationale when, say, half the firms in an industry form a joint venture in research, agreeing to share any patents that may result, thus excluding the other firms in the industry from any benefits? Would a requirement that outsiders be given access to new technology "on reasonable terms" reduce the incentives for investing in joint research projects? These and similar questions have had to be addressed by the courts and, eventually, by Congress. Since answering them necessarily involves speculations about the future competitive impact of these arrangements, rulings and laws have frequently been controversial.[16]

7.3.3 U.S. Patent Activity in the Twentieth Century

How important has the patent system been to technological advancement and industrial growth? Has its significance changed over time? Since we have only a count of patents but no measure of the significance of individual patents, our answers to these questions necessarily have to be tentative. Case studies show that there are many instances in which the development of basic technologies, and of industries founded on them, hinged on some key patents. Here, however, we are concerned only with the aggregate picture.

In Table 7.1 we show the annual average number of patents applied for and granted for successive five-year periods, since the turn of the century. From

TABLE 7.1 *Patent applications, patents issued, and recipients; annual averages for five-year periods, 1901–83*

Years	Average number of applications	Average number of patents issued	Percentage of patents[a] issued to		
			U.S. Individuals	U.S. Corporations	Others[b]
1901–05	49,357	28,750	81.7	7.1	1.2
1906–10	60,199	34,312	79.4	19.4	1.2
1910–15	67,873	37,248	75.3	23.1	1.6
1916–20	70,327	38,929	72.3	26.3	1.6
1921–25	81,081	40,795	69.1	28.5	2.4
1926–30	87,099	43,872	57.7	39.3	3.0
1931–35	63,613	47,850	47.3	48.1	4.6
1936–40	63,943	40,235	42.3	52.0	5.7
1941–45	53,083	32,933	37.1	57.8	5.1
1946–50	72,017	28,815	40.9	54.4	4.7
1951–55	70,330	38,530	40.7	52.1	7.2
1956–60	76,956	47,494	32.3	56.4	11.4
1961–65	87,216	51,994	26.9	58.7	14.4
1966–70	95,248	65,029	22.6	58.6	18.8
1971–75	102,082	75,106	23.2	51.4	25.4
1976–80	101,800	62,460	20.8	48.2	31.0
1981–83[c]	106,567	60,167	20.2	44.9	34.8

[a] Until 1920, percentage distribution refers to first year of each period.
[b] U.S. government and foreign patentees.
[c] Latest available data are for a three-year period.
Sources: U.S. Department of Commerce, *Historical Statistics of the United States, 1789 to 1957* (Washington, DC: U.S. Government Printing Office, 1960), and *Statistical Abstract of the United States*, various annual volumes.

these figures it appears that patent activity has gone through three phases: a period of relatively moderate growth, which lasted until the mid-1930s; a fifteen-year period, including the tail end of the Great Depression, World War II and its aftermath, during which the number of patents issued each year declined markedly; and a phase of vigorous growth since the 1950s.

The data also reflect the shift from independent inventors to corporations, which we discussed in Chapter 6. Another notable feature is the variation in the ratio between patent applications and patents granted. It ranges from a low of 40 per cent in 1946–50 to a high of 75 per cent in 1931–5. Unless we assume that there was some systematic change in the quality of applications, these changes have to be attributed to differences in the stringency of examination by the Patent Office. The fact that the highest ratio was achieved during the depth of the Great Depression adds at least a bit of circumstantial evidence in favor of this conjecture.

Finally, the sharp increase in the proportion of patents issued to foreigners since the early 1960s is worth noting. During 1961–65, foreign-held patents accounted for 12 per cent of all new patents granted; by the 1980s, about one-third of all patents were issued to foreigners. This development is no doubt due to a growing penetration of the American market by foreign industrial products and the rise in direct investment in the United States by foreign multinational corporations. It has also been claimed, however, that especially the Japanese have engaged in "patent overkill," obtaining protection for many ideas that "are not worth the paper they are written on."[17] Be that as it may, we must observe also that the trend has been matched by the growing number of patents obtained abroad by American individuals and firms.

These numbers do not tell us anything about possible changes in the relationship between patent activity and industrial growth. We have observed on several occasions that there are great differences in the extent to which particular industries rely on patent protection. In the aggregate, it appears as though growth in patent activity and in manufacturing output moved roughly apace in the first four decades of the century, but despite some careful analyses by economists, the evidence is not very strong.[18] Developments since World War II are illustrated in Fig. 7.1, where we have related an index of patents issued to U.S. individuals and corporations to an index of manufacturing output, with both sets of figures calculated as five-year moving averages in order to smooth out shorter-term fluctuations. It can be seen that, except for the first decade after the war, patenting grew at a much slower rate than did manufacturing output. Since 1975, the number of patents issued annually has actually declined. We conclude that in numbers, if not necessarily in quality, the relative significance of patents to industrial growth has declined. In a well-known study of patent activity, Professor Schmookler offered a number of explanations for this trend, including a shift from purely empirical work to more science-based invention, a less favorable judicial and legislative treatment of corporate patent activity, and the development of other means for protecting

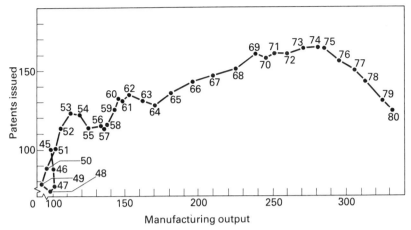

FIG. 7.1 Relationship between manufacturing output and patents issued to U.S. inventors, 5-year moving averages, 1945–80 (indices, 1945 = 100).
Sources: See Table 7.1.

inventions.[19] Whatever the reasons, the apparent decline in the economic importance of patents to aggregate industrial production has not caused the patent system to become a less contentious institution. Therefore, we want next to examine the nature of the patent holder's monopoly, and then we shall turn to a brief survey of the major arguments in the controversy.

7.4 The Inventor's Monopoly

According to the law, the holder of a patent has the exclusive right for 17 years "to vend, use or sell" the invention. The implication is clear: the patentee's monopoly has value only to the extent that he or someone else sees a commercial potential for the idea. The point is often overlooked in arguments about the social rationale for the patent system.

The incentive effects that are supposed to result from the grant of time-limited monopolies ultimately must be evaluated not in terms of the number of inventions made, but in terms of the effect of secure property rights to an idea on investment in development and innovation.

In his discussion of the development of psychoactive drugs, Professor S. H. Snyder provides a fine example of what can happen when such protection is not available:

> "The usefulness of lithium was appreciated by many research psychiatrists by the mid-1960s. However, since it is a common salt and can't be patented, major pharmaceutical companies were unwilling to invest heavily in the development of lithium for clinical use . . . Thus a full 20 years elapsed between the first publication of lithium's therapeutic effect and its introduction into American psychiatry . . ."[20]

In practice, a patent holder faces a number of possibilities for drawing benefits from his invention, some of them complementary and some mutually exclusive. The most important choices are: (1) The inventor can raise the necessary capital for development and innovation and thus become an entrepreneur; (2) he or she can sell the invention to another party for a one-time payment; (3) he or she can license the invention against the promise of royalties, i.e., an agreed-upon share of the economic benefits derived by the innovator, or against the partner's promise also to make his patents available in similar fashion; and (4) the inventor may decide neither to use nor to sell the invention.

7.4.1   The Inventor-innovator

One of the original arguments for giving inventors a time-limited monopoly on their idea was that this would enable them to find investors who would stake them to the cost of developing, producing, and marketing their inventions. The history of major inventions, especially in the nineteenth century, is replete with examples of patent holders who followed precisely this path.[21] And despite the growth of corporate inventive activity, the inventor-entrepreneur is still a common feature today. This is especially so in new fields of technology, such as electronics, where the potential for new products appears large and where development and entry costs are relatively low.

If the inventor is successful in turning out a workable product and if there is demand for this product, we can describe his position with the standard model for a monopolist (see Fig. 7.2). Shown are the demand curve D and its corresponding marginal revenue curve, MR, as well as the firm's average total cost (ATC) and marginal cost (MC). Short-run profit-maximizing output will be at Q^*, where marginal cost is equal to marginal revenue; the price charged will be P^*, and the monopolist's total profit will be equal to $CP^* \times Q^*$, shown as the outlined rectangle in the diagram.

All the economist's usual observations about the allocative inefficiency of monopolies apply: fewer resources are absorbed into the manufacture of the product and its price will be higher than would be the case if patent protection did not prevent the entry of other firms. One additional observation is worth making: If competitors were allowed to enter the market, and the innovating firm's cost remain the same, the result would not necessarily be to eliminate all of the inventor's economic profit. Everything then depends on what happens to demand for the product. One possibility is that imitators force the monopolist to lower his price, but that his demand curve is not affected, because the marketing efforts of the new competitor(s) have created additional demand. Under this assumption, entry would tend to force the price down, but only to P_c, the point where the marginal cost curve intersects the demand curve. The firm's economic profit would then be equal to the area $C'P_c \times Q_c$.

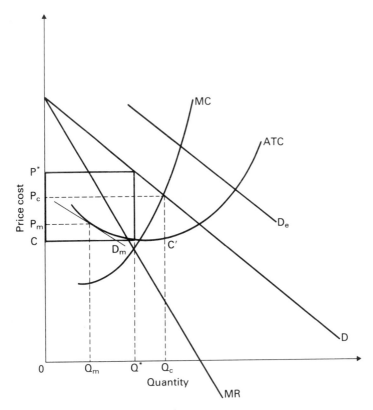

FIG. 7.2 Position of a patent monopoly before and after entry of imitators.

Alternatively, one could imagine that the combined marketing and advertising of all firms increase total demand to the point where the original monopolist actually faces a new, higher demand curve such as D_e. The fact that firms in newly-developed and growing product markets do not play a zero-sum game for some fixed amount of total sales is well known. An extreme, but not at all hypothetical, case of intermediate products is the one where the patent holder for a superior new product confronts total resistance from industrial customers, because they do not want to become dependent on one supplier. Thus, for example, automobile manufacturers were unwilling to make the modifications to wheel rims necessary for adopting tubeless tires, as long as such tires were available only from the original patentee, B. F. Goodrich. Only by conceding the invention to its competitors could the firm generate *any* demand for the new product.

Defenders of the patent system who claim that an inventor-entrepreneur would never get any profit at all if it were not for patent protection, ignore these and other possibilities. Whether the assumptions underlying the models are justified and whether the *ceteris paribus* (other things, especially costs, remaining equal) condition holds in a particular case is a matter for empirical investigation, as is the question how long it will take before new entrants begin to erode the inventor's monopoly. Eventually, when a product market has matured and total demand is stagnant, we might visualize a situation like the one illustrated by demand curve D_m in the diagram. Readers will recognize this as the equilibrium position of the firm in monopolistic competition, where the market price obtained by the seller of a (differentiated) product is indeed equal to average total costs. This solution begs the question whether such mature markets are not likely to be oligopolistic, in which case entirely different models of firm behavior would be appropriate. Relaxing additional assumptions quickly makes the theoretical case indeterminate . . . which is one of the reasons for controversy.

What if an existing firm follows the pattern described above, by introducing a new, patented product? The arguments for granting it a time-limited monopoly remain essentially the same, although they may be tempered by additional considerations. Presumably, multi-product corporations have marketing and distribution networks in place, thus reducing the cost of introducing a new product as well as the economic consequences of failure. Furthermore, it can be argued that such businesses can maintain their monopoly positions beyond the original life of a patent by directing their R&D effort at producing patentable, follow-up inventions. These and other considerations give rise to many of the contemporary criticisms of the patent system. Here we want to conclude only that, in principle, a corporation that establishes a new line of business, based on patents, faces all the hazards of an inventor-entrepreneur. If, as is often claimed, large firms tend to be less innovative than smaller ones, there must be other factors that offset their apparent advantages. This is a matter we shall have to consider in the next chapter.

7.4.2   Arm's-length Sale of Inventions

The inability to raise the capital for developing an idea, risk-aversion, or other considerations may induce an inventor to sell a patented idea in an arm's-length transaction, i.e., for a one-time payment of a stipulated sum. In particular, we would expect to find such transactions between independent inventors and corporations that have the resources and facilities for development. There have been many spectacular examples of the outright sale of inventions that brought seller and purchaser huge economic benefits. In 1899, Leo Baekeland, famous mainly for the invention and development of Bakelite, the first plastic material, sold his idea for a photographic paper that allowed making prints under artificial light to Eastman Kodak for $750,000, at that time a fabulous price. On the other hand, many inventors who sold their ideas felt later that they were not compensated adequately, because their inventions yielded unexpectedly large benefits. In recent years, for example, a former employee filed a lawsuit against Sears, Roebuck & Co., to get additional compensation for a socket wrench he had invented and which proved a major commercial success.

Economists would regard the existence of an efficient market for inventions as an important feature of a well-functioning system. But arm's-length transactions face a host of difficulties. For one thing, the purchaser must make his decision in the face of considerable ignorance about the invention's features. After all, if the seller provided all the necessary information, "the cat would be out of the bag," and there would be little reason for the buyer to pay anything, especially if he does not expect to have any continuing relationship with the seller. There have been many instances in which independent inventors who tried to sell an idea to a large corporation later claimed that the deal fell through because the firm had in fact "stolen" their idea. As a consequence, some large companies refuse to talk to independents as a matter of principle, feeling that the small chance of meeting up with a useful invention is more than outweighed by the poor public relations and the cost of legal action in cases where the inventor claims infringement.

Given the absence of anything approaching full information, the market's efficiency may be impaired also by the methods whereby prices are arrived at. For the case of any one invention, the agreed-upon price probably reflects some sort of subjective valuations by buyer and seller, as well as their respective bargaining power. But the record of actual prices, as far as they become public knowledge, forms the signals that will influence future transactions. If potential sellers feel that, as a group, they have been "preyed upon" by buyers, they may not even consider drawing benefits from their inventions in this fashion, resorting to other, perhaps less efficient, methods. The opposite is true for potential buyers.

Given these difficulties, firms that have produced inventions connected with, but somewhat peripheral to, their current structure may decide to integrate forward or backward, or to diversify their operations in order to internalize the potential benefits. Thus the inherent problems of this particular market for information could well have contributed to the growth of large corporations beyond what would otherwise have been considered desirable.

Another source of potential trouble lies in the typical employment contracts of invention workers. These contracts usually stipulate that any patents obtained by the employee must be assigned to the company that hired him and pays his or her salary. But what if the individual makes an invention that has nothing to do with the employer's technology or line of business? Should the inventor be entitled to sell such an idea to a third party or is the employer's claim all-embracing? If the dividing line between "inside" and "outside" inventions were always clear-cut, such problems would not arise. In practice, however, many cases have had to be decided by the courts.

7.4.3 Licensing and Royalties

The most common form in which patented inventions are shared is licensing, i.e., the sale of the idea against periodic payments, frequently based on the amount of revenues derived from its commercialization. On the face of it, this is riskier than the outright sale (at whatever price), because the receipt of a reward depends on the assignee's technical and economic success. Where one of the partners to such an agreement is an independent inventor, this consideration may carry substantial weight. In practice, however, licensing is an activity carried on primarily by corporations, many of which maintain extensive networks of such agreements, in which the mutual exchange of patents takes the place of royalty payments.

The cross-licensing of patents among firms represents a means of reconciling various components of a given technology, and it helps to avoid wasteful duplication of effort. For that reason, it contributes in principle to the efficient working of the economy. On the other hand, however, licensing arrangements have also proven to be one of the most effective means of cartelizing industries and markets.[22] They may be used to lock out competitors, and they have often been tied in with provisions concerning other aspects of firm conduct, such as sales quotas, market area assignments, and pricing. The practices are clearly illegal in the United States, but American corporations often have to contend with the fact that agreements of this type are perfectly legal in many other countries. International licensing may raise strategic and defense issues and therefore has been the subject of continuing governmental attempts at surveillance.

From the individual firm's viewpoint, ongoing licensing agreements also create some liabilities. Most important is the fact that a dissolution of such a relationship, for whatever reason, still leaves the former partner, or partners, with all the technology and know-how acquired during the relationship. And this information may produce spill-over effects that strengthen the ex-partner firm as a competitor, even though it may not infringe on any existing patents. Nowhere are these hazards more apparent than in situations where the partner is a foreign firm, subject to a different patent jurisdiction. Efforts on the part of corporations to avoid problems by internalizing all key technology have been cited as one of the main reasons for the proliferation of multinational firms in manufacturing.

7.4.4   The Non-use of Patents

One of the most controversial options legally available to an inventor is to do nothing at all with an invention. While most people would regard the decision of a land owner to let his plot lie idle, because he is speculating on some more profitable future use, as entirely defensible, they view the social and economic consequences of idle inventions with considerable suspicion. Needless to say, we would also expect independent inventors who find no market for their ideas to claim that they were being "frozen out" by existing economic interests.

In this connection, we must first set aside the stories about unused ideas that belong to the realm of popular myths, such as the 100 mile-per-gallon carburettor that, according to recurrent rumors and even news stories, is being withheld by avaricious automobile and oil company interests. What we are left with, then, is the fact that many corporations protect the technology they are currently utilizing by accumulating hundreds of patents that form a protective fence around products and processes. This makes it increasingly difficult for competitors to invent around these patents and leads, it is argued, to wasteful investment in applied research.

Under current antitrust law and relevant judicial decisions, the accumulation of patents is legal when it is the result of a company's own R&D efforts. Only the building of protective fences through the buying up of other firms' patents may be considered a violation of the law. From the legal point of view this seems perfectly reasonable, but the economist realizes that patent accumulation probably is a game in which the rich get richer, and the rest get left out. Having built up the capability of producing patents in a given field of technology, a corporation may find that the benefits of further strengthening its protective fence may be low, but so is the marginal cost of obtaining additional patents. Arguably even more important is the deterrent effect the practice may have on potential competitors, who would confront very high costs in their attempts to overcome the entrenched firm's advantages.

These are speculations that would have to be substantiated by specific evidence. But even if it were true that the pyramiding of patents by large corporations produces some undesirable economic results, there still remains the question what should be done about it without producing even less desirable secondary effects. There seems to exist no way to force patent holders to develop their inventions; if, for example, specific tax incentives were offered, development and innovation might be sustained only because of these tax benefits. If penalties were imposed, the resulting slow-down in patenting may include ideas that might have been very useful in addition to useless ones. A policy of selectively picking "key inventions" and forcing their development raises even more questions. Not only is there no valid presumption that legislators or bureaucrats are better at picking "winners" than are business decision-makers, but there is also the strong possibility that the process would quickly become subject to political and special-interest group pressures.

That the non-use of patents may result precisely from a faulty understanding of "the public interest" is illustrated by the history of government-financed applied research. Until 1980, patents resulting from federally funded inventive activity were in the public domain—free for the taking by anyone who wanted to develop them. The rationale seemed persuasive: if the government used tax moneys to finance inventions, then no private firm should be allowed a monopoly. Against this stood the view that if all producers have equal access to an invention, none of them will want to develop it, because there is little promise of profit in a marketable product that any competitor can copy under legal protection. In actual fact, large numbers of patents that were potentially of great benefit remained idle under the old law.[23]

It took some time for this realization to overcome the legislature's conception of the public interest, but in 1980 the law was amended to allow small businesses, universities, and non-profit organizations to retain patents on federally funded inventions.[24] Later on, bills extending these provisions to large firms were introduced and passed. As a result, there has been a renewed flourishing of University-industry cooperation in the development of new processes and products. Many non-profit organizations that derived at least partial research support from the government formed for-profit subsidiaries to work on the commercialization of new ideas. And federal funding was probably allocated more rationally by recipients because of the prospect of direct economic benefits. Certainly, the interests of the country have been served better than they had been under the old arrangements.

7.5 Economic Evaluations of the Patent System

Having discussed the patent system's most important features and the position of a patentee, we can turn to a summary of the controversy about the system. In the interest of efficient presentation, we shall list first the main considerations adduced by those who support patents as an economic institution; we shall turn to the most telling arguments against patents; and finally, we shall consider some proposals for reform. This approach is a matter of convenience only. Not all supporters or critics would subscribe to all the arguments, nor do all those who find the present system wanting provide clear remedies.

Although there exists an extensive economic literature on the patent system, most of this work represents variations on the theme with which we are already familiar: If there is demand for his invention, the patentee (or the entity to whom he has transferred his rights) enjoys a monopoly position. This implies *allocative inefficiency*. But, under a number of perfectly reasonable assumptions, it can also be shown that the existence of the system—though not of each individual patent or group of patents—contributes to the economy's *dynamic efficiency*. It is unlikely that better theories or more empirical research will resolve this fundamental conflict.

7.5.1 *Main Arguments in Favor of the Patent System*

Those who think patents are a useful feature of our economic system are most likely to draw on the following arguments:

(1) Well-defined and protected property rights are essential to a market economy, in which rational self-interest guides the behavior of individuals. The legal protection of intellectual property contributes to the economy's smooth functioning, because it creates greater certainty about the status and role of participants in transactions.

(2) Although patents confer monopoly rights, the very fact that the technological bases for these rights are made public contributes to the body of

generally accessible information. Not only does the patent record document the advancement of useful knowledge, it also helps to avoid the waste of having people invest in the search for information that already exists. Besides, the time limitation of the monopoly assures that anyone can utilize all the information contained in a patent at the end of the protection period.

(3) The patent system provides the necessary incentives for further investment in technological advancement. This is a two-pronged argument: on the one hand, it implies that the assurance of legal protection is required to induce development and innovation; and on the other, existing patents (and monopoly positions) are assumed to motivate others to come up with even better inventions in order to attack existing monopolies.

(4) Even in the age of large-scale corporate inventing, patent protection is essential, because many modern technologies require large investments and long time periods for the development and commercialization of new ideas. At least some firms in some industries would have little reason to expend funds on applied research, experimentation, pilot plants, etc., if they did not have the assurance that others are prevented from simply taking all the information thus produced. And outside financiers would be unlikely to commit funds to ventures the inherent uncertainty of whose outcomes is increased even further by the hazards of imitation.

(5) To the extent that patents cover successful process innovations, lower costs of production and lower market prices will result even if the patentee behaves like a rational monopolist (i.e., maximizes short-run profit). This argument assumes, of course, that such cost-reducing advances would not have occurred without patent protection.

(6) The patent law encourages the development of improved products, because it allows firms to extend their monopoly positions through improvement patents. Having established a market on the basis of some major product innovation, a dynamically efficient firm will try to forestall the entry of competitors by making product improvements.[25]

Summing up, we recognize a common feature in all of these arguments: they assume that other means of appropriating new technical information would not be sufficient to motivate all the advances made under patent protection. This is, of course, an assumption that cannot be put to an empirical test.

7.5.2   Arguments against Patents

(1) Patents create monopolies, and all monopolies involve a misallocation of society's resources. Even under the best of circumstances, firms' monopoly positions are very likely to extend beyond the implications of the protected invention itself. One example of this is the creation of de facto cartels through cross-licensing.

(2) A socially optimal system of knowledge production must reflect the fact

that the marginal cost of using existing information is zero. The originators of new ideas can benefit from them in ways other than by charging a price for the information itself; therefore, the creation of "artificial" property rights is wasteful.[26]

(3) Patent holders may capitalize on inventions by suppressing their development, even though these inventions would benefit the public. Even if the patentee has no economic incentive to innovate, others might. Unused, and unusable, information represents an even greater waste than information used only by a monopolist.

(4) Patents also lead to waste by inducing others to invent around protected monopoly positions. This practice involves an unknown but substantial cost to society, because it rarely results in genuinely superior products. The common corporate strategy of fencing in utilized technology by means of numerous fringe patents adds to this cost.

(5) Because there is no legal presumption of the validity of a patent, the equal legal burden of proof falling upon patentee and alleged infringer is anything but equal in economic terms. Given the differences in wealth position between individuals and firms, or even between large firms and small firms, it is possible for one party to a conflict to "squeeze" the other in protracted lawsuits. Therefore, the patent law often fails today even with respect to what might be regarded as its only justification—the protection of the small inventor.

(6) In a modern industrial economy, patent protection is unnecessary as an incentive for technological effort, because inventors can rely on other technical and institutional factors to achieve quasi-rents, such as (a) imitation lags, (b) the original inventor-innovator's lead in markets, (c) the extensive know-how required for the utilization of many technologies, (d) customers' "brand loyalty," (e) scale economies, and so on.

7.5.3 Proposals for Reform of the Patent System

The above lists of arguments pro and con patents, which we could have extended even further, suggest that some defenders and attackers are con-cerned with the very concept of the patent as a legal institution, whereas others deal only with certain aspects of the law and the behavior they are likely to induce. It is not surprising, therefore, that over the years numerous proposals for reforms of the patent law and its administration should have been made by individuals and by what one authority called "an interminable procession of blue-ribbon commissions and special legislative committees,"[27] Despite a lot of legislation, however, the essence of the patent system has remained untouched.

Suggestions for changes reflect in part features of other countries' patent laws and in part original ideas on how the system might be made to function more to the proponents' liking. The following are among the most important proposals:

(1) In order to avoid both the granting of large numbers of trivial patents and the burden on a patentee of proving the validity of his patent, the law should be changed to establish more stringent criteria and to require a careful, expert examination of all petitions. With well over 100,000 applications arriving at the Patent Office each year, this would obviously require an increase in the size and an improvement in the quality of the Office's staff. One would expect, however, that once such a reform was in place, a higher degree of self-screening of ideas would result in a lower number of petitions.

Nevertheless, the experience of countries with strict examination procedures shows that there is a cost involved in this reform. In the German Federal Republic, for example, the average lag between application and the issuance of a patent has been reported to be in excess of five years.[28] Under these conditions, controversies over priority assume greater importance, and the period of actual protection is stretched beyond what was intended in the law.

(2) Another set of proposals deals with the length of time for which patents should be granted. Some critics think that the uniform protection of seventeen years fails to discriminate among different types of inventions, especially with respect to their likely economic importance. A number of more or less elaborate schemes have been suggested for varying the length of protection. They all raise the same question: who is to decide, in advance of development and commercialization, how a given invention should be classified? Only in the case of so-called improvement patents might one be able to make any reasonable judgments.

(3) Some reform proposals concern the commercial use of a developed invention before a patent is taken out. Where inventor-innovators are already deriving economic benefits, later patent applications are taken to reflect an *ex post facto* attempt legally to monopolize an established market. It is suggested that strict criteria be set to avoid this possibility. This sounds fair enough until one considers the bureaucratic problems that are bound to arise in determining exactly when an (as yet unpatented) invention was made and when commercial use began.

(4) A more radical reform proposal suggests compulsory licensing as a remedy for the non-use of patents. If a patentee does not utilize an invention within some specified period, and if he refuses to license another party, this party may apply to the courts for the granting of a compulsory licence, if certain criteria are met. Several countries, including Britain and Japan, have compulsory-licensing laws. Their experience shows, however, that the number of applications made is likely to be very small. This may be due to the cost of legal proceedings, to uncertainty about the fees or royalties to be set, or to the fact that the mere existence of the law discourages patentees from refusing to license voluntarily. Furthermore, there is the possibility that firms would opt for greater secrecy or other means of protecting their inventions, thus reducing the information function of the patent system.[29]

(5) Concern with the accumulation of patents and non-use has also triggered proposals for annual taxes or fees, to be paid by the patentee in order to maintain the validity of the patent. Some proponents suggest that fees be progressive over time, so that maintenance becomes more and more expensive. Supposedly, this feature of the law would discourage frivolous patenting as well as the protective accumulation of patents. With respect to the latter, however, one guesses that fees would have to be very high in order to cause the abandonment of patents that provide a fence around some firm's utilized technology; such high fees would not, however, be socially desirable or equitable when it comes to individual inventor-entrepreneurs or small firms. Maintenance fees are part of the patent systems of a number of countries, including Great Britain, Switzerland, and Germany. Evidence from them suggests that about half the patents are abandoned by non-payment within seven or eight years and that fewer than 10 per cent are kept in force for their full legal life.[30]

Whatever economists may think about the desirability of these various reforms, political resistance has prevented the introduction of any of them in the United States. Here, too, we observe that the interests and expectations created by the existing patent system, of which the interests of the patent bar are a major and influential force, militate against a substantial revision. In the face of these attitudes, proposals to do away with patents altogether, even if one thought such a revolutionary move could be justified on economic grounds, can hardly be taken seriously.

7.6 Concluding Observations

In his summary evaluation of the economic evidence pro and con the patent system, Professor Machlup concludes that all the arguments, though they purport to be based on reasoned judgments, are in fact made on the basis of unstated assumptions about the working of the economy. And most of them do not offer any evidence that these assumptions hold true in the real world. He summarizes his review by stating:

> "No economist, on the basis of present knowledge, could possibly state with certainty that the patent system, as it now operates, confers a net benefit or a net loss on society . . . If one does not know whether a system 'as a whole' (in contrast to certain features of it) is good or bad, the safest 'policy conclusion' is to 'muddle through'—either with it, if one has long lived with it, or without it, if one has lived without it."[31]

Although this evaluation was made a quarter century ago, neither additional theoretical developments nor the accumulation of more empirical evidence have changed its sound common sense. The American patent system has evolved under unique historical and economic conditions. The fact that other nations' patent laws have different underlying philosophies and different features reflects their particular experience. We must not conclude that social institutions can be as readily transferred from country to country as can technology. Having said this, we must hasten to add that international differences in patent law, just like differences in other laws, do create problems for trade, investment, and technology transfer. But it would be as utopian to expect nations to agree on a uniform patent system as it would be to expect them to adopt a common system of taxation or trade regulation.

Notes

1. In a conversation with the author, the chief executive officer of a corporation well known for its aggressiveness in a tough market explained why his firm hardly ever resorted to patent protection for its inventions: "If we haven't come up with a better idea by the time we're marketing a product, we're in serious trouble anyway. For us, patents would be mostly a record of what we've done in the past." Such statements should not be taken too literally, but they do reflect an attitude that is not uncommon in certain, technologically progressive industries.

2. Thus, for example, a study compared the number of inventions made by the pharmaceutical industries of countries which did offer product patents on new drugs and those that did not. "Superior" performance was found for the latter group of countries, but the investigators ignored the fact that most of these had comprehensive national health plans. Where such schemes exist, the inclusion of a drug in the list of products available "free" to patients (upon perscription by a physician) surely gives the manufacturer a degree of monopoly protection greater than that provided by a patent in an open market. Cf. Blair, J. M., *Economic Concentration: Structure, Behavior and Public Policy* (New York: Harcourt Brace, 1972), pp. 388-91.

3. For an up-to-date evaluation, see Scherer, F. M., *Industrial Market Structure and Economic Performance*, 2nd ed. (Boston, MA: Houghton Mifflin, 1980), Ch. 16.

4. Asch, P., *Industrial Organization and Antitrust Policy*, rev. ed. (New York: Wiley, 1983), p. 366.

5. That ambitious inventors may believe that they have overcome the laws of physics is illustrated by the prolonged court battle of one Joseph Newman, who claims to have invented an "Energy Generation System Having Higher Energy Output than Input." The Patent Office had unjustifiably and unfairly rejected his petition, Mr. Newman maintained in his lawsuits to reverse this decision. Zimmerman, R. G., "Inventor's Energy Machine is Stalled again in U.S. Court," *The Plain Dealer*, March 15, 1985.

6. Scherer, *op. cit.*, p. 440.

7. Details of the case can be found in Rae, J. B., *The American Automobile*, (Chicago, IL: University of Chicago Press, 1965), pp. 33–8.

8. Byrn, E. W., *The Progress of Invention in the Nineteenth Century* (New York: Munn & Co., 1900), pp. 76–9.

9. *Ibid.*

10. Posner, R., *Economic Analysis of Law* (Boston, MA: Little, Brown, 1973), p. 32.

11. Machlup, F., *An Economic Review of the Patent System*, Study of the Subcommittee on Patents, Trademarks, and Copyrights of the Committee on the Judiciary, United States Senate, Eighty-Fifth Congress, Second Session, Study No. 15 (Washington, DC: U.S. Government Printing Office, 1958).

12. Sherwood, M., "The Origins and Development of the American Patent System," *American Scientist*, September–October 1983.

13. An Act to amend the patent and trademark laws, Public Law 96-517—Dec. 12, 1980, 94 Stat. 3015, §117.

14. Sherwood, *op. cit.*, p. 502.

15. Large, A. J., "Congress is in Midst of Making Many Changes in Patent Laws," *The Wall Street Journal*, July 16, 1982, p. 15.

16. Baxter, W. F., "Antitrust Law and Technological Innovation," *Issues in Science and Technology*, Winter 1985.

17. "Japanese Thrive on Patent Overkill," *New Scientist*, March 18, 1982, p. 719.

18. See, for example, Schmookler, J., *Invention and Economic Growth* (Cambridge, MA: Harvard

University Press, 1960); and Nordhaus, W. D., *Invention, Growth, and Welfare* (Cambridge, MA: M.I.T. Press, 1969).

19. Schmookler, *op. cit.*, pp. 30–2.

20. Snyder, S. H., "Medicated Minds," *Science 84*, November 1984, p. 142.

21. For details, see Byrn, *op. cit.* A popular account of more than a dozen such cases can be found in Fuller, E., *Tinkers and Genius: The Story of the Yankee Inventors* (New York: Hastings, 1955).

22. For examples, see Scherer, *op. cit.*, pp. 452–3.

23. Large, A. J., "Public Money and Private Gain," *The Wall Street Journal*, March 15, 1979.

24. *Congressional Quarterly*, November 29, 1980, p. 3443.

25. Thus the success of the Polaroid Corporation in maintaining its monopoly on instant-developing photography for over two decades has been attributed to the ability of its R&D organization to produce a continuing stream of product improvements and cost-reducing innovations.

26. It is a matter of some curiosity that most authors making this argument do not extend it, by analogy, to copyright protection. In fact, a casual survey of their books typically showed no index entries for the term, copyright.

27. Scherer, *op. cit.*, p. 439.

28. Grefermann, K., *et al.*, *Patentwesen und technischer Fortschritt*, vol. I (Göttingen: Otto Schwartz & Co., 1974), p. 21.

29. For an interesting survey of the situation in Britain, see Taylor, C. T., and Silberston, A., *The Economic Impact of the Patent System* (Cambridge: Cambridge University Press, 1973).

30. Nordhaus, *op. cit.*, pp. 14–5.

31. Machlup, *op. cit.*, pp. 79–80.

CHAPTER 8

Development and Innovation

In this chapter we shall deal with the core of the technological change process, the events that lead from the selection of ideas for development to the actual innovation. It has been said that invention is, after all, "the less important part of the story of technological progress."[1] This statement has economic meaning in at least two respects: (1) although the existence of a pool of technical ideas is a necessary condition for advances, decisions on *which* ideas appear worthy of development will determine the output of innovative activity, i.e., the directions of technological change; and (2) in terms of monetary equivalents, by far the greatest proportion of R&D inputs is absorbed by the development process. In the United States, development expenditures typically account for over 75 per cent of aggregate R&D spending.

In the following sections, we shall look first at the characteristics of development and innovation as economic activities; we shall then consider some historical evidence concerning these activities; and we shall turn, finally, to an examination of the processes from the perspective of an individual enterprise.

8.1 Concepts and Definitions

Judging from the flood of exhortations by outside observers as well as from the testimony of (successful) business executives themselves, being innovative is not only a mark of distinction but *the* most important determinant of a firm's competitive survival. There is no denying the general validity of such statements, but we should be careful in interpreting their implications from an economic perspective.

Two points must be made at the outset: (1) The emphasis on innovativeness as a survival characteristic assumes, at least implicitly, that a firm's competitive performance is satisfactory with regard to other determinants—the ability to turn out an adequate volume of products that meet specifications or customers' expectations, reliability in keeping to promised delivery deadlines, the provision of after-sales service, and so on. (2) Innovativeness does not necessarily mean making changes in process or product technology; in a market economy, it means doing things differently from one's competitors in order to gain an advantage over them. There may be times in the evolution of industries and markets when strategies aimed at technological advances deserve the highest priority, but there may be others when innovation in matters of industry organization, in the development of labor relations, in accounting or in marketing are more important. These alternatives are clearly part of Schumpeter's list of "new combinations" (see Chapter 1, p. 2). They have been properly emphasized also by perceptive authorities on the tasks of management, one of whom put the matter in provocative fashion: "Deliberate emphasis on innovation may be needed most where technological changes are least spectacular."[2] One type of innovation, questionable in terms of the economy's efficient functioning but understandable from the individual firm's or industry's viewpoint, may involve the obtaining of a new form of governmental protection against competition!

Our concern, however, is with *technological* development and innovation. Even in this seemingly clearcut frame of reference, we face some ambiguities and disagreements among students of the subject which often affect the nature of empirical findings. But, as one of them has pointed out, "The choice must be between discussing these matters with concepts that are necessarily somewhat vague and not discussing them at all."[3] When we define an innovation as the first "commercial" application of a process or the first production of a new output, we immediately confront the problem of what is meant by the words *first* and *commercial*. As we shall see in the next chapter, a product or process hardly ever remains unchanged as it is diffused; therefore, "firsts" abound even after an original innovation has occurred, and many of these turn out to be at least as significant, technically and economically, as the basic innovator's contribution. Precisely *when* development, pilot-plant production, and the breaking-in of full-scale production facilities have reached the point where one can speak of the "commercialization" of a new process or product is a controversial matter as well. In contemporary industrial practice we find a wide range of approaches: some firms announce commercial production as soon as the first units of output come off the line, while others adopt a much more conservative approach. Nevertheless, the development work on major innovations very often has to continue after commercial start-up, because many problems cannot be identified in advance. Thus, for example, a case study of twenty major innovation projects showed that, of over 800 identifiable technical "events" that had to be completed for full success, approximately one-third occurred *after* the projects had been initiated on a commercial basis.[4] As the recent history of computer hardware and software development shows, there are serious hazards in premature announcements of "commercial" production. But even in cases of less sophisticated technologies, firms may run into serious trouble by assuming that customers will want to participate in the de-bugging of new products.

One obvious conclusion from these observations is that we probably have to restrict our study to major, highly visible innovations, those that turned out to have a clear and discernible impact on the founding and growth of firms, industries, and markets. But there is general agreement that these account at best for about half all observed technological advance.

A second set of conceptual difficulties arises frequently when we try to trace an innovation to some one, specific invention. This is possible only for a minority of cases. In many others, we find that the chain from idea to application has missing links—or too many links. The antecedents of major innovations are typically spread across time and a variety of technical fields. Therefore, even carefully worked-out chronologies may reveal no more than the most important interconnections among events. The picture is further complicated by multiple, independent inventions, by long lags, by the pursuit of technical dead ends, by competitive development work, and by situations in which one developer proceeded in total ignorance of another's parallel efforts.

Thus it is not too surprising that especially for important innovations, such as the automobile, the helicopter, or the jet engine, the intellectual and technical genealogy becomes difficult to trace. Various nations and companies frequently can lay some defensible claims to priority, because there was no "straight shot" from invention to development to innovation.

We confront similar problems in connection with the concept of *development*. According to the present-day governmental definition, this includes expenditures involving the design, construction, and testing of prototypes of new products, as well as those for operating pilot production facilities. On the other hand, this definition excludes such activities as market research, test marketing, and engineering follow-up improvements in commercial production. The economist would like to take a broader view, even though reliable statistical data may not be available. From the decision-maker's point of view, the total costs of bringing a new product or process to the innovation stage is made up of both, the expenditures on technical development as such and the outlays for investigating the economic viability of a development project. In terms of likely impacts on the economy as a whole, however, it may well be that these expenditures are spread across several firms or even several industries. Thus, for example, development work on possible applications of certain modern inventions, such as lasers, carbon fibers and holography, is being carried on in many industries and has resulted in a variety of innovations.

In historical perspective, another difficulty arises from the fact that new ideas may go through *incubation periods*, during which all sorts of technical work is carried on by someone, but no clear commercial interest in applications had emerged. Only after initial technical problems have been solved or after a potential demand is recognized does the *commercial development period* begin. But the distinction between these two phases involves hindsight: after all, those who committed resources to explorations during the incubation period did so in the expectation of an eventual pay-off, and not to lay the groundwork for someone else's successful innovation. Here as elsewhere, the question of the extent to which findings can be appropriated arises. It is not surprising, in any event, that individuals and firms often attempt to surround their development work with considerable secrecy.

Finally, we must recognize that the technical evolution of a new product or process is an ongoing activity. The very fact that an initial innovation was commercially successful will invite efforts at improvement, refinement, scale-up, and at the creation of new variants. In some instances, we can identify the results of such efforts, as for example in the case of the horsepower, weight, speed, or fuel consumption of automobiles. In others, the dimensions of further development are not so readily measured, especially when they concern production techniques rather than the characteristics of the product. Nevertheless, the concepts of *product life cycles* and of *technology cycles* are generally accepted. These are meant to aid in tracing the evolution of technologies and markets for identifiable products or processes, from their infancy to maturity. Here, too, we often face some ambiguities in defining when an "old", product has been replaced by a "new" one. Everyone would agree that the slide rule has been replaced by a clear-cut product innovation, the electronic calculator. On the other hand, although the transistor has displaced the vacuum tube in portable radios and their weight, dimensions, and quality have changed as a consequence, it is not at all clear whether one should consider transistorized radios a new product or simply a substantial refinement of an existing one.

These, then, are some examples of the conceptual and definitional problems one encounters in studying development and innovation. Even finely-spun taxonomies are unlikely to be of any great help in resolving the issues at stake. We shall avoid them, in any event. Instead, a two-pronged approach to pursuing the subject seems reasonable: On the one hand, in general discussions and surveys a certain degree of vagueness is unavoidable, and dividing lines between activities, and outputs, are likely to remain fuzzy. Thus one may have to settle, for example, for some common-sense understanding of what one means by an automobile or by the automobile industry, without becoming bogged down in precise definitions of boundaries around these concepts. On the other hand, in specific investigations or case studies of development and innovation, one has to be careful to establish clearly what one is observing or measuring, even though this procedure brings with it the risk of making findings less than directly comparable to those of other studies.

8.2 Some Historical Evidence

A historical perspective forms a necessary complement to the economic analysis of technological change. Historical data form the bases for many of our attempts at generalization, and case studies of past innovations enable us to get a better understanding of how the character of inventing and innovating has changed with the changing economic environment.

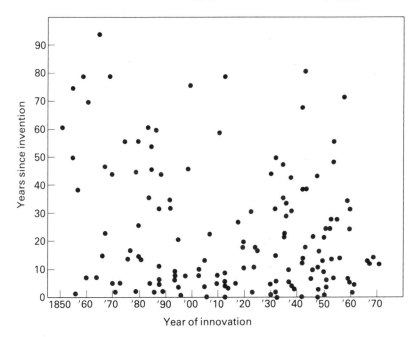

FIG. 8.1 Lag between invention and major innovations, 1850-1971.
Source: See Note 5.

8.2.1 *Lags between Invention and Innovation*

How long has it taken for major innovations to emerge from technically important inventions? Has there been any reduction of the lag between key inventions and innovations because of the advent of organized, corporate R&D? In Fig. 8.1 we summarize the evidence from a variety of sources, for 140 major innovations made in years from 1850 to 1971.[5] On the vertical axis, the number of years that elapsed between invention and innovation is measured. A picture of great variability emerges from these data. For 20 innovations, the lag was 50 years or longer, for nine it was one year or less. But even if we were to eliminate these extreme cases, we would still have great difficulty in discerning any sort of pattern, nor would the calculation of an average lag have any great meaning. Only a case-by-case examination would show whether there are any common factors that determine differences in invention-innovation lags.

The evidence with respect to our second question also appears inconclusive. At least from the innovations included in the survey, it would be difficult to argue that the speed with which inventions are turned into innovations has been increased substantially by the advent of modern, organized R&D. But recalling our discussion of types of invention in Chapter 6, we may guess that inventions leading to major innovations of the kind that would have appeared in this list are not necessarily the corporate laboratories' most important product. If this is so, one would expect their advantage in the efficient conversion of ideas into technical and commercial reality to lie with other kinds of innovation.

The apparent drop-off in the number of observations after 1960 does not mean that the rate of innovation has slowed down; rather, the researchers, who mostly assembled the data in the 1970s, were careful to avoid premature judgments on whether a given innovation was indeed "major" or "basic." Innovations that we recognize now as major, such as the compact disk, fiber optics, and others do not yet appear on the list.

Finally, we must make a point that will concern us at greater length in the next chapter: the year of commercial introduction tells nothing about the economic impact of an innovation. Thus, for example, the introduction of television is currently dated as having occurred in 1936, but the economically significant diffusion of the product did not begin until after World War II.

8.2.2   Nineteenth-Century Invention and Innovation—A Case Study[6]

As soon as we dig beneath summary statistics into the detailed histories of individual innovations, we find much greater complexity than might be suggested by data on key inventions and innovations. The case of the sewing machine provides a prototypical model for much of technical and economic progress in the nineteenth century, and it also has its modern-day parallels. In the collection of statistics from which Fig. 8.1 was derived, the first invention of a sewing machine is dated 1790, and commercial introduction, 1851. Between these two years, many inventors and entrepreneurs attempted to produce a genuinely workable machine, but few of them succeeded.

The 1790 invention was made by an Englishman, Thomas Saint, who took out patents for a machine designed to sew leather but did not succeed in developing the product. A similar machine was invented at roughly the same time by an Austrian, Josef Madersperger, with the same lack of success. The first U.S. patent for a sewing machine was granted in 1826, but there is no record of any development effort.

In 1830, the French inventor Thimonnier patented a machine, the first to include the practical idea of putting the eye in the point of the needle. By 1841 he had produced eight working models made from wood, which were tested in the manufacture of uniforms for the French army. Like other labor-saving innovations before and since, Thimonnier's machines were smashed by an angry mob of tailors and seamstresses who feared for their jobs. Thereafter he seems to have abandoned any attempts to continue production.

Between 1832 and 1835, W. Hunt of New York worked on a lock-stitch machine but ran into insurmountable technical problems. He turned his inventive skills to a much simpler device that proved eminently successful, the safety pin. In 1842 a patent was granted to J. J. Grenough for a machine with a double-pointed needle that was drawn back and forth through the material by a pair of traveling pincers. In 1843, a patent on a sewing machine with stationary needle was obtained by one B. W. Bean; in this invention, the cloth was to be gathered in crimps or folds and forced over the needle. Neither of these ideas proved workable.

An 1846 patent granted to Elias Howe might be considered the forerunner of the ultimate technical solution, at least in so far as the needle was carried on a vibrating lever which also transported the thread, with a second thread looped up from a shuttle below the work surface. The cloth had to be held to a "baster plate" by means of pins and had to be advanced manually. Howe had built a prototype in 1845, but he was too poor to develop this further until a former schoolmate advanced him $500, in exchange for which he obtained a half interest in the invention. A second machine was completed in 1845, and the patent was based on this version. Howe sewed two suits on it, one for himself and one for his partner. In a public competition, he handily beat five seamstresses, but he could not find any investors interested in the invention. Efforts to obtain capital in England brought no greater success; however, a prospective investor, William Thomas, apparently stole Howe's ideas and patented them in his own name. Financially desperate, Howe worked on development as Thomas's hired hand, but he soon returned to the United States. Meanwhile, a number of American inventors had started to copy features of his machine. At this point, some financiers came forth to help Howe with lawsuits against the infringers. Eventually, these suits proved successful, and manufacturers had to start paying royalties to Howe. By 1863, his income was estimated at $4,000 a day. He formed his own manufacturing company and produced Howe-type machines well into the 1880s.

Other patents foreshadowing the final, successful invention were those for a continuous cloth-feed mechanism (1849), for a stationary bobbin instead of a shuttle (1852), and for a four-motion feed bar (1854). The inventor of these last two items, Wilson, formed a partnership with a financier, Wheeler, and the Wheeler & Wilson Company had produced some 800 machines by 1853. One problem common to Howe's and Wilson's machines was their high price, compared to the wages of seamstresses.

In 1851, Isaac M. Singer had obtained a patent on a machine incorporating all the features necessary for a resounding commercial success: relatively low costs of production, sturdiness, a vertical standard with horizontal, needle-bearing arm above a large work table, a foot treadle instead of a hand crank, and the ability to sew leather as well as cloth.

Also in 1851, Grover and Baker patented a double chain-stitch machine. Both they and Singer started manufacturing companies in 1853, and there began a vigorous rivalry among the various types of sewing machines, each of whose producers claimed some technical advantages over the others. The results were confusion of the potential customers and, worse yet for the producers, strong downward pressure on prices. Therefore, in 1856 the manufacturers formed a cartel, "for the protection of their mutual interests."

Soon, however, the Singer machine proved itself vastly superior to all the others. When the original patent expired in 1877, it had become the dominant product in the market. Thousands of patents relating to sewing machines were issued in subsequent decades, but none of them was sufficiently innovative to overcome the Singer Company's leading position.

Here, then, we have a case illustrating many of the characteristics of major innovations: competing, almost simultaneous, solutions to certain basic technical problems; inventors' difficulties in holding on to information while trying to raise capital for development and commercialization; a rather rapid transition from ideas to production *if* the necessary funds could be obtained; the inventor becoming an entrepreneur and founding a firm based on his technical ideas; infringement suits and market competition among technical variants, which is ended by a collusive agreement; and, finally, the emergence of a technically and commercially superior version of the competing innovations.

To what extent have changes in the sources of technological advancement, in the size and diversification of firms, and in the structure of markets, altered the ways in which *major* new products are developed and introduced? Despite obvious differences, one may conclude that transformations have not been as radical as is often suggested. The introduction of the automobile in the early twentieth century offers striking parallels to the story of the sewing machine, and—though with different contours and dimensions—even the contemporary market for small computers illustrates once again many of the features we observed in our case study.

8.2.3   Development and Innovation after World War I

Continuing our examination of the historical record, we now look in somewhat greater detail at a group of major innovations of the past six decades. In Table 8.1, we present a summary of relevant data for 38 significant new products and processes. They were selected because the relevant information was readily available. Therefore, they should be taken as representative cases rather than as *the* most important technological advances or as a random sample of all such advances.

Nevertheless, it is remarkable that 18 of the inventors who provided the key ideas underlying these innovations were independents, and that another 12 did their applied research at universities. These findings must be interpreted with caution, however, because in many cases significant follow-up inventions were made by the innovating firms' employees in the process of further applied research and during development. With few exceptions, the development work and commercialization were done by established businesses or by companies founded especially for this purpose by established firms. The Kinetic Chemicals Corporation, formed as a joint venture by General Motors and Du Pont for the purpose of developing refrigerants, and the Dow-Corning Company, which developed silicone for Dow Chemical and Corning Glass, are examples of the latter pattern. Only a few firms, like the Harwood Self-winding Watch Company and the Polaroid Corporation, represent start-ups by inventor-entrepreneurs. There were, however, some small established firms whose fortunes rose only after they had become major innovators, such as the Haloid Corporation with xerography. And some other innovators like the German motor vehicle manufacturer N.S.U., went bankrupt, because the product was not sufficiently developed before commercialization.

As notable as this variety in the arrangements whereby inventions were turned into innovations are the great differences in invention-innovation lags. It is worth observing, though, that these lags for the 9 innovations that derived clearly from "in-house" inventions of the innovating company were considerably shorter than for the others. We must not regard our findings as conclusive evidence, but perhaps corporate R&D establishments do have an advantage in pushing their own inventions to the commercialization stage.

That our list includes a large number of independent inventors is in keeping with the results of more comprehensive studies,[7] which generally found that independents have continued to be important sources of ideas leading to major innovations. Any further judgments on this matter would have to differentiate

TABLE 8.1 *Origins of selected major innovations, 1920–67*

Innovation	Year	Innovator (country)	Key Inventor(s)	Status	Year
Triode-valve radio	1920	Westinghouse (U.S.)	De Forest	Ind.	1912
Insulin	1923	Connaught Labs. (Can.)	F. G. Banting	Univ.	1921
Continuous hot strip rolling	1923	Armco Steel (U.S.)	Employees of a Bohemian mill	Ind.	1892
Self-winding watch	1928	Harwood Self-winding Watch Co. (U.K.)	J. Harwood	Ind.	1922
Synthetic detergents	1930	I. G. Farben (Ger.)	Krafft	Univ.	1886
Freon refrigerants	1931	Kinetic Chemicals Corp. (U.S.)	Midgley and Hume	Empl.	1930
Crease-resist. fabrics	1932	Tootal Broadhurst Lee (U.K.)	R. S. Willow *et al.*	Empl.	1926
Plexiglas	1935	Rohm & Haas (U.S.)	W. Chalmers	Univ.	1929
Kodachrome	1935	Eastman Kodak (U.S.)	Godowsky & Mannes	Ind.	1923
Radar	1935	Societe Francaise Radio Electrique (F.)	H. Hertz Hüllmeyer	Univ. Ind.	1887 1904
Television	1936	R.C.A. (U.S.)	V. Zworykin P. Farnsworth	Empl. Ind.	1919 1929
Catalytic cracking	1937	Sun Oil Co., Socony-Mobil (U.S.)	E. Houdry	Ind.	1922
Nylon	1938	Du Pont Corp. (U.S.)	W. H. Carothers	Empl.	1934

Continued

TABLE 8.1 *Continued*

Innovation	Year	Innovator (country)	Key Inventor(s)	Status	Year
Fluorescent lamp	1938	Westinghouse, G.E., Sylvania (U.S.)	P. Cooper-Hewitt	Ind.	1896
Helicopter	1937	Focke-Wulf (Ger.)	Many inventors		
Jet engine	1943	Rolls Royce (U.K.)	F. Whittle	Gov.	1929
Turbojet engine	1944	Junkers Co. (Ger.)	H. von Ohain	Univ.	1934
Mechanical cotton picker	1942	International Harvester Co. (U.S.)	A. Campbell	Ind.	1889
Penicillin	1942	Kemball, Bishop (U.K.)	A. Fleming	Univ.	1929
DDT	1942	J. R. Geigy Co. (Swiss)	P. Müller *et al.*	Empl.	1939
Silicon	1943	Dow-Corning Co. (U.S.)	F. S. Kipping	Univ.	1904
Ball-point pen	1944	Eterpen Co. (Argentina)	L. J. & G. Biro	Ind.	1938
Streptomycin	1946	Merck & Co. (U.S.)	S. A. Waksman	Univ.	1943
Long-playing record	1948	C.B.S. (U.S.)	P. Goldmark	Empl.	1945
Automatic transmission	1939	General Motors (U.S.)	H. Föttinger E. A. Thompson	Ind. Empl.	1904 1930s
Polaroid camera	1948	Polaroid Corp. (U.S.)	E. H. Land	Ind.	1937
Xerography	1950	Haloid Corp. (U.S.)	C. Carlson	Ind.	1937
Terylene	1950	I.C.I. (U.K.)	J. R. Whinfield, J. T. Dickson	Empls.	1941
Transistor	1951	Bell Labs. (U.S.)	Shockley, Barden and Brittain	Empls.	1947
Electronic dig. computer	1951	Remington Rand (U.S.)	J. Mauchley, J. P. Eckert	Univ.	1944
Power steering	1951	Chrysler Co. (U.S.)	H. Vickers, F. W. Davis	Inds.	1926
Continuous casting steel	1952	Mannesmann A.G. (Ger.)	S. Junghans	Ind.	1927
Oxygen steel-making	1952	VOEST A.G. (Austria)	R. Durrer *et al.*	Univ.	1939
Float glass	1959	Pilkington Bros. (U.K.)	A. Pilkington	Empl.	1952
Contraceptive pill	1960	Searle Drug Co. (U.S.)	R. Marker	Univ.	1950s
Hovercraft	1960	Saunders-Roe (U.K.)	D. K. Warner C. Cockerell	Ind. Ind.	1928 1953
Laser	1967	Hughes Aircraft (U.S.)	C. H. Townes	Univ.	1954
Rotary-piston engine	1967	N.S.U. (Ger.)	F. Wankel	Ind.	1954

Note: "Status" indicates whether the inventor was an independent (Ind.), a university (Univ.) or government (Gov.) employee, or the employee of the innovating firm (Empl.). Some inventors designated as independents were employees of firms in other lines of business at the time they made their inventions.

Sources: Jewkes, J., Sawers, D., and Stillerman, R., *The Sources of Invention*, 2nd ed. (New York: Norton, 1969); Van Duijn, J. J., *The Long Wave in Economic Life* (London: George Allen & Unwin, 1983) Ch. X; "20 Discoveries that Changed our Lives," *Science 84*, November 1984.

among industries; the resource requirements for applied research in some of them, like the metallurgical industries, are such that corporate efforts tend to dominate invention and innovation. Finally, we must emphasize that more detailed studies of the innovations on the list show virtually no instances in which an independent "came knocking at the door" of the innovating firm after he had done all his work. In many instances, inventors had established all sorts of industrial contacts and may even have received some financing from potential purchasers of their ideas.

None of these observations says anything about the more general role of corporate R&D organizations in generating large numbers of smaller and improvement inventions, as well as in developing key inventions. Their ability to maintain a portfolio of projects, to speed up or slow down specific ones as the situation demands, to draw on a broad array of in-house as well as on outside consultants, and—last but not least—their resilience in surviving even substantial failures, gives them a clear advantage over other types of ventures. When we add to this the fact that governmental funds for applied research and development projects are more likely to go to well-established firms with a track record in their respective fields than to comparative newcomers, no matter how good their ideas may be, we have another reason why organized R&D has come to be thought of as the key source of technological advances.

8.2.4 Major Post-World War II Innovations, by Industry

Which industries have been most innovative in the past thirty years? Any attempt to answer this question runs up against difficulties. Even after one has used some judgment in identifying major innovations, there still remains the problem of weighing the significance of major advances in technology against the impact of the incremental improvements that have played an important role in many fields. Furthermore, a mere count of innovations says little about their effects on the growth and competitiveness of industries. One innovation, the transistor, transformed a whole host of product technologies; other innovations, perhaps equally significant for the innovator from a technical and economic point of view, may have had a much narrower range of effects.

With these caveats in mind, we present the data in Table 8.2. They show three industries well ahead of all others in the generation of major innovations. Not too surprisingly, the electrical equipment and communications sector leads the list, followed closely by the chemical and machinery industries. In evaluating the meaning of these statistics, we must also keep in mind that there are considerable variations in the coverage of processes and products, as well as in the number of firms included in each industry. Obviously, a category like "machinery" or "motor vehicles and other transportation equipment" encompasses more technologies and more companies than, say, the category "petroleum refining and extraction."

TABLE 8.2   *Major U.S. innovations, by industry,*
1953–73

Industry	Number of innovations	Per cent of total
Electric equipment, communication	53	17
Chemicals and allied products	45	15
Machinery	44	14
Professional & scient. instruments	29	9
Stone, clay & glass products	18	6
Motor vehicles & other transport eq.	18	6
Primary metals	17	5
Rubber and plastic products	15	5
Aircraft and missiles	11	4
Fabricated metal products	10	3
Petroleum extraction & refining	5	2
Textiles and apparel	4	1
Paper and allied products	4	1
Food and kindred products	2	1
Lumber, wood products, furniture	2	1
Non-manufacturers industries	33	11
Totals	310	100

Source: National Science Board, *Science Indicators 1976*
(Washington, DC: U.S. Government Printing Office, 1977),
Table 4-20 (p. 269).

TABLE 8.3   *Sources underlying major U.S. innovations,*
1953–73

Source	Frequency	Per cent of innovations*
Same profit center that produced the innovation	152	62
Same enterprise, but not same profit center	59	24
Independent inventor	46	19
Government laboratory	13	5
Professional/scientific and government publications	6	2
University	19	8

* 246 innovations covered; multiple responses were accepted,
therefore percentages add to more than 100.
Source: National Science Board, *Science Indicators 1976*
(Washington, DC: U.S. Government Printing Office, 1977),
Table 4-27 (p. 275).

Let us keep in mind, finally, that the relevant decision unit in a market economy is the firm. One innovation, even if it were not classified as major, may turn around the fortunes of an individual enterprise. Decision-makers are not impressed by industry composites, but by their own and others' ability to stay ahead by doing something different from the competition. Even in industrial sectors that are generally regarded as mature or stagnant, there frequently exist opportunities for firms to reap the benefits of innovative strategies.[8]

Table 8.3 shows the sources of invention underlying 246 of the 310 innovations summarized in Table 8.2. According to these data, some two-thirds of the inventions were made in the innovating enterprises, with the rest coming from outsiders. A number of innovations had multiple sources. It is interesting to note that independent inventors make up almost one-fifth of the sources; this is not far off their share in patents granted.

8.3 Project Selection and the Management of Innovation

Business decisions about the direction of, and level of commitment to, R&D are not made in a vacuum; rather, they reflect two sets of influences: (1) the specific pressures or opportunities that trigger innovative efforts, and (2) the more general context of managerial strategies, of which technological innovation is only one component. These influences operate under the constraints of both, the firm's existing structure and its environment—in the sense in which we have defined these terms in Chapter 5 (pp. 89–90). To the extent that a given firm is engaged in several distinct lines of business, these represent a third dimension of context; all of these lines will have some elements of environment and structure in common, while others will be unique to them.

Figure 8.2 is an attempt to illustrate these notions in stylized fashion. The interaction among all the components of the diagram is suggested by the

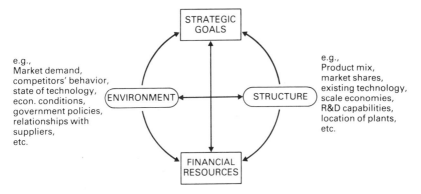

FIG. 8.2 Key factors influencing the innovative behavior of firms.

arrows. From everything we have said so far, it should be clear that by *strategic goals* we do not mean the maximum profit of the microeconomic model. Rather, the setting of these goals will be influenced by considerations of structure and environment, and the goals will change with the evolution of the firm and its basic technology. Thus, for example, an operational goal in the early stages of new-product introduction may be to maximize performance per dollar of price; at a time when there are various technical approaches and substantially different products competing for the same market, the struggle is for emergence as the technically superior product. In a later stage of market development, the ability to produce a differentiated product reliably and in large enough quantities, and to provide the necessary services, may be the most important goal. And when products and markets have matured, and competition is mainly on the basis of price, reduction of unit costs is often seen as the overriding strategic goal.

Looming in the background are considerations of the firm's financial resources for implementing major strategic moves. These resources may be self-generated, in the form of retained earnings and cash flows from depreciation, or they may derive from outside suppliers of funds, i.e., additional equity investors or creditors. Needless to say, many strategic projects other than technological innovations compete for these resources. Major marketing campaigns, the development of new distribution systems, reorganizations of the firm, expansions of capacity on the basis of existing technology, acquisitions of other businesses, and a host of other projects may lay claim to resources.

8.3.1   *Pressures, Opportunities, and Decision Processes*

How does management select innovation projects, and how are decisions about them made once they have been initiated? There are probably as many answers to this question as there are types of organization and styles of decision-making. Therefore, in trying to cull some generalizations from this real-world variety, we run the risk of presenting a picture that does not actually portray any one situation. The risk is worth taking, however, if we keep this reservation in mind as we outline the main features of decision processes.

Since expected returns from research and development efforts are virtually impossible to estimate, most firms appear to maintain a budgetary allocation to R&D that bears some more or less stable relationship to company sales, total profits, or some other measure of overall economic activity. Deviations from these rough rules of thumb occur when a particularly promising project requires additional resources or when financial exigencies seem to make reductions unavoidable. The desire for stability of allocations, even if these are based on no more than rules of thumb or on some comparative industry standards, is understandable. For one thing, top executives in publicly-held corporations think—with some justification—that their reported expenditures for R&D form an important element in financial analysts' and investors' evaluations of the firm's longer-term prospects. This also means that what kind of work is actually done under the heading of R&D may vary greatly according to circumstances. The president of one medium-size corporation with highly cyclical sales commented to the author: "When business is booming, we've got all our technical people working out on the shop floor, but we wouldn't dare report a reduction in R&D spending during those periods." A second consideration in making stable allocations is that frequent gearing-up or scaling-down of R&D activities can be very expensive in terms of both, cost-effectiveness and employee relations. This is demonstrated especially by the experience of corporations whose R&D budgets depend heavily on government contracts; fluctuations in contract awards often force them to engage in massive hiring and firing programs.[9]

What determines the directions of R&D effort? The concept of specific "pressures," as shown in Fig. 8.3, has two roots. On the one hand, it means that environmental or structural changes will convince managements that they better "do something" in order to maintain competitive positions. On the other hand, the accumulation of favorable information about a particular technical opportunity or about a market development may provide sufficient evidence in the hands of a project's advocates to persuade top decision-makers that a commitment should be made. In many instances, such pressure is very direct, as for example when a firm's established customers call for a change in product or process. Once a project has been initiated, technical and economic appraisals on the basis of accumulated information form the process of development. And eventually, a decision has to be made whether to invest in commercialization or not. The extent to which non-objective factors impinge on the process is suggested by the observations of experienced practitioners:

> "Personalities, likes and dislikes, production problems real and imaginary, costs, uncertainty of the market, unknown service requirements, intangible customer reactions, all swarm around the new product when it is weakest. This is the period of greatest need for the protection of a guardian angel and the will of a champion to assist in bridging the swamp of hazards between the laboratory development and factory production."[10]

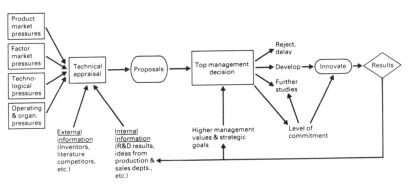

FIG. 8.3 Decisions leading to major technological innovations.
Source: Adapted from Gold, B., Peirce, W. S., and Rosegger, G., "Diffusion of Major Technological Innovations in U.S. Iron and Steel Manufacturing," *Journal of Industrial Economics*, July 1970.

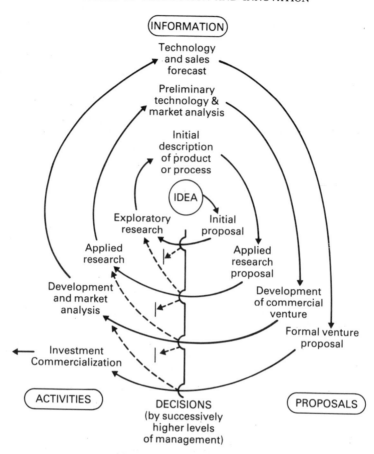

FIG. 8.4 Decision cycles for major innovations.
Source: Adapted from Blickwede, D. J., "On Managing R&D in the Steel Industry," *Proceedings, 1969 National Steel Industry Economics Seminar* (New York: American Iron and Steel Institute, 1969).

Between initiation and commercialization, a project typically is subjected to periodic evaluations. Figure 8.4 illustrates this process as a series of decision cycles, with opportunities at each stage to stop the project, to return it to the previous cycle for more information, or to push it onto the next phase. In discussing this decision model, the corporate director of research who developed it emphasized that one should not take the neatness of such a flow diagram too literally. Seldom is the path of major development projects so transparent and uncluttered. Furthermore, at each decision point there also are opportunities to intensify or reduce the effort with which a project is being pursued, from turning it into a crash program to putting it "on the back burner," where it may be allowed to linger and perhaps even die.

Stylized as this brief survey was, it permits some general observations about the role of R&D in corporations:

(1) Technology-orientated decisions continuously compete with all other decisions for top managements' attention, just as they compete for allocations of resources.

(2) Decisions are not made episodically, on a once-and-for-all basis; rather, they involve reactions to the accumulation of (positive or negative) information about particular projects, as well as to the inevitable internal politics of organizations.

(3) The chances of success for major innovation projects depend not only on what happens inside the firm, but also on developments in its environment, such as changing assessments of market potentials and of the behavior of competitors.

(4) Given these considerations, it is not surprising that decisions cannot be made on the basis of formulae, rigid evaluation models, or calculations of expected rates of return. When neither the initial costs of a venture nor the future stream of benefits generated by it is known with anything approaching predictable ranges of outcome, reliance on purely quantitative evaluations is bound to produce the kind of conservatism for which many large corporations have been criticized.[11] The Appendix to this chapter deals with these matters from the perspective of an experienced manager of corporate research and development.

Only projects carried on through continuous infusions of public funds may be an exception to these observations, since they will tend to be pursued almost regardless of intermediate results and changing evaluations. Where *political* commitments to development have been made, and where final outcomes are not subject to the test of the marketplace, formal evaluation models yield results that become self-fulfilling prophecies.[12] In the last decade, the U.S. government's financing of projects aimed at the development of alternative energy sources provides a host of examples for the effects of premature commitments on the behavior of private decision-making units.[13] Little guidance for the management of privately-funded R&D can be derived from experience with public projects.

8.3.2 The Broader Context of Innovation Management

If we want to get a better understanding of actual, economy-wide patterns of technological change, we have to look beyond the narrow framework of individual decisions about development and innovation. In particular, we must consider the factors that might influence overall managerial strategies in this area. This is so because investment in *major* innovations cannot be justified in terms of the standard criteria of financial management. The innovator succeeds by ignoring the rules that apply to the ordinary conduct of business and to incremental changes in products and processes. On the other hand, the greater certainty surrounding the gradual advancement of technology goes a long way toward explaining why decision-makers might prefer more or less routine changes to attempts at breakthroughs. Top management values and goals therefore play an important part in explaining the behavior of firms.

In an intensive analysis of managerial strategies, Professor Gold[14] established a series of hypotheses about the role of technological change in organizations. Recognizing that major innovation is but one among an array of devices for promoting the objectives of a business, he proposes the following general observations;

(1) In most firms, top management tends to have a more or less stable ranking of the means for the achievement of goals, such as target returns on investment, market share, security of assets, stability of operations, or some combination of these. Rankings are bound to be influenced also by executives' personal preferences with respect to work and leisure (peace of mind).

(2) Given a choice, most managements will opt for a continuation of well-tried strategies, because these appear to involve minimal risks for the established structure of organizations as well as for relations with their environment. Therefore, modest improvements will be preferred to radical ones, limited capacity expansions to big leaps, and gradual cost reduction programs to operational revolutions.

(3) The generation of major technological advances is likely to rank quite low in this hierarchy of means, because it involves heavy investments and high risks, not only to the firm but also to the personal careers of decision-makers.

(4) Strong commitments to a strategy of radical innovation will be made only if
   (a) less risky methods for promoting organizational goals have proven inadequate;
   (b) external forces (such as governmental pressure for change or the availability of subsidies) change the relationship between expected costs and benefits;
   (c) technological advances by competitors threaten the firm; or
   (d) the ongoing internal R&D programs yield some unexpected, seemingly high-payoff results.

(5) Nevertheless, managers claim to believe that technological change is a fact of life and that it can be ignored only at the risk of endangering the long-run survival of the business.

Seen in this way, investment in major innovation is not a uniquely worthwhile, no less a preferred, strategy but generally has to overcome higher hurdles than alternative strategies. Desirable as it may be for the economy as a whole, rapid technological change therefore may not rank high in the portfolio of private firms. No wonder, then, that outside observers of the corporate scene have felt compelled to issue "a call for vision in managing technology,"[15] pointing to the need for decision-makers to revise their attitudes in the face of growing international competition and rapidly changing industrial technologies.

There are influences other than managerial values and goals that must be considered in assessing innovative strategies. One of these has to do with the very size of modern corporations and the complexities of decision-making. It is well known that the way in which an organization is set up has a strong effect on management's ability to design and implement strategies. The more hierarchical and bureaucratic a firm's decision-making arrangements, the less the likelihood of radical change. Before condemning these arrangements out of hand, however, we must recall that they may be regarded as essential for the carrying-out of the organization's routine operations.

A second influence has been proposed as a direct consequence of massive, highly organized R&D efforts—too many ideas.[16] In such situations, the mere sorting-out of proposals may absorb too much of executives' time and thus create a climate in which everyone eventually perceives that ideas are not particularly welcome at the top management levels. In addition, experience with seemingly outstanding technical ideas, the development of strong markets for which takes a long time, may reinforce such attitudes.[17] Another frequently advanced explanation is that corporations do not sufficiently reward employees for the *advocacy* of successful innovations, while penalties for failures are quick in coming.[18] Where such conditions prevail, people will adopt an attitude of "not rocking the boat."

We could extend the list of diagnoses, but we hope that the point has been made: Although technological progress is one of the hallmarks of a healthy economy, one should count more on competitive pressures and on external events than on any inherent organizational proclivity for change, when it comes to stimulating major innovative efforts. In business firms as in other social organizations, radical change is perceived as a threat to well-established modes of behavior as well as to the status of individuals and groups.[19]

Our whole preceding discussion of successful major innovations seems to fly in the face of these generalizations. But we must recall that our judgments of success are always made with the wisdom of hindsight, and that we know much less about failures, unless they were really spectacular.[20] If we accept Schumpeter's notion of innovation as a "process of creative destruction," then we should not be surprised that, on the whole and on average, the strategies of firms are conservative rather than revolutionary. Innovator-entrepreneurs, whether they operate as independents or in established organizations, are the exception rather than the rule even in a market economy.

Notes

1. Jewkes, J., Sawreres, D., and Stillerman, R., *The Sources of Invention*, 2nd ed. (New York: Norton, 1969), p. 152.

2. Drucker, P. F., *The Practice of Management* (New York: Harper, 1954), p. 70.

3. Jewkes *et al.*, *op. cit.*, p. 25.

4. Carlson, J. W., "Aspects of the Diffusion of Technology in the United States," paper presented at the fifth meeting of the Senior Economic Advisers, United Nations, Economic Commission for Europe; Geneva, Switzerland, 2 October 1967.

5. The data on which this chart is based were collected from a variety of sources and presented in tabular form in van Duijn, J. J., *The Long Wave in Economic Life* (London: George Allen & Unwin, 1983), pp. 176–9.

6. The information for this brief history was summarized from information in Byrn, E. W., *The Progress of Invention in the Nineteenth Century* (New York: Munn, 1900), Chapter XV; and in Brandon, R., *A Capitalist Romance: Singer and the Sewing Machine* (Philadelphia, PA: Lippincott, 1977).

7. See, for example, Hamberg, D., "Invention in the Industrial Research Laboratory," *Journal of Political Economy*, April 1963; and Enos, J. L., "Invention and Innovation in the Petroleum Refining Industry," in National Bureau of Economic Research, *The Rate and Direction of Inventive Activity: Economic and Social Factors* (Princeton, NJ: Princeton University Press, 1962).

8. A number of interesting case studies is presented in Harrigan, K. R., *Strategies for Declining Businesses* (Lexington, MA: Lexington Books—D. C. Heath, 1980).

9. Mansfield, E., *The Economics of Technological Change* (New York: Norton, 1968), p. 62.

10. Furnas, C. C., ed. *Research in Industry* (New York: Van Nostrand, 1948), pp. 379–80.

11. See, for example, Hayes, R. H., and Abernathy, W. J., "Managing Our Way to Economic Decline," *Harvard Business Review*, July–August, 1980.

12. Nevertheless, huge margins of error are common. It is not surprising that so-called "cost over-runs" occur when the original estimates in evaluation models were based on no more than hunches, or on the private interests of the proponents. Thus, for example, one study found that in a number of military hardware development projects, actual costs exceeded estimated costs by anywhere from 70 to 400 per cent, and the actual times of completion exceeded the estimated times by 50 per cent, on average. Marshall, A. W., and Meckling, W. H., "Predictability of Costs, Time, and Success of Development," in National Bureau of Economic Research, *op. cit.*

13. A careful assessment of one such case can be found in Weinberg, A. M., "Reflections on the Energy Wars," *American Scientist*, March-April 1978.

14. Gold, B., "The Framework of Decision for Major Technological Innovation," in Baier, K., and Rescher, N., *Values and the Future* (New York: Free Press, 1969).

15. Foster, R. N., "A Call for Vision in Managing Technology," *Business Week*, May 24, 1982. An excellent collection of papers dealing with various aspects of corporate innovation can be found in Tushman, M. L., and Moore, W. L., eds., *Readings in the Management of Innovation* (Boston, MA: Pitman, 1982).

16. Haeffner, E. A., "The Innovation Process," *Technology Review*, March–April 1973. This is not, of course, a universal problem. A considerable time ago, the director of a very successful corporate research laboratory was reported to have complained, "It is a constant irritation and disappointment to me that so few ideas are presented to us from which to select." Quoted in Furnas, C. C., *op. cit.*, p. 107.

17. One such example is discussed in Tannenbaum, J. A., "Carbon Fiber Finds Diverse New Uses, but Can You Afford a $1,200 Bicycle?" *The Wall Street Journal*, July 17, 1975.

18. Schwartz, J. J., "How an Organization Decides to Innovate," *Wharton Quarterly*, Spring 1974.

19. An excellent case study of such resistance is E. E. Morison's "Gunfire at Sea," in his *Men, Machines, and Modern Times* (Cambridge, MA: M.I.T. Press, 1966).

20. Allan, J. H., "Decisions that Went Awry," *New York Times*, July 2, 1972.

Appendix: Innovation in a Large Corporation*

by Dr. John R. Coltman, Director of Research Planning (Retired), Westinghouse Electric Corporation.

At the heart of the industrial age is technological innovation. This is the process of applying science and technology in an inventive manner so as to place new products and new ways of doing things into the hands of the public.

Lately there has been a good deal of concern expressed about the possible failing of the innovative powers of industry in the United States. I have spent most of my career closely associated with the process. On my retirement, Westinghouse asked me to spend some time looking at the way we have carried out this process in the past in the hopes of deriving some guidance for the future. I thought you might like to hear about some of the conclusions I have gleaned from these studies.

Innovation must be distinguished from invention. To be successful, the innovation must command a market and a profit that is commensurate with the status and ambitions of the innovator. Many, perhaps most, innovations are the results of efforts by individual entrepreneurs. One hears about those which are successful but no one knows how to count the innumerable failures, so that it is difficult to compare the hit rates of such individuals with those of large industry. In either case, we know it is a low-probability process—most attempts at innovation either fail outright or lead to very modest returns. And very often the returns go not to the pioneer, but to those who come later and pursue the business in a particularly effective manner. So there is a very large content of business acumen, timing, execution and sometimes just pure luck needed along with the invention itself in order to make an innovation succeed.

Most large industrial corporations have a quite diverse product line, often covering a very wide range of technologies and serving very different markets. To handle this complex, it is common practice to set up separate divisions, each having a responsibility for a particular product line. The manager of such a division is expected to make a profit and to assure the future health and growth of his division. While he may be encouraged to think about new products, his incentives to engage in innovation are not large. Financing a new product attempt detracts from his profit. Moreover, new products ordinarily take many years to come to fruition, and the benefits, if any, are more likely to accrue to the division manager's successor than to him. Under these circumstances, it is not surprising that most corporations find it desirable to set up some central organization designed to encourage new product development. The standard approach is to have a central research and development laboratory. This lab is

*Dr. Coltman is best known for his invention and development of the X-ray Image Amplifier, standard equipment in every hospital radiological department. His observations on corporate innovation first appeared in *The Case Alumnus*, Summer–Autumn 1982. They are reproduced here, slightly abridged, with Dr. Coltman's kind permission.

usually charged with the responsibility of understanding the chemical and physical phenomena of importance to the company's products, of solving problems relating to product performance or manufacture, of reducing product cost, and if there is time, thinking about new products. The trouble with this is pretty much the same as with that of the division—the researcher ordinarily finds it more gratifying and certainly less risky to work on present problems with good chances of solution than to go out on limbs with propositions nobody seems to want.

Nevertheless, innovation does occur, and when it does, it is usually the result of the actions of a particular individual. He is often given the name of "champion"—a person who espouses an idea and devotes most of his working hours to thinking about little else. While the champion is usually described as a technologist with a technological idea that he is sure will be a winner, it more often occurs in the large corporation that the champion comes from the business end—somebody who recognizes a business opportunity and pushes towards its realization.

It is helpful to distinguish between these two ways of initiating innovation—what one might call technology push versus market pull. Of course, both technology and market are necessary for successful innovation—the distinction lies in which comes first. The resulting process in each case often takes a very different course.

Let me give you a couple of examples from Westinghouse's experiences. The first one is an example of market pull. The key step was the recognition, on the part of a manager in our Elevator Division, that electric stairways were expensive to build as each one was a custom-engineered job and service was a headache for the customer and the supplier because of the great variation in product. He was aware that planning of new urban transit systems would call for many escalators of large and varying length. He asked his engineers and the mechanical design people at the central product design laboratory for an economical solution to this problem. What came out was the modular escalator—an arrangement where individual motors spaced along the flight would share the load of driving the steps rather than depending on a single massive drive unit at the bottom. With this arrangement, an escalator of any desired length could be made from standard parts. These could easily be made available from stock for service and repair. There were several inventions made on the mechanical execution of this idea that provided good patent protection. The development was carried off in record time and an initial order from the Washington, D.C. Metro System was the start of a revised product line, a totally changed-over factory and a present dominant share of the market. While the basic idea was certainly not profound, nor the technology dazzling, there was a real advantage to the customer and to the producer.

An example of technology-push innovation is the oxygen analyzer. This started at the Research Laboratories during investigations of solid ceramics as electrolytes for fuel cells—a subject which is still very active. The potential generated across a thin layer of certain oxide ceramics is a direct measure of the difference in oxygen concentration on either side of the layer. The usefulness of an instrument based on this principle was a subject passionately embraced by one of our chemists. In 1962, he persuaded a fledgling new product department to build and sell such instruments for laboratory use, for industrial process monitoring and even for medical applications in respiration studies. The product limped along in the marketplace for several years. Then our chemist persuaded our Industrial Controls Division that an important application lay in the monitoring of combustion products as a means of controlling proper combustion feeds. What was needed, however, was a probe that could operate directly in the stack. After a good deal of research and development, a practical probe was produced. This came along at the time when energy conservation was being intensively pushed and it was demonstrated very soon that the use of such an oxygen probe could effect large economies in boiler operation. It has been twenty years since Westinghouse first offered an oxygen analyzer for sale. This year, we formed a new division to handle just combustion control.

Persistence, then, is an important element, and a champion is usually required for this. But things start really to happen only if the innovation finds that key niche in the marketplace in which it can perform a needed service better than its predecessor.

Over the years, Westinghouse has maintained several forms of centralized new product organizations in addition to the Research Laboratories. These organizations have taken different forms and operated in different ways. Their success rates and the impact they had on the composition, were subject to large variations.

A study of these organizations and how they fared seems to point to some fairly clear lessons. The major one is this: the chance of success of a new product in Westinghouse is tremendously enhanced if the attempt is carried out in partnership with an established organization which has a stake in the success. That partner may be a going division of the corporation or it may be a customer who is interested in the product or it may be a government agency like the Department of Defense. In almost every case where the internal new product organization tried to go it alone, it met with failure, whereas a fairly large proportion of cooperative efforts succeeded. Why should this be so?

The most common cause of failure of an innovation is not a technological failure but a wrong estimate of the value of the innovation to the customer. Procuring the support of a future customer or of a division already serving a customer is a strong indication that the estimate has some basis in fact. In some cases, the prognostication is self-fulfilling. The future customer who has invested in a development for his own benefit will do what he can to make the development succeed and to use it for his own benefit. This applies to external customers as well as to that somewhat similar relationship that exists between a central new-product organization and a corporate division for whom they are trying to develop a product.

A cost-sharing partnership, then, has a powerful influence. It helps to assure better planning. Each partner must specify what he really expects to accomplish and the course he expects to follow. There is also a very human desire not to let a partner down. Almost all new product efforts of any technological complexity go through periods when the product performance seems desperately wanting or the estimates of market acceptance turn gloomy or the expenditures have risen to painful levels at a time when the cash position of the sponsor is perilously low. In these periods, it is easy for a "single proprietor" to abandon the effort. When two independent units work together, there is a mutual obligation that often carries the project through these dangerous low periods.

The organizational scheme within Westinghouse that appeared to have the best success record in commercial innovation was the maintenance of a central organization with the responsibility of stimulating new product ideas among established company divisions. This organization had self-funded capabilities that it could offer divisions to help in the design and testing of a new product. It brought to the division not only an idea but a means to help carry out the needed product design and early manufacturing information. Before a project was initiated, however, a development plan was to be mutually drawn up, and approved and committed to at the vice-presidential level. This process provided strong stimulus to many operating divisions. Money was made available to those who wanted to enter into something new, but the recipient also had to make an investment and the availability of help was dependent on having a sound plan and a commitment to the future. And of course, the money originally came from taxing the recipients.

From what I have observed in our corporation, the golden rule for an innovation group is this: "Do only with others what you might like to do by yourself."

CHAPTER 9

The Diffusion of Innovations

Although innovation is the key event in the technological change process, the *economic* impact of new products and processes depends on the speed with which they are diffused among potential owners or users. In this chapter, we shall examine diffusion as an economic phenomenon, offer some hypotheses about the determinants of the rate of diffusion, and look at the ways in which individual firms react to the flow of new technological possibilities. The focus of our inquiry is the spread of innovations in industry, but we shall also make some brief observations about the diffusion of consumer goods.

The theory of diffusion attempts to answer the question why new, and presumably superior, products and processes are not adopted immediately by all firms who might benefit from them. In doing so, the theory has to deal with both, factors that influence the *demand* of potential adopters for innovations and elements of the *supply* of innovations that might influence patterns of spread. A survey of the extensive literature on the subject suggests that, on the whole, economists as well as other social scientists have been more successful in explaining the demand side of diffusion than in dealing with supply factors.[1]

Before we begin our discussion, some comments on terminology are necessary. As in the preceding paragraphs, we shall use the terms *diffusion* and *spread of innovations* interchangeably. Many authors also write of *technology transfer*, but there seems to be a tendency to reserve this term for the spread of technology from one industry to another, or among different economies. As we hope will become clear from the content of this chapter, speaking of diffusion in industry as *imitation* is not really appropriate, because the word tends to belittle the frequently substantial difficulties of adopting an innovation into an existing organization and production system, no matter how successful it may have been elsewhere.

In other social contexts, diffusion may be equivalent to the *spread of information*, but what matters from the economist's viewpoint is the *spread of physical items or of techniques and practices*. The availability of information, as well as its improvement over time, are a necessary but not sufficient condition for diffusion in the economic sense. Indeed, technological advances in communication have meant that awareness of the existence of industrial innovations tends to spread so rapidly that it cannot be used, by itself, to explain the reactions of potential adopters.[2]

Finally, we must emphasize that our concern is with the *time dimension of the diffusion process*, i.e., with the speed with which innovations spread through the economic system—within firms (intra-firm diffusion), among firms (inter-firm diffusion), among industries, and among consumers. Economic geographers, anthropologists, and others also have studied the *spatial patterns of diffusion*, i.e., the ways in which new products and processes spread geographically.[3]

9.1   Diffusion as a Social Process—General Models

The spread of new products, processes, and organizational techniques is only one species of diffusion as a social phenomenon. Indeed, economists were relative latecomers to the study of the subject, which has been explored by social scientists and others in a variety of contexts. Therefore, it is useful first to make a brief survey of diffusion as a universal social process, in order to see how far the general theoretical models are applicable to the study of diffusion in the industrial setting or how they might have to be modified.

9.1.1   *A Sociological View of Diffusion*

In an effort to describe diffusion in an all-encompassing fashion, sociologists have defined the process as involving "(1) *acceptance*, (2) *over time*, (3) of some specific *item*—an idea or practice, (4) by individuals, groups or other *adopting units*, linked (5) to specific *channels of communication*, (6) to a *social structure*, and (7) to a given system of values, or *culture*."[4]

Although this definition is general enough to cover technological innovations, we recognize immediately that the latter have some unique features that will require further refinement in our concept of diffusion. For one thing, "acceptance" of an innovation implies some very specific activities on the adopter's part, many of them involving high risks and the commitment of scarce resources. And for another, the nature of "the item" is likely to change in the process of diffusion, so that potential adopters are confronted with different information at different stages in this process. These are matters to which we shall return in a subsequent section.

9.1.2   *Is there a General "Law" of Diffusion?*

Efforts to build formal models of diffusion as a social process have derived guidance mainly from the natural sciences and from fields like epidemiology, which are concerned with "spread by contact." However, one of the main contributors to the general theory of diffusion issued a caution about the limitations of analogies:

> "The use of the word 'diffusion' in the social sciences indicates the awareness of some similarities between the spread of, say, a technological artifact and the spread of a solute through a solvent. Of course it may be argued that the use of a metaphor does not establish the reality of the connection between situations compared and, in fact, may be seriously misleading . . ."[5]

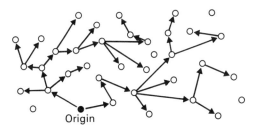

(a) Spread by contact

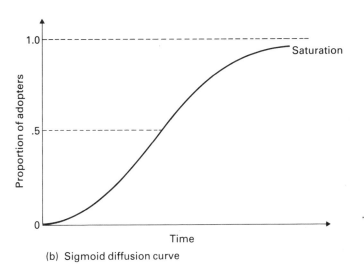

(b) Sigmoid diffusion curve

FIG. 9.1 Standard diffusion model.

If we accept the notion of *contagion* as underlying all spread processes, then we may view each adopter as a "node" from which the item being diffused can be transferred to other potential adopters, and so on, until the *population of potential adopters* is saturated. As the stylized illustration of Fig. 9.1.a suggests, the probability of an adopter contacting a potential adopter will increase during the early stages of the process but will decline as the number of "susceptible" units declines. Given the fact that we are dealing with a social phenomenon, we would not expect saturation to be the same as 100 per cent exhaustion of the population of potential adopters. Just as in the case of epidemics, where not all members of a population will succumb to the contagious disease, some potential recipients of an innovation may never actually become adopters.

In a general way, the process can be described by the equation

$$dx/dt = ax(1 - x),$$

where x is the proportion of all units that have "contacted" the item already, t stands for time, and a is a parameter indicating the "potency of spread."[6] This model gives rise to S-shaped, so-called logistic, diffusion curves (See Fig. 9.1.b). Whether logistic or other kinds of sigmoid functions best describe actual diffusion processes has been a matter of some controversy among statisticians in the various social sciences, but there is general agreement about the shape of the curve—the proportion of adopters rising first at an accelerating and then at a declining rate, until saturation has been achieved.

The notions underlying the model are inherently plausible, and the diffusion of many technological innovations does show an S-shaped pattern. But this cannot conceal some serious conceptual and operational problems in applying the general "law" in the economic setting. First of all, experience shows that we must not presume the existence of a fixed population of potential adopters for new products and processes. Both, the evolution of innovations during the process of diffusion and changes in structural as well as environmental factors on the demand side will determine who, at any given time, is a potential adopter. "Saturation" thus becomes an elusive concept. The availability of a major product or process innovation may, for example, cause firms to enter an industry to which they did not previously belong. An analogous observation can be made for new consumer products. For example, it would have been difficult to predict as recently as a decade ago that the adopters of small, electronic calculators would include housewives, who use them to keep running totals of their expenditures as they fill their shopping carts with groceries! Forecasts about potential adopters are, implicitly, forecasts about the development of technology, and these are notoriously unreliable.

A second problem arises from the fact that even in the industrial setting adoption decisions are not necessarily guided by rational criteria only. Just as in the case of innovating organizations themselves, resistance even to apparently advantageous kinds of change may come into play. On the other hand, investigators have also recognized the existence of "band wagon effects," i.e., adoption decisions provoked solely by the fact that competitors have already made a move and perhaps even by their "boasting and heroics" in technical publications.[7] Under such conditions, the meaning of "contact" is ambiguous at best, well as it may serve in the context of the spread of diseases, ideas, or news items.

Third, hindsight observation of roughly S-shaped diffusion patterns gives us no clues as to the time dimension of ongoing spread processes. Consider, for example, the diffusion paths of fourteen major innovations in the U.S. iron and steel industry, during the first fifteen years after their commercial introduction (Fig. 9.2). Given the long lead times between adoption decisions and production start-up in this industry, a fifteen-year period is not an unduly long time

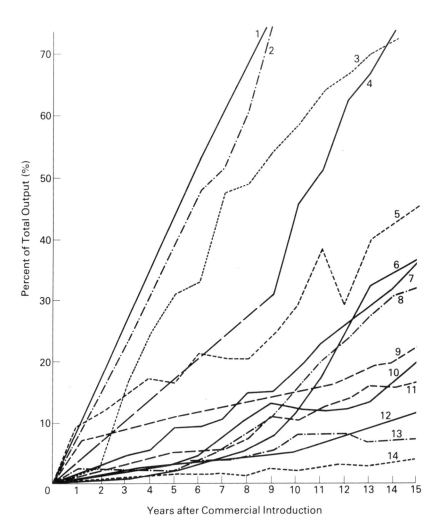

1. Bessemer Furnace (1865)
2. Cont. Cold Rolling, Sheets (1927)
3. Electrolytic Tinplating (1940)
4. Continuous Hot Strip Mill (1926)
5. Cont. Cold Rolling, Strip (1930)
6. Basic Oxygen Furnace (1954)
7. Pelletizing (1956)

8. Continuous Miner (1948)
9. Washing Coking Coal (1889)
10. Machine Loading, Coal (1923)
11. By-product Coking (1895)
12. Machine Cutting, Coal (1882)
13. Open Hearth (1870)
14. Strip Mining, Coal (1914)

FIG. 9.2 Output of new technology as per cent of total output during first 15 years after indicated year of initial commercial use.

Source: Gold, B., Peirce, W. S., and Rosegger, G., "Diffusion of Major Technological Innovations in U.S. Iron and Steel Manufacturing," *Journal of Industrial Economics*, July 1970.

for firms to make evaluations and take action. But the diagram suggests that it would have been very difficult for decision-makers to draw useful information from early diffusion data. Four innovations spready very rapidly, exceeding shares of 70 per cent of total output within 15 years. Another four reached 30 to 50 per cent of output during this time span, whereas the other six diffused more slowly. Nevertheless several of them later on came to dominate production in the industry. Early recognition of their technological and economic potential might have given adopters a competitive advantage. Eventually, every one of the curves by force followed a more or less S-shaped pattern—but over vastly different periods.

Finally, we must recognize that the great bulk of all innovations is substitutive in the broadest sense of that term, i.e., new products and processes displace or replace existing technology. The steamship was a radically new product, but its introduction had to overcome resistance from the economic interests that had coalesced around the sailing vessel. And while it would be misleading to see the automobile simply as a replacement for horse-drawn carriages or railroads, motor vehicles nevertheless forced these other modes of transport from their traditional markets. In other words, only rarely will we encounter innovations so radical that they perform previously unknown functions or satisfy entirely new kinds of demand.

All of this suggests that the spread of technological innovations is a phenomenon *sui generis*, requiring theories and empirical approaches that go beyond the general "social law" of diffusion.

9.2   Diffusion in the Industrial Setting

The most important characteristic of diffusion in the industrial setting is that it requires not only the transmission and passive reception of items, but an active commitment on the part of the receptor. As we shall argue in a subsequent section, from inside a firm the decision to adopt an existing new product or process may not look qualitatively different from a decision to innovate. But before we turn to this issue, we want to consider some more general economic explanations of diffusion.

9.2.1   *Vintage-model Explanations*

Let us first consider the diffusion of techniques in the (greatly simplified) framework of a given industry. We realize, of course, that what is a process innovation to the user industry consists of new products for the suppliers of industrial equipment. Conversely, virtually all changes in products will require adaptations of processes. Assume that, in a given period, the (single-plant) firms in that industry embody the best technology available at the time when each of them was built, and that the vintage characteristics of their capital stock can be differentiated solely on the basis of their respective variable costs per unit of output. Thus, the "state-of-the-art" plant would have the lowest average variable cost, and the oldest would be the marginal plant, i.e., it would just be able to cover average variable cost at whatever price it can obtain for its product. All firms other than the marginal one would earn varying amounts of contribution to overhead and profit (the difference between their total variable costs and their total revenue).

In the short run, these firms could be likened to farms with land of differing fertility: the firm with the lowest direct costs (the most "fertile" capital) earning the highest quasi-rents, and the marginal firm's capital stock analogous to no-rent (marginal) land. In order for the state-of-the-art firm's technique to be diffused to the rest of the firms, other things remaining equal, this technique would have to meet a very stringent criterion: A firm would not consider adoption unless the *total* cost per unit of output of the new technique is lower than *variable* cost per unit of its present technique. Diffusion might take place only to the firms with the very oldest plant and equipment.

But other things are not likely to remain equal. What events might trigger a more rapid diffusion of the best technique? One possibility is that some of the older firm's capital stock breaks down beyond repair because of physical deterioration, so that there is no choice but to replace it. We would not, however, expect this substantially to speed up diffusion in most situations. Only in mature industries with stagnating demand and virtually undifferentiated products might such replacement be a considerable factor.

A second, and more likely, possibility is that relative input prices change, making older plant and equipment obsolete even though it is still serviceable. For example, a rise in wages under industry-wide collective bargaining or a sudden increase in energy prices might disturb the short-run equilibrium we have described above, leading to the wholesale adoption of new techniques.

Third, and equally plausibly, the equilibrium might be upset because of downward pressure on product prices, triggered either by the strategic behavior of one of the low-cost firms or by the entry of new competitors, such as foreign manufacturers. Even though the members of our industry are selling differentiated products, they are not likely to be impervious to such pressure. Loss of market share may convince them that the time had come to adopt the available, lowest-cost techniques.

Finally, institutional changes may trigger the diffusion of new products and processes. The most obvious examples are provided by governmental regulations mandating changes. Needless to say, other kinds of regulations may also retard technical change.

This highly stylized model of factors influencing inter-firm diffusion has value mainly because it highlights the kinds of events that one frequently observes in the real world. But we must also recognize its shortcomings. The notion of a single "best technique" is difficult to sustain, because it ignores the greatly different circumstances (size, cost structure, product mix, etc.) of an industry's member firms. The assumption that firms will always replace their existing equipment with the best available machinery is suspect; empirical evidence shows that typically a variety of machines, embodying techniques of different vintages, might be considered as replacements. Finally we must observe that, despite their plausibility, there is nothing in any of the scenarios described above that would necessarily lead to S-shaped diffusion curves. In order to establish conditions that might result in a sigmoid pattern, we have to bring the role of information into our simple model.

9.2.2 Possible Extensions of the Logistic Model

Let us start with a hypothesis that, taken by itself, is trivial: The rate at which an innovation is diffused depends on the *expected economic advantage* it gives adopters, compared to their present position. That advantage may consist of higher returns on investment through cost savings, increased sales, higher prices for an improved product, or some combination of these. It is an *expected* advantage in the formal sense, i.e., it represents the net present value of a future stream of monetary benefits, discounted by the probability that these benefits will actually occur. Since these probabilities have to be arrived at subjectively, we may think of them as no more than the assessment of decision-makers of the chances that a given decision will yield the anticipated results. If adoption ever were a "sure thing," the probability of success would be 1.0. But if the probability is, say, only .7, decision-makers might well consider a project too risky, even if success meant a great improvement in the rate of return. If we wanted to explore the attitude of different firms toward the same probabilities further, we would have to consider their disutility for losses, which will depend primarily on the firm's wealth position. Thus, for example, a diversified firm with assets of $800 million might consider a .6 probability of success (that is, a .4 probability of failure) for a $2 million project acceptable, while a small business with assets of $4 million would be likely to reject such a project as too risky. All of this is not meant to suggest that managers always, or even occasionally, think of their decision problems in such a formalistic way. The concept of expected value is a mental construct that helps us to theorize about these problems. Furthermore, the analysis sidesteps the possibility of a divergence between the interests of the firm and the utility functions of decision-makers, who may, for example, prefer a quiet life to the uncertain prospects of higher income for their businesses and themselves.

For our purposes it is not necessary that we pursue this matter any further. Instead, we assume that, whatever their subjective evaluations of probabilities, decision-makers will make improved assessments as they obtain more and better information about a new product or technique. In other words, they will feel more confident in sorting likely winners from losers. If this is so, then we would expect the diffusion curve to be roughly S-shaped. We have emphasized already that during the early stages of the introduction of major innovations there is great uncertainty—about technical performance in general, about which of several competing approaches to the same functional requirements will prove economically superior, and about the consequences of adoption among the pioneers. During this phase, which, as we have seen earlier, may last quite a long time, we would expect diffusion to be relatively slow.

Eventually, however, standard versions of a new technology do emerge, "bugs" are worked out by early adopters, market results are reported, and thus the quality of information available to later adopters improves. At this point, diffusion will tend to accelerate, as decision-makers in more and more firms have convinced themselves of the economic advantages of adoption. At the same time, the costs of adoption may decline because of scale economies in the manufacture of equipment or products.

Sooner or later, the apparent benefits of adoption will tend to be dissipated by the widespread availability of very good information about the innovation and by the effects of competition among those who have adopted it. Latecomers will be forced to take up the innovation as a purely defensive strategy, in order to survive in the competitive game. Diffusion slows down, and ultimately there are no more incentives for adoption. Again, however, we must emphasize that this does not mean that the innovation has reached 100 per cent penetration.

While this kind of model helps us to rationalize the existence of sigmoid diffusion curves, it has other implications that are difficult to verify empirically. For example, our assumptions would lead us to expect rapid acceptance of major innovations among large, wealthy firms and slow diffusion among small, specialized, and cash-poor businesses. There is no strong evidence to support this conclusion. Furthermore, there are many instances in which spectacular failures among one or two early adopters so becloud the available information that a more significant number of successful adoptions tends to be ignored. More generally, the problem with our efforts to build a general theory of diffusion along these lines is that the "quality" of all relevant information is in the eye of the beholder. In other words, nothing but a real-time analysis of the actual decision processes leading to adoption or rejection of innovations in individual firms would enable an observer to confirm or reject the model we have outlined. This would mean having access to all the records documenting how and on the basis of what information successive decisions were arrived at. Needless to say, such data are generally held in confidence by companies, and few researchers have been able to follow this approach, promising as it might look.[8]

Our hypothesis about the role of changes in information could explain the existence of sigmoid diffusion curves, but so could a large number of competing hypotheses.[9] This fact, together with the difficulties we mentioned in section 9.1.2, above, explains why most empirical studies do not even pretend to test some version of the "general law" of diffusion. Instead, they restrict themselves to examining the significance of *specific* factors that might help to explain the observed spread patterns for *specific* innovations. A number of these factors appear to play a role in many different industries and therefore deserve a closer look. Before we turn to them, however, we must briefly address the question of how diffusion should be measured.

9.2.3   *Measures of Diffusion*

So far, we were content to speak of "items" or "techniques" being diffused. If one wants to examine the spread of innovations empirically, one has to be more precise. What sorts of data are relevant depends very much on the purpose of an investigation. Thus, for example, the interest of a firm that wants to know how many of its competitors have already tried out a new process will be different from a government agency wishing to check on compliance with some mandate concerning product characteristics.

From the economist's point of view, three measures of diffusion are relevant:

(1) If one is interested in the speed with which innovations spread from enterprise to enterprise, one will want to concentrate on the adoption decisions of individual firms. The distinction between adopters and non-adopters may be useful in examining the influence of such factors as the competitive structure of an industry, the characteristics of individual firms (large vs. small, single-product vs. diversified, etc.), or the types of decision-makers and decision-making processes—in other words, the "openness" of organizations to innovations.[10] It is important to recognize, however, that measuring how many firms have adopted an innovation does not tell one anything about the exent to which they have committed themselves. They may be trying out new products or processes on a small scale, or they may have invested in a complete switch-over to an innovation.

(2) If one wishes to assess the extent to which innovations have affected industries by replacing or displacing existing processes and products, one would concentrate on the capacity or output effects of diffusion. In that case, the changes in the percentages of total capacity or of total output accounted for by the innovation would be the relevant measure. By the same reasoning, this would also be the appropriate indicator of the intra-firm diffusion of innovations.

(3) A third focus of interest is the aggregate growth of new products and of new industries as a result of major innovations. Here the rise in the absolute value of output, or the share of industry sales in GNP or some other measure of economic performance is appropriate. In the case of consumer products, the number (or percentage) of all households having adopted an innovation would serve the same purpose.

In marketing studies, total-expenditure measures are used to reflect diffusion. For individual businesses, concerned with market penetration or market share, this is useful information. But we know that total expenditure (or, from the firm's point of view, total revenue) is the product of price × quantity sold. When diffusion is accompanied by declines in the price of a new product, as it frequently tends to be, this measure understates the extent of spread. For example, total spending on television sets or on electronic calculators grew much less rapidly than did the number of units sold.[11]

9.3   Factors Influencing Diffusion Rates

When we turn from efforts to establish a universally valid theory of diffusion to a consideration of what influences the spread of individual innovations, we find that the empirical literature presents a bewildering array of hypotheses, clues, and suggestions. It would not be unusual to find studies which rely on as many as a dozen different factors that they regard as significant for the spread of a particular new process or product. This state of affairs is explained by both, the nature of the subject and the present state of our understanding. We make no attempt here to summarize all of the variables that appear to have influenced diffusion in one situation or another. Rather, we have attempted to cull from various studies those factors that seem to recur in many of them. For our purposes, we can group them into four major categories:

(1) factors related to the characteristics of the innovation;

(2) factors attributable to the structural characteristics of adopters and non-adopters;

(3) factors having to do with the mechanism whereby diffusion takes place in a particular setting; and

(4) those originating from firms' and industries' institutional environment.

Our concern in this classification is with major innovations. For reasons to which we have referred already, we need not make a distinction between new products and new processes. To be sure, environmental (competitive) conditions may weigh more heavily in case of the former, and structural factors may receive major weight for the latter, but these are differences in degree rather than in substance.

9.3.1   *Characteristics of the Innovation*

A recurrent observation that will hardly occasion great surprise is that innovations requiring relatively low levels of commitment and that promise only incremental improvements are more likely to be adopted than those involving large amounts of resources and major change-overs in traditional production methods. Beyond this rather obvious aspect of the characteristics of innovation, the following appear significant:

(a) *Origin of the Innovation.* The speed of diffusion may be influenced by where an innovation originated. Some innovators, such as equipment manufacturers and suppliers of input materials have an obvious economic interest in seeing their new products adopted by as many firms as possible. Similarly, a customer firm may have made an innovation that it wants its suppliers to use.

On the other hand, if the innovator was a competing business or a company in a different industry, we would not expect these to exert a strong push on potential adopters. In some of the management literature, the "not invented here" syndrome has also received considerable attention. The allegation is that large organizations with their own tradition of innovativeness are reluctant to take up new technology developed elsewhere.

(b) *Expected Effects on Other Inputs*. Innovations are frequently classified as labor-, capital-, materials-, or energy-saving. We know already that whether such physical effects are translated into corresponding economic ones depends on a variety of additional factors. Diffusion rates appear to be affected in many cases by the current market conditions for the inputs that would be saved by adopting the innovation. Thus, for example, the run-up of energy prices in the 1970s led to the rapid spread of a number of energy-conserving techniques that until then had lingered unnoticed, as well as triggering the search for new techniques. Not too surprisingly, a number of studies also found that differences among countries in the diffusion rates for specific types of innovation can be explained by differences in relative factor endowments.

(c) *Location of the Innovation in the Existing Production Structure*. Managements have different attitudes toward the riskiness of adoption, depending on how the innovation in question might affect the existing production system. In general, one would expect new processes that will not affect the current flow of production to be accepted most readily. Thus, for example, the installation of equipment for the purpose of backward or forward integration entails low risks of disruption. On the other hand, a new technique that completely replaces a currently functioning step in a production sequence and therefore requires an all-or-nothing commitment will be viewed with much greater caution. Similarly, innovations that affect the total operations of a plant, such as new materials-handling or inventory-control systems, will receive careful scrutiny before being adopted. In general, innovations that can be introduced gradually and thus enable firms to acquire information in the process of adoption will be diffused more rapidly than those whose introduction requires complete reliance on pre-decision information.

(d) *Changes in the Innovation*. We have emphasized on several occasions that major innovations undergo transformation in the process of diffusion. As each adopting firm fits a new process or product into its production structure, it tends to make qualitative and quantitative changes in equipment, refine a product or add new features, and thus to create additional information for later adopters. One of the most common features of this process is the scaling-up of new process equipment. While early versions may have been of interest only to small plants, later versions of greater capacity will bring large plants into the group of potential adopters. Qualitative changes frequently explain interindustry diffusion. Thus, a process or a new input material that was refined during diffusion in one type of production, may suddenly appear suitable for an entirely different type. It is important to recognize, though, that the expectation of rapid changes in an innovation can actually retard its spread: decision-makers may always find it worthwhile to postpone adoption until the next generation of the new technology comes along.

(e) *Complementarities among Innovations.* Frequently, the full benefits of adopting an innovation can be reaped only if ancillary or complementary innovations are adopted simultaneously. Thus, what may appear to be a series of different innovations is in fact perceived as a technical package by potential adopters. An example of this was the introduction of tubeless tires, which required changes in the design of the wheels as well as in the techniques for producing them. The greater the novelty or complexity of such a package, the more decision-makers will want to accumulate information before adopting it.

9.3.2   Characteristics of Potential Adopters

By adopting an innovation, firms establish the linkage between the innovation's technical potential and its actual economic effects. But whether adoption appears attractive or not, depends not only on this potential but also on the technological and economic characteristics of the firms. Therefore, the apparent advantages of a new process or product always remain an abstraction that has to be evaluated within the framework of a potential adopter's existing structure. This fact alone would explain why not all firms in an industry are automatic candidates for the adoption of major innovations. Some businesses may be situated such that they become pioneers; others may find it useful to monitor the innovation's evolution but to postpone a decision until their own circumstances have changed; and yet others may never become adopters, because the innovation simply does not fit into their particular context. This classification of firms is influenced by what the authors of an authoritative study have called "a formidable list of factors."[12] Only the most important are listed here.

(a) *Technological Specificity of the Existing System.* At any given time, the production system of a firm embodies a more or less integrated set of techniques, a given scale of operations, and methods of organization and control. We refer to all these arrangements as the technological specificity of a system. This will exert a strong influence on the attractiveness of particular product or process innovations. For example, a technique that will improve output rates may not be considered for adoption if the firm already has excess capacity at the production stage affected. Similarly, innovations that require extensive modification of all preceding and succeeding stages may be bypassed, no matter how beneficial they may look in the abstract.

This kind of specificity can also extend beyond individual firms, to a whole technology. Where the standardization of certain components is a necessary aspect of such a technology, or where standardization has evolved over time, innovations may be difficult if not impossible to introduce. An example of the former case is provided by air traffic control systems: adoption of major new techniques tends to be an all-or-nothing proposition, because little benefit would derive unless all airports and all aircraft are equipped with compatible systems. The role of evolutionary standardization is illustrated by the type-writer keyboard; alternative, ergonomically more efficient, designs have been proposed on numerous occasions, but even the most modern computers still incorporate the traditional layout of letter keys.

(b) *The Firm's Financial Position.* Even if an innovation appears technically and economically attractive, a lack of access to funds may prevent a firm from adopting it. We can frequently observe a vicious cycle: a business is in financial difficulties because its techniques or products are no longer competitive; yet this very condition means that sources of additional capital are drying up, and thus the firm falls further behind in the marketplace. Conversely, there have been instances where the adoption of major innovations became a counsel of despair, the firm staking all on one more try at survival. It would be convenient to conclude from these observations that profitable, cash-rich businesses will always be among the early adopters, but such is not the case. There is the danger of assuming all is well because existing products act as what have been referred to as "cash cows," and thus overlooking the longer-term prospects of new products and new markets.

(c) *Technological Capability.* We have emphasized the fact that the adoption of an innovation typically involves more than mere imitation. Major innova-tions must be adapted to fit into a firm's production system. This may require a plant- or firm-specific technological advances, scaling-up, or scaling-down. Whether R&D departments are capable of doing the necessary internal development work, whether technicians and workers with the necessary know-how are available, and whether personnel has the experience required to start up new facilities—these are factors that will influence decision-makers' assessments of the cost of adoption. Some of them may conclude that an innovation is simply too big or too complex to be digested without endangering the whole firm.

(d) *Market Position and Alternative Strategies.* Each firm in an industry occupies a specific place in the competitive spectrum. Its strengths and weaknesses with respect to particular products, or *vis-a-vis* particular com-petitors, will influence the ranking of innovation adoption in the hierarchy of strategies open to management. The acquisition of another existing business, an expansion of marketing efforts, or even the investment of resources in the improvement of an old technology, might be considered more promising than adoption of a major innovation. Ideally, each firm would maintain a "strategic portfolio" of old and new products, but this state of affairs is easier to prescribe than to implement within the constraints of an ongoing operation.

(e) *Managerial Attitudes.* Ultimately, it may well be that the personal characteristics of top managers play a dominant role in adoption decisions. Unfortunately, the determination and measurement of the relevant attributes is extremely difficult. Efforts to relate attitudes toward innovations to such factors as the decision-makers' age, their education and professional backgrounds, their careers within a firm, and the expected duration of their tenure at the top, have resulted in some highly suggestive evidence but not in any firm conclusions. Nor is it entirely clear whether owner-managers tend to behave differently from managerial employees. The basic problem with the search for social or psychological factors in innovativeness is a common one in all investigations of this type: they ultimately rest on hindsight interpretations of actual behavior but have little predictive content. Why individuals interpret the same information in completely different ways is a question that remains largely unanswered.

(f) *Age of Firms and Industries.* In one of the classic investigations of readiness for change, Professor Kuznets suggested that the age of firms and industries in itself is a major factor in explaining their attitudes toward innovations. He wrote:

> "As an industry starts from small beginnings and develops rapidly to substantial output, it is enabled to do so mainly by progress in technical conditions of production. But the effects of technical progress show an unmistakable tendency to slacken due either to retardation in technical progress itself or the pressure of exhaustion of resources, or both. Added to that is the check exercised by groups of productive activity whose industrial arts do not improve as rapidly and as significantly as in the industry in question."[13]

Economists and economic historians have dealt with this problem in considerable detail, but the question is far from settled: are the attitudes of potential adopters of innovations affected in a systematic way by the maturity of the industry to which they belong? There is a lot of evidence suggesting that this question should be answered in the affirmative, but there are also many instances in which an industry has been pronounced mature and technologically stagnant, only to experience another spurt of growth.[14] Here, as in so many other areas of technological change, prediction on the basis of past patterns is a hazardous business.

9.3.3   The Process of Diffusion

While we have argued that mere information transfer is not analogous to diffusion, the mechanism whereby such information is spread will nevertheless exert an influence on adoption rates. The technology of generating and communicating information has improved greatly over the past half century, but the sources and channels of its distribution nevertheless remain important factors in explaining diffusion. The reasons for this observation become clearer when we consider what might be involved in the accumulation of information that is regarded as sufficient for a decision by the managers of an individual business.

(a) *External vs. Internal Information.* By definition, potential adopters of an innovation receive initial information from outside their organization. This information may range in character from a public good to knowledge protected by property rights. Typically, public goods-type information will deal with the abstract characteristics of an innovation or with the results of its application elsewhere. It gives decision-makers no more than clues about the innovation's interest to them. That the institutions and mechanisms through which private-property information becomes available to firms will have a strong influence on diffusion needs no further elaboration; we have dealt with these matters in the preceding chapters. Equally important, however, is the balance between all forms of external information and the data the firm itself has to generate in order to evaluate innovations. Once again, decision-makers are confronted with a dilemma that we have referred to before: as diffusion proceeds, the quantity and quality of information available through external channels improves, reducing the need to commit resources for internal investigations. But as this process goes on, the prospective benefits of adoption are also reduced. Generalizations about the respective roles of external and internal information are made more difficult by the fact that we observe considerable differences in the "technological openness" of industries. In some, new technical knowledge is shared rather freely, whereas in others a tradition of secrecy prevails.

(b) *External Interests in Diffusion.* The cost of acquiring information is often mitigated by the fact that some outside agent has an interest in rapid diffusion. As we have mentioned above, the most obvious cases of this type involve the suppliers of industrial equipment or of input materials. However, ideas and pressure from customers (potential users) also frequently play an important role.[14] Particularly interesting are situations in which sellers and buyers of innovations have to rely on the expertise of third parties. Thus, for example, the adoption of new medical technology by hospitals hinges on the decisions of physicians, who thus become the targets for the selling efforts of equipment manufacturers. More generally, the role of technical consultants and similar agents in diffusion poses some questions that have been little explored so far. The issue in all such cases centers upon the behavior of economic units that do not have to bear the direct economic consequences of decisions.

(c) *International Diffusion.* A host of separate problems is raised by the international diffusion of innovations. We shall deal with these in a later chapter. Here we only need to mention that the mechanisms and channels of spread probably play an even more important part in influencing diffusion patterns than they do within economies. Thus, multinational corporations have been found to be particularly effective agents for the transfer of new technology, while some of the processes working well within economies run up against difficulties in diffusion among countries.

9.3.4 *The Role of the Environment*

Just as institutional factors influence the rates of invention, development and innovation, they also affect the speed of diffusion. Not surprisingly, there are great differences among industries with respect to the environment's role in the adoption decisions of firms. Only a few general considerations will be mentioned here.

(a) *The Patent System*. Orderliness requires that we mention the influence of secure intellectual property rights in the present context, but we need not repeat our observations of Chapter 7. At one end of the continuum of possibilities, one would expect the existence of a strong patent to prevent diffusion of a basic innovation for the duration of legal protection. At the other end, the absence of such protection for an inventor-innovator of a successful new product or process presumably would lead to rapid adoption by others.

(b) *Laws and Governmental Regulations*. Governments may accelerate or retard diffusion, either in expressed pursuit of some social objective, or inadvertently. Indeed, it would be difficult to think of any laws affecting business, from taxation to environmental protection, that will not also affect the adoption of new technology. When rules mandate or prohibit the use of certain products and processes, the implications are obvious. Less transparent are those situations in which the acceleration or retardation of diffusion occurs as a side effect. Thus, for example, requirements for installing costly pollution-control equipment may hasten firms' decisions to replace old facilities with new, because the additional investment in equipment tacked on to marginal plants cannot be justified. Another interesting illustration of rapid diffusion induced by policies aimed at a different objective was provided by airline regulation. As long as route assignments and fares were strictly controlled by a government agency, airlines competed mainly on the basis of travel speed, comfort, and "frills." Therefore, they were forced to adopt the most up-to-date aircraft types in order to stay ahead of, or at least match, the services offered by their rivals on a given route.[15] Deregulation has changed this picture, price competition substantially replacing various forms of non-price competition.

(c) *Specification-writing Agencies, Insurance Companies, etc.* A number of non-governmental institutions may also affect diffusion rates. In many industries, the use of new products or of the products of new processes for specific applications depends on approval by specification-writing agencies. Thus, for example, a new type of steel or a steel of known metallurgical characteristics made by a new technique may not be used in, say, ships, pressure vessels, or bridges until it has been tested and approved by the appropriate body. Conversely, such organizations may also accelerate diffusion. Thus, earlier in this century, the setting of hundreds of component standards by the Society of Automotive Engineers led to the rapid spread of certain types of motor vehicle parts among all manufacturers. Insurance companies frequently influence diffusion, because they may refuse to write policies for final products, equipment or plants incorporating an innovation until they have examined all features relevant to their risk.

(d) *Labor Unions*. The story of labor resistance to technological change is too well known to bear repeating. From the original French *saboteurs*, who used their *sabots* (wooden shoes) to destroy the weaving machines that threatened their livelihood, to today's efforts by unions to retard process innovations through featherbedding and other means, workers have often exerted an influence on diffusion. It is worth remembering, however, that the attitudes of organized labor have varied greatly over time, and from industry to industry. Thus, in the 1930s and 1940s the United Mine Workers under the leadership of John L. Lewis accepted the wholesale mechanization of coal-mines, while the railroad and printing trades unions were notorious for their stubborn rejection of innovations and their efforts to prevent employers from reaping the benefits of technological advances.[16] Over the long run, none of these efforts have proved very effective, just as none of the predictions of large and permanent unemployment on account of labor-saving innovations have come true. In recent years, major advances like programmed automation and robotization have once again raised the spectre of widespread technological unemployment; however, the impact of international competition on many of the industries affected appears to have persuaded labor leaders that the rationalization of production was necessary if American firms were to survive in the marketplace. On a less visible plane, we must observe also that crafts unions, especially, have often acted as strong political pressure groups to assure the survival of their jobs in the face of technological progress. Thus, for example, the building trades have displayed great interest in maintaining local building codes that prevent the introduction of factory-type component manufacture to replace on-site construction work.

What kinds of institutional factors influence diffusion rates in particular cases is an empirical question. Understandably, managers have a tendency to attribute most of their difficulties in adopting innovations to obstacles in their firms' environment. Meanwhile, much of the management literature tends to focus on variables endogenous to businesses in explaining or criticizing an apparent lack of technological progressiveness. Keeping in mind our several earlier discussions of the interplay between structure and environment, we conclude that the truth probably lies somewhere between these two views, but that it cannot in any event be established through sweeping generalizations.

9.4   A Synoptic Model of Diffusion in Industry

Although a great variety of substantive factors might affect firms' decision to adopt, or not to adopt, an innovation, we can nevertheless provide a characteristic model of the process (Fig. 9.3). Such a model has to start with the act of innovation itself. Usually, all sorts of technical information about a new product or process are floating about even before one firm becomes the innovator that faces all economic consequences of pioneering. The initial assessment of the innovation by others will be influenced by the general state of relevant technological knowledge, as well as by data about similar or analogous innovative efforts that failed on account of technical or economic reasons.

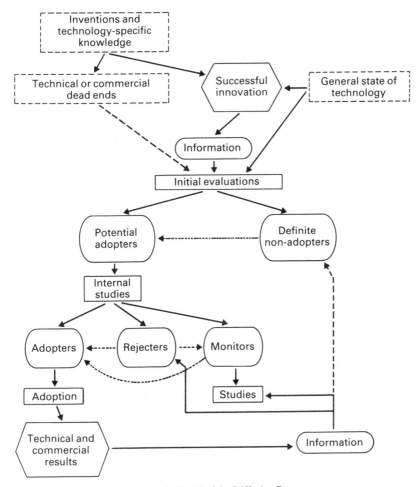

FIG. 9.3 Synoptic Model of the Diffusion Process.

On this basis, decision-makers will make their first evaluations. Subject to the influence of some combination of the factors discussed in the preceding section, many will conclude that—at the present time—the innovation definitely should not be adopted; others will join the ranks of potential adopters; and yet others will decide actively to monitor developments before making a commitment. The technical and economic results achieved by the adopters then constitute a new information base for the initial non-adopters and monitors, triggering a new round of assessments and decisions. The dotted lines between the three groups are meant to suggest the possibility that—over time—firms may shift from one group to the other.

This dynamic view of the diffusion process enables us to see the population of (realistically defined) potential adopters as changing over time, as criteria for

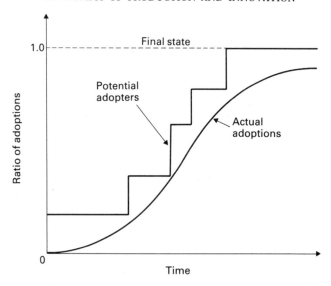

FIG. 9.4 Diffusion with change in the population of potential adopters.
Source: Gold, B., Peirce, W. S., Rosegger, G., and Perlman, M., *Technological Progress and Industrial Leadership* (Lexington, MA: Lexington Books—D. C. Heath, 1984), p. 47.

adoption change and as the innovation itself evolves technologically. As Fig. 9.4 is meant to illustrate, such a view implies that "saturation" may be greater at some early stage in the diffusion process than in later ones. It also suggests that fast or slow diffusion rates cannot be judged as desirable or undesirable until the causes for the behavior of potential adopters are determined. Some investigators even have raised the question whether any attempts to measure overall, long-term diffusion as a ratio of adopters to potential adopters is meaningful, when this is "a ratio for which the appropriate denominator is difficult to find."[17] No general model of the diffusion process can capture all the variations that exist from industry to industry, but it does provide a conceptual base for the examination of specific cases.

9.5   Brief Comment on the Diffusion of Consumer Innovations

Three major differences among the factors influencing diffusion in industry and those affecting the diffusion of consumer products are noteworthy. First, the primary criteria for industrial decisions appear more generally susceptible to evaluation in terms of technical performance parameters and economic measures of benefits and costs, although less objective criteria may enter the decision process when the former do not yield conclusive results. Second, evaluation processes in industry are of necessity more intensive and, as we mentioned above, frequently involve considerable additional R&D effort. In the case of household decisions to adopt a new product, the influence of such evaluations on observed diffusion rates tends to have less explanatory power than changes in (relative) product prices and in household incomes.[18] And third, such decisions in industry are likely to have more serious consequences, in terms of the economic performance and perhaps even the survival of firms.

Of course, consumer products cover a broad range of possibilities with respect to each of these three distinctions. Thus, the more serious the implications of household decisions, especially with respect to the total cost of adoption relative to household incomes, the more consumers are likely to incur (implicit or explicit) search costs or to defer to the decisions of experts. This is most obvious in the case of critical health problems, when decisions about new therapeutic techniques or medications are turned over to the attending physician. But even in situations where the consequences of badly informed judgments are less potentially serious, consumers may place great reliance on intermediaries, such as external information services, experienced friends, or even individual sales people who have earned their trust.

When all this has been said, however, there remain vast areas of consumer response to innovative products in which subjective factors and non-economic motives play a dominant role. The quality of available information (including advertising), peer group pressure ("keeping up with the Joneses"), and what Thorstein Veblen called the preference for "conspicuous consumption," all are likely to enter into household decisions. The marketing efforts of manufacturers and distributors will of course cater to these propensities. This does not mean that consumers are powerless pawns in the game of persuasion, for if such contentions were true, new products—especially those marketed by major firms with the necessary experience and resources—would fail only rarely. Corporate decision-makers may dream of such a happy state of affairs, but they are not likely to encounter it in real life.

In recent years, we have witnessed lengthy debates about the "social desirability" of high levels of consumer responsiveness to innovative products, and therefore their rapid diffusion. Although these debates have produced attacks on marketing in general, on "unnecessary" product differentiation, and on the so-called "throw-away society," they have not shed much light on the basic issues. Some people may place a high value on the durability of products and be willing to pay for this characteristic, whereas others express a preference for less durable, cheaper products. There is little evidence to suggest that consumers as a group do not know what they want, or that they are the easy prey of hucksters. To the extent that consumers might need "protection" against the consequences of their own decisions, there is also little evidence that governmental rules do a particularly effective job of providing such protection. This is not the place to consider the problems of regulating product characteristics in any detail, but we need only to observe the ongoing controversy about so-called "passive restraints" in automobiles to get some flavor of the difficulties raised when a decision is made to impose rules requiring technological fixes upon a reluctant public.

Having stressed some basic differences in the determinants of diffusion in industry and among households, we can conclude by emphasizing their conceptual unity: both involve the *physical spread* of some innovation among potential adopters; and the speed of this spread is influenced by the acquisition and interpretation of information, with decisions focussed on the expected benefits and costs of adoption.

Notes

1. A comprehensive survey of diffusion as a social phenomenon can be found in Rogers, E. M., *Diffusion of Innovations*, 3rd ed. (New York: The Free Press, 1983).
2. Rosegger, G., "Diffusion Research in the Industrial Setting: Some Conceptual Clarifications," *Technological Forecasting and Social Change*, 9 (1976). For an empirical study, see Gold, B., Rosegger, G., and Boylan, M. G., *Evaluating Technological Innovations* (Lexington, MA: Lexington Books—D. C. Heath, 1980), pp. 147–50.
3. See Hägerstrand, T., *Innovation Diffusion as a Spatial Process* (Chicago, IL: University of Chicago Press, 1967).
4. Katz, E., Levin, M. L., and Hamilton, H., "Traditions of Research on the Diffusion of Innovation," *American Sociological Review*, April 1963.
5. Rapoport, A., "The Diffusion Problem in Mass Behavior," *General Systems Yearbook, 1956*.
6. *Ibid.*
7. Price, D. J. deS., "The Structures of Publication in Science and Technology," in Gruber, W. H. and Marquis, D. G., *Factors in the Transfer of Technology* (Cambridge, MA: M.I.T. Press, 1969).
8. For one of the rare examples of this type of study, see Skeddle, R. W., "Expected and Emerging Results of a Major Technological Innovation—Float Glass," *Omega*, 8/5 (1980).
9. A survey of models can be found in Stoneman, P., *The Economic Analysis of Technological Change* (Oxford: Oxford University Press, 1983), Part II.
10. Results of investigations along this line are reported in Mansfield, E., *Industrial Research and Technological Innovation* (New York: Norton, 1968).
11. The spread patterns for a number of consumer and capital goods are reported in Fisher, J. C. and Pry, R. H., "A Simple Substitution Model of Technological Change," *Technological Forecasting and Social Change*, 3 (1971).
12. Nabseth, J. and Ray, G. F., *The Diffusion of New Industrial Processes* (Cambridge: Cambridge University Press, 1974), p. 12.
13. Kuznets, S., "Retardation of Industrial Growth," *Journal of Economic and Business History*, August 1929; reprinted in Kuznets, S., *Economic Change* (New York: Norton, 1953).
14. See v. Hippel, E., "Successful Industrial Products from Customer Ideas," *Journal of Marketing*, January 1978.
15. Phillips, A., "Air Transportation in the United States," in Capron, W. M. (ed.), *Technological Change in Regulated Industries* (Washington, DC: Brookings, 1971).
16. For case studies and some general observations, see Weinstein, P. A. (ed.), *Featherbedding and Technological Change* (Boston, MA: D. C. Heath, 1965).
17. Nabseth and Ray, *op. cit.*, p. 298.
18. Bonus, H., "Quasi-Engel Curves, Diffusion, and the Ownership of Major Consumer Durables," *Journal of Political Economy*, 81 (1973).

CHAPTER 10

The Effects of Technological Change, I

This is the first of two chapters concerned with the economic impact of technological change. When we consider how societies and cultures have been transformed by major innovations like the steam engine, the automobile, radio, and television, we are forced to preface our investigations with a word of caution: only a materialist of the purest persuasion would claim that economic factors alone can explain these transformations. No field of human thought and endeavor has been left untouched by advances in technology. And most observers would agree that the last century has seen more radical changes in all aspects of life than virtually any other period.

While historians have rightly stressed the elements of continuity in mankind's efforts to deal with its own new artifacts, many of them also point to the fact that the recent clustering of major technological developments has led to quantum jumps in what traditionally has been a more or less evolutionary process, thus raising entirely new problems of adjustment. An author illustrates this by referring to progress in one of man's oldest arts, navigation: A Phoenician or Greek sailor would have felt quite capable, two thousand years later, of handling the caravels of Columbus; and three centuries later, one of Columbus's sailors could have adapted himself to Lord Nelson's frigates; but transplant a seaman from the *Victory* to a modern aircraft carrier, and he "would think he had been whisked into the world of magic."[1] Yet we could claim that at least the sailor would have had a frame of reference within which to understand the implications of the new technology. But what about nuclear energy or genetic engineering?

In this broader perspective, an explanation of the economic effects of technological innovations would seem a relatively modest undertaking. Nevertheless, the subject could fill (and has filled) many books. We can do no more than to highlight what we consider some of its more important aspects. By convention, economic theorizing has been organized around the impact of technological change on output, employment, and investment; on living standards and the distribution of incomes; on the structure of industries and markets; and on the international competitiveness of economies. But, as one student of the field has pointed out, empirical investigations quickly reveal that these impacts have many more dimensions and that no organizing principle will suit all purposes.[2] Since we want to conduct a brief survey, our choice of topics is eclectic. In the present chapter, we look first at efforts to assess the aggregate impact of technological change, but this will be no more than a quick glance; our main attention then turns to microeconomics, i.e., the effects of change on plants, firms, and industries, and to the side effects of technical progress.

10.1   Technological Change and Economic Growth

The term, economic growth, has been used in so many different contexts that we must state at the outset what we mean when we speak of growth: it is an increase in the economy's *aggregate capacity to produce goods and services*. In Chapter 2, we modeled growth as an outward movement of the production possibilities frontier (see Fig. 2.2). If an economy currently operates inside the frontier, i.e., has underutilized capacity, and then moves on to the frontier, the resulting increase in aggregate output does not represent growth—even though it is often designated as such by leaders of governments seeking credit for their policies.

Furthermore, the fact that growth has occurred does not automatically imply that people's real incomes will have risen, on average. Many a less-developed country has achieved quite substantial growth rates, only to see the higher output swallowed up by increases in population! Finally, even when per capita output has risen, this tells us nothing about how the benefits were shared, i.e., about the effects of growth on income distribution.

10.1.1   *The Growth Record of the United States*

In Fig. 10.1 we present some statistics relevant to an assessment of the U.S. growth record in the last few decades. Estimates of average annual growth in real output since the turn of the century range between 3.3 and 3.6 per cent. Compounded at the rate of 3.4 per cent, aggregate output would increase by 40 per cent in every decade, but such long-term averages are somewhat misleading. Although the statistical data for the earlier periods are not very reliable, there is every indication that growth rates were higher than they have been in the more recent past. Slower population growth has meant, however, that per capita output and income have more than kept pace with the increases in aggregate performance.

The long-run effect of growth on income distribution is less clearcut, mainly because institutional changes such as the development of Social Security and private pension funds, of a variety of income transfer programs, as well as changes in the composition of the labor force render longer-term comparisons

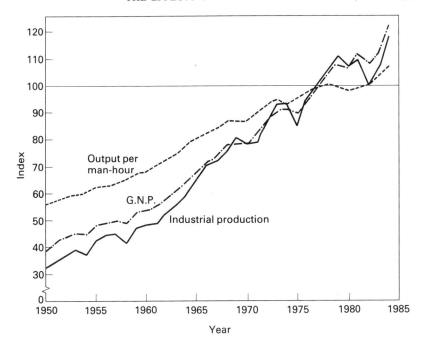

FIG. 10.1 U.S. gross national product (in constant dollars), industrial production, and non-farm output per man-hour, 1950-1984. (Indices, 1977 = 100).
Source: Council of Economic Advisers, *Economic Report of the President 1984* (Washington, DC: U.S. Government Printing Office, 1985).

problematical. But even if the distribution of income has changed only marginally, as many investigators have estimated, there can be little doubt that the real incomes even of the lowest groups have risen remarkably. That this development has not eradicated the problems of poverty, which seem to be with us as much as ever, emphasizes the fact that we are dealing with a relative concept: America's poor are disadvantaged in comparison to the average citizen in this country; that they may look well off to average citizens in other countries is quite irrelevant.

Growth rates cannot be judged by any absolute standard but only relative to earlier periods or to the performance of other economies. In terms of long-run trends, the United States has outperformed virtually every other major industrial country with the exception of Japan, which boasts a long-term average growth rate of around 4 per cent. Germany with 2.9 per cent, Great Britain with 1.9 per cent, and France with 1.7 per cent, rank well behind this country in twentieth-century growth. However, in recent years a number of major economies have outstripped the United States in industrial production (see Table 10.1).

TABLE 10.1   Indices of industrial production, major industrial countries, 1960–83
(1967 = 100)

Year	United States	Canada	Japan	France	West Germany	Italy	United Kingdom	European Community*
1960	66.2	63.1	43.0	70	78.4	59.2	83.9	74.4
1961	66.7	65.6	51.2	73	82.8	66.5	84.2	78.1
1962	72.2	71.2	55.4	78	86.1	71.9	85.0	81.3
1963	76.5	75.7	61.7	86	88.9	78.4	87.8	84.8
1964	81.7	82.6	71.4	90	96.6	79.2	95.0	91.0
1965	89.8	89.7	74.2	93	102.1	82.8	97.8	94.7
1966	97.8	96.2	83.8	98	103.0	93.3	99.3	98.4
1967	100.0	100.0	100.0	100	100.0	100.0	100.0	100.0
1968	106.3	106.4	115.2	104	109.2	106.4	107.6	107.4
1969	111.1	113.7	133.4	114	123.2	110.5	111.3	117.6
1970	107.8	115.3	151.8	120	131.1	117.6	111.8	123.3
1971	109.6	121.5	155.7	128	133.6	117.5	111.2	126.1
1972	119.7	130.7	167.0	135	138.7	122.7	113.2	131.7
1973	129.8	144.6	190.5	145	147.7	134.6	123.3	141.4
1974	129.3	149.2	183.1	148	145.1	140.6	120.8	142.3
1975	117.8	140.3	163.9	139	137.1	127.6	114.4	132.8
1976	130.5	148.5	182.0	149	149.1	143.5	118.1	142.6
1977	138.2	152.7	189.7	152	152.0	145.1	124.2	145.9
1978	146.1	157.8	201.1	155	154.1	147.9	127.8	149.7
1979	152.5	167.6	215.2	163	161.5	157.6	132.8	156.8
1980	147.0	165.1	225.2	161	162.0	166.5	124.1	155.8
1981	151.0	165.9	227.5	160	159.1	163.8	119.5	152.1
1982	138.6	149.5	228.4	158	154.5	158.8	121.7	149.7
1983	147.6	157.6	236.5	159	155.7	153.7	125.7	151.1

* Consists of Belgium, Luxembourg, Denmark, France, Greece, Ireland, Italy, Netherlands, United Kingdom, and West Germany. Data for Greece included since 1981.

Source: Council of Economic Advisers, Economic Report of the President 1984 (Washington, DC: U.S. Government Printing Office, 1985).

10.1.2   *The Technology Component in Growth*

Our earlier discussions enable us to list the factors which, in principle, could contribute to economic growth: (a) increases in the quantity of labor (although, if all other inputs were to remain constant, we would expect the eventual onset of diminishing returns and perhaps even of negative returns); (b) improvements in the quality of labor through education and training; (c) increases in the economy's stock of capital, private and public; (d) the discovery and exploitation of new natural resources; (e) the development of more efficient institutional and organizational arrangements; and (f) improvements in productive techniques and the introduction of new products—in other words, technological advancement.

When we turn to measuring the relative contribution of each factor, and especially that of technological progress, we face problems. For one thing, the necessary data may be difficult to come by. And for another, it is next to impossible—without making severely restrictive assumptions—to account for the interdependence among the factors. For example, additions to the capital stock are almost always going to embody technological advances, these advances will necessarily affect the quality of the labor force, which in turn will have an influence on the probability of further technical improvements, and so on.

Empirical investigations have to find a way out of this dilemma. One approach is to select more readily definable variables and to use these as surrogates for the above determinants of growth. Thus, one comprehensive study lists several dozen measurable indicators of "processes relating to economic growth."[3] Such a grab-bag of statistics is interesting in its own right, but it does not tell us anything about the relative importance of technological change in bringing about economic growth.

A second, and more widely used, approach relies on the concept of an *aggregate production function* of the form.

$$Q = f(K, L, \ldots),$$

where Q is the economy's total output, K is the aggregate capital input and L the labor input into production, with other variables added as required by the assumptions underlying the model to be estimated. Many versions of such models have been developed, and depending on their structure they yield different results.[4] Some assume, clearly counter-factually, that all technological change is disembodied and is strictly a function of time. A second category of models assumes that all new technology is embodied in the capital stock, in which case the rate of technological progress is reflected solely in the vintage structure of this stock. Yet another approach asks what output growth would have been if only the quantity, but not the quality, of inputs had changed and then attributes the difference between this hypothetical growth and the actually observed growth, the "unexplained residual," to improvements in technology.

None of these methods can deal very satisfactorily with the impact of new products, of changes in the quality of existing products, or of new institutional arrangements. No wonder that the numbers arrived at via aggregate production functions have been called "measures of our ignorance." Non-economist researchers have attributed the shortcomings of these models to their very design, in which "the primacy of these so-called factors of production was axiomatic"[5], despite the contribution of economists like Schumpeter, who clearly demonstrated that changes in the *qualitative* characteristics of inputs were more important in explaining growth than increases in their quantities. Nevertheless, there exists general agreement that, no matter what model is used as a basis for estimation, technological advancement accounts for well over half of the observed economic growth. It would be difficult, however, to draw any inferences for economic analysis or policy formulation from this conclusion. We know that neither the impacts of new technology nor the effects of government policies fall evenly, like snow, upon the economic landscape, although this is the impression one might get from macroeconomic analyses. In fact, long-term growth and improvements in productivity vary greatly among industries. With the aggregate picture of growth composed of the vastly different performance patterns of individual industries, investigations which focus on the role of innovations in these industries or on sectors of technology ultimately have provided more useful insights into the process of technological change than have efforts at aggregate assessment, albeit at a loss in generality.[6]

10.2 Microeconomic Effects—Elementary Theory

Since the aggregate results of technological change are thought to be generally beneficial for economic growth, it is frequently assumed that each individual innovation mirrors macroeconomic impacts at the microeconomic level, as follows:

(a) The major *physical* effect of innovations is to yield either new products (which automatically mean higher profits to the adopter, and more efficient production or a higher standard of living), or new processes (whose diffusion implies increased factor productivity).

(b) By their very nature, increases in productivity and expansions in capacity result in lower unit costs of production.

(c) Lower unit costs and successful new products yield increased returns on investment and lead to the growth of firms, thus constituting the main incentives for further efforts at improving technology.

(d) Since improved productivity also means resource conservation and since growth is a desirable societal goal, there is an inherent congruence between the objectives of firms and those of the economy as a whole, and—even more important—between decision-makers' expectations and the actual results of innovative activity.

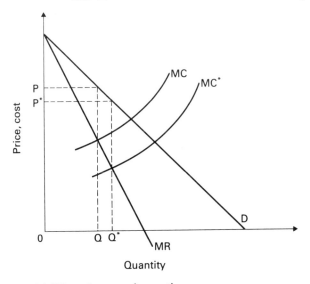

(a) Effect of process innovation

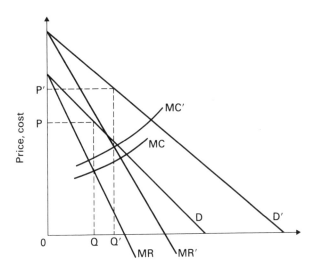

(b) Effect of successful product improvement

FIG. 10.2 Short-run effects of innovations.

The standard model for demonstrating the first three of these inferences for process improvements is shown in Fig. 10.2.a. Given demand and marginal revenue curves for a product, MC represent cost conditions before a process innovation has been adopted. Output will be at Q, and price at P. After introduction of the innovation, marginal costs shift to MC*, the profit-maximizing quantity is now Q*, and price has been lowered to P*.

Figure 10.2.b shows the analogous model for product improvements. Here the MC curve shifts upward to MC', reflecting the increased cost of production. But the new product characteristics induce an outward shift in demand to D' which more than offsets the cost increase.

These stylized versions of the impact of technological change fit nicely into the theory of the profit-maximizing firm. Unfortunately, however, the available empirical evidence suggests that such simple linkages of cause and effect are probably the rare exception rather than the rule. It is not difficult to surmise why this should be so. First, the model treats the *results* of the adoption of an innovation as conforming to the *goals* of the adopting firm. But whether the expectations that triggered investment in an innovation are actually fulfilled, and for how long, are crucial questions in the assessment of actual effects. Second, the model assumes a direct correspondence between the *physical* effects of an innovation on the production system and its *economic* effects on the firm. But we have seen already, in our discussion in Chapter 5, that only under certain conditions do input-productivity improvements translate themselves into analogous cost reductions. And third, the model implicitly assumes that the markets for inputs and outputs will remain unchanged when an individual firm adopts innovations; what is missing in this partial-equilibrium framework is a link between the behavior of firms and the behavior of industries, as well as any suggestion of the role that the passage of time might play in influencing the nature of effects. It is not surprising, therefore, that the basic microeconomic theory has little relevance to empirical research, plausible as its postulates and conclusions may look.

10.3 A More Complex View of Likely Effects

If we want to move beyond an elementary theoretical framework for the analysis of the effects of technological change, we must recognize four crucial elements in the movement from adoption decisions to the ultimate effects of innovation:

(a) Investment in innovations may be triggered by a variety of motives, of which demonstrable cost savings or market expansion are but two.

(b) In the case of major innovations, uncertainty implies possible gaps between expectations and results on the one hand, and between physical results and financial results on the other.

(c) The reasons for divergences between technical and economic results may be found either within the structure of the adopting firm or in its environment.

(d) When major innovations are diffused, this environment is bound to change and therefore it will modify initial economic results over time, even if they were entirely in line with expectations.

We shall deal with these matters in order.

10.3.1 *The Variety of Goals in Innovation*

In order properly to interpret the effects of technological advances, we must recognize first that the generation and adoption of innovations in industry can have a number of quite distinct objectives. The following have been suggested:[7]

(a) Modifications in the physical and chemical properties of input materials as well as the introduction of new materials, with the goals of
 i. offsetting actual or potential shortages, declining materials quality, or increases in the (relative) price of a material;
 ii. reducing transportation costs;
 iii. reducing the generation of waste products, unmarketable byproducts, or adverse effects on the working environment; or
 iv. improving the characteristics or appearance of the final product.

Examples of innovative efforts in pursuit of these goals include the beneficiation of low-grade ores, the partial processing of materials before they are moved from their source to their place of use, the elimination of environmentally damaging substances in fuels, or the substitution of lighter materials for heavier ones.

(b) Changes in the design and scale of equipment, production units, and plants in order to:
 i. improve specific technical performance parameters, such as speed, precision, reliability, safety, yield, or downtime for maintenance and repairs;
 ii. increase capacity, eliminate bottlenecks in production, or achieve better balance among production stages in a vertically integrated sequence;
 iii. set up facilities for the production of new or modified products; or
 iv. adapt facilities to the changes in materials inputs undertaken for any of the reasons suggested under (a), above.

Machine tools working to closer tolerances, more powerful cranes, or improved refractories in furnaces are examples of this type of innovation. Adaptations required, say, to substitute plastic for steel components in automobile manufacturing illustrate why it is difficult to separate product from process innovations.

(c) Improvements in control systems, with the goals of
 i. achieving more automatic operation;
 ii. assuring minimal deviations from desired operating conditions; or
 iii. making possible rapid changes in production levels and product mix, in response to changing market demands.

The numerical control of machine tools, the introduction of continuous process control and feedback systems, and the more recent innovation of flexible manufacturing systems come to mind as illustrations.

(d) New products and changes in the design of existing products, in order to
 i. exploit newly emerging markets;
 ii. penetrate existing markets more effectively; or
 iii. maintain market shares against competitive inroads.

Although each of these operational goals could be subsumed under that ultimate catch-all, profitability, their separate consideration is essential if one wants to analyze the different directions and intensities of actual effects. At the same time, we must realize that not all innovations will fit neatly into one of the taxonomic boxes. Indeed, it is the mark of major technological changes that they spill over into several of the above categories. The point is, in any event, that the pursuit of these various goals by firms is based on very specific expectations about the benefits to be derived. There can be no presumption that the same benefits would accrue to another firm, or that other firms might not achieve the same objectives by different means.

10.3.2   Gaps between Expectations and Physical Results

Presumably, no management will engage in the risky business of innovating or adopting innovations unless it expects an improvement in terms of at least one of the variables by which its performance is evaluated, be they on the cost or revenue side. The first requirement, therefore, is that the physical-technical results of an innovation are up to expectations. As we saw in the preceding chapter, firms will gather external information and undertake whatever internal R&D is necessary to evaluate projects.

However, no matter how carefully such evaluations are carried out, the actual physical performance of an innovation within the context of a particular production system will be subject to a lot of uncertainty. Even more important, in general only the technical results will be observable in an unequivocal fashion, while the economic effects of all but the most important innovations tend to merge into a firm's ongoing operations. Only where adoption involves the setting up of distinct new facilities, organizational entities, or product lines, would we expect to be able to observe economic effects uncontaminated by noise from other parts of the system. As one expert points out:

> "The overwhelming majority of business investments are of [the] segmental or component type—replacements, improvements, expansions or some combination thereof. They become a part—usually a small part—of an existing operation. Since it is impossible in most cases to compute their separate revenue generation and operating cost incurments after they are in service, it is even more impossible to predict these magnitudes before the projects are acquired."[8]

Although this view has not gone uncontested by those who believe that *ex ante* project evaluations can do better than is suggested by this statement,[9] the point is that most managements have only the technical success or failure of an innovation as a sure yardstick for the soundness of their decisions. This also explains why they are quite willing to commit additional resources after adoption, in order to make an innovation come up, more or less, to expectations. In a competitive environment, decision-makers appear to be carried along by the belief that, on average and in the long run, technical advances will also produce desirable economic results . . . or at least that falling too far behind in the adoption of innovations may have undesirable economic consequences for a business.

In practice, only clearcut cases of failure in the marketplace give unequivocal economic signals. In other cases, human nature and the politics of organizations frequently lead to what has been called "the teleological fiction," i.e., after-the-fact evaluations which tend to confirm decision-makers' initial judgments about an innovation. With a little additional effort, the expenditure of some additional funds, and an appropriate revision of one's recollections, post-audits tend to show that a project was brought to a successful conclusion, in line with original intentions. Alternatively, new products or processes may be left to linger until they die a natural death, everyone having lost interest in them. The more bureaucratic an organization, the more likely this is to happen. Government-financed innovative efforts that do not have to operate under the constraints of the marketplace and of accountability to the owners of a business are most likely to fall into the category of self-fulfilling prophecies.

These observations notwithstanding, it is easy to see why managerial attention in the evaluation of the effects of innovative undertakings is focussed on their physical results, in the hope that if they turn out roughly as expected, they will also pay off economically.

10.3.3 *Physical vs. Economic Effects*

The expectation that physical improvements will lead to analogous economic benefits hinges on the assumption that other variables, such as the prices of inputs and outputs, will not change on account of an innovation. Although this assumption is not in accord with actual experience, especially in the case of major innovations, technical analyses frequently are conducted in such a partial-equilibrium framework. Written by engineers, such reports tend to show that there is a one-to-one correspondence between an input saving and its cost effects. Upon reading a lot of the literature, one wag suggested the following research project: survey the issues of some technical journal over several decades and add up all the cost savings claimed for successive innovations affecting some particular technology or set of operations. He claimed that, had all the expected economic benefits materialized, many plants would be operating eventually with negative costs!

This may be a caricature, but the point is well taken. In the absence of clear data, it is always tempting to deduce the economic implications of innovations from their physical results. Reality often does not justify such a simple faith. The divergence between technical and economic success can be due to two fundamental reasons: A failure to take into account all the internal (structural) adjustments necessitated by the introduction of an innovation, or a failure properly to assess or predict changes in the firm's environment.

In discussing the productivity and cost network as a basis for performance evaluation (Chapter 5), we emphasized the interactions among the various components of an operating system. The introduction of an innovation at any stage in this system may affect performance and costs not only in subsequent but also in preceding stages. An example of how the expected economic benefits of a technically successful innovation can be reduced through such a network effects is provided by the introduction of the basic oxygen process (BOP) in some of the older American steel mills. The new process could accept scrap charges of no more than 30 per cent, while its predecessor, the open hearth process, was completely flexible with respect to molten iron vs. scrap charges. Depending on their product mix and output rates, mills might generate more home scrap (i.e., waste from their own operations) than could be worked up by the BOP, with the result that they had to keep at least some of the old, and much less efficient, open hearth furnaces in production, in addition incurring the energy-cost penalties of running these furnaces on up to 90 per cent cold-scrap feeds. Eventually, three or four years after the introduction of the BOP, these problems were solved through appropriate changes in the total production system. Until then the net economic benefits of investment in this major process innovation looked discouraging, even though it performed entirely up to expectations.[10]

10.3.4 *Environmental Influences on Expected Economic Effects*

Changes in institutional arrangements, in governmental regulations, or in the behavior of competitors may invalidate the assumptions on which expectations about an innovation's economic benefits were formed. To the extent that such changes are totally unpredictable, as for example the 1973–74 run-up of oil prices by the OPEC cartel, there is not much a firm can do, except to make the adjustments necessitated by the new conditions.

In the case of the introduction and diffusion of major innovations, however, the most important changes tend to occur in (relative) input or output prices *on account of* the innovation. And the direction, if not the magnitude, of such changes often can be predicted and taken into account in the assessment of likely effects. If decision-makers evaluate expected economic effects of a process innovation on the basis of current input prices, they are assuming that inputs will remain in perfectly price-elastic supply, at these prices, to an individual firm. Early adopters may well be justified in this assumption, at least for a while. But if the innovation is diffused widely, thus changing the market demand for various inputs, prices will change. Very late adopters thus may be forced to take up the innovation for purely defensive reasons, and not because they expect great benefits.

We may speculate about at least some of the possible interactions between diffusion and market effects:[11]

(a) If the prime physical effect of an innovation is an increase in the scale of operations, market effects will depend on the impact of scale-up by many firms on resource markets and on supply-demand relationships in output markets.

The recent increases in the size of bulk carriers (oil tankers, iron-ore vessels, etc.) provide a fine example of how a market can be transformed by a widely diffused innovation.

(b) If the prime physical effect of an innovation is an increase in labor productivity, expected economic benefits may be offset by rising wage rates. The total impact on unit costs will depend, among other factors, on the share of labor costs in total cost, and on the degree of rivalry in output markets.

(c) If the technological change results in substitutions among input materials, we may expect market effects on the materials being saved to accentuate physical effects, because reduced demand for them will tend to result in lower prices. Conversely, increased demand for the substitutes may raise their prices.

(d) Rapid diffusion of new types of equipment and machinery obviously will affect the opportunity cost of acquiring them. Not only would we expect their prices to remain firm in a seller's market, but long lead times between the placement of orders and the receipt of deliveries will further affect opportunity costs. Even more important, these cost effects will tend to affect the rates at which old equipment becomes obsolete.

From the individual adopting firm's viewpoint, uncertainty about these market effects implies the probability that even a technically successful innovation may not yield the expected economic results. For the economy as a whole, however, these effects are part of the process whereby innovations are absorbed gradually by the system, their benefits being diffused from adopters to other units.

10.4   Levels and Timing of Effects

We can bring some order to the multiplicity of possible effects of innovations if we recognize three basic aspects of the absorption process:

(1) The impacts of major technological changes will manifest itself in different ways at different levels—ranging from the production units directly affected to the economy at large.

(2) The nature of these impacts at each level will change over time.

(3) Therefore, the beneficiaries of technological innovation will also change.

This view of the process is in keeping with the Schumpeterian theory, which perceives of an innovation as disturbing an existing technological and organizational state, sending ripples of effects throughout the system from its point of impact, until a (more or less stable) new state is reached. With technological innovations occurring almost continuously in different sectors of the economy, the notion that this state represents an equilibrium is no more than a mental construct. A particularly instructive example of these ripple effects will be found in the Appendix to this chapter.

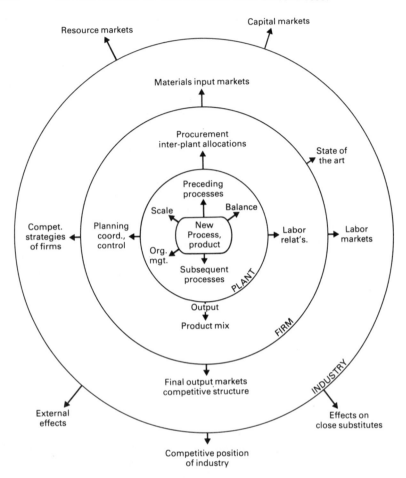

Fig. 10.3 Levels of effects of technological changes.

10.4.1 *The Spread of Effects*

In Fig. 10.3, we present a stylized version of the way in which an innovation affects different levels in the economy.

(a) At the initial point of impact, i.e., a particular production unit or department of an existing plant, we will generally find a preoccupation with the technical and physical performance characteristics of an innovation. The job of people at this level is to make the innovation work as expected. Of course the same primary goals would exist if an entirely new plant is built to manufacture a new product or to utilize a new process.

(b) At the plant level, evaluation of effects will shift to a concern with such matters as production flows, the interconnections among production stages, and the implications for labor assignments. The primary criteria by which managers at this level are evaluated are likely to be their ability to meet production targets and to keep costs under control. Therefore, they will bend every effort to get through the process of learning as rapidly as possible, so that expectations might be met. Strategic considerations, such as those of pricing, product mix, etc., will rarely enter into the assessment of effects at the plant level.

(c) When we move to the level of the firm, we encounter concerns with a different set of effects because the range of decision-makers' discretion and responsibility tends to be wider. Questions of input procurement, of the allocation of production to individual plants, of labor relations, and of competitive strategies begin to weigh heavily in the assessment of an innovation's impact. In other words, neither physical performance nor cost effects, taken by themselves, are sufficient criteria for determining the success or failure of an innovation at this level. In fact, to the extent that corporate top executives are not technically trained or have no experience with the production side of operations, the detailed data on improvements as a consequence of a major innovation will tend to be of little meaning and interest to them.

(d) The effects of major innovations tend to manifest themselves in yet different ways at the level of an industry. Shifts in market shares, as well as the entry or exit of firms, may change the competitive structure. Labor markets, materials markets, and the nature of competition may be affected. Even more important, the competitiveness of the whole industry vis-a-vis substitute products or foreign rivals will be influenced by technological advances.

At this level, public-interest assessments of new technologies are also likely to enter into the picture. For example, governmental concern with anti-trust implications of changed industry structure or with the characteristics of new products may become important aspects of evaluation. In any event, criteria for assessing the impacts of new technology on a whole industry will vary substantially from those used at lower levels of aggregation.

(e) Finally, when the impact of major innovations is assessed from the perspective of the economy as a whole, most micro-economic criteria yield their place to more comprehensive yardsticks, such as the effects on aggregate employment, on the sectoral and regional distribution of economic activity, on the country's balance of trade, and so on. Needless to say, an increasing number of political and social considerations will enter into evaluations at this level.

The point of this brief discussion of the scheme suggested by Fig. 10.3 was not to provide a complete checklist of effects, but rather to give substance to our contention that it is impossible to speak of *the* impact of a major innovation without taking into account the different criteria by which it is likely to be assessed at various levels. This observation also takes us a long way toward understanding why the introduction of innovations runs into conflicting reactions from various groups at interest—some welcoming the resulting changes enthusiastically, and others resisting them with all means at their disposal.[12]

10.4.2   Time and Changes in Beneficiaries

How long it takes for the process of absorption to work itself through the various levels depends on the nature of the innovation and on the economic sector initially affected by it, as well as on the speed of diffusion. But whenever we speak of economic progress or of advances in living standards as a result of technological innovations, we recognize the fact that originally localized impacts will be spread through the economic system and in the process absorbed by it.

Although the great variety of experience hardly permits any generalizations about this process, we may suggest the following sequence of beneficiaries from innovation:

(a) Successful innovations will first benefit the owners of businesses in the form of higher returns on their investment; simultaneously, employee-managers presumably also will reap financial rewards.

(b) The employees of innovative firms may benefit from less arduous work at constant incomes.

(c) Employees may also benefit from increased real incomes.

(d) Suppliers of capital and other inputs will benefit from expansion in the form of increased demand for their particular products.

(e) Competition and expansions of demand will benefit consumers through lower relative prices.

(f) New products and wider ranges of choice among existing products will enhance aggregate welfare.

(g) Innovations will offset the adverse effects of resource depletion on real incomes and living standards.

Stated in such stark terms, this list of beneficiaries sounds somewhat utopian. Yet it suggests precisely the mechanisms whereby the benefits of technological progress are absorbed. It also should make us properly modest in our efforts to assess the total impact of major innovations: beyond a certain point, absorption of new technologies is so complete that no one can trace all of its economic and social ramifications. We only have to attempt to enumerate the transformations brought about by, say, the automobile, to realize that no one discipline or perspective could yield anything approaching satisfactory answers.

If a competitive economy absorbs the effects of technological advances in roughly the fashion suggested above, we would not be surprised by the essential stability of the functional distribution of incomes (the shares of aggregate income going to labor, interest, rents, and profit) over extended periods of time. This stability also tends to be reflected, in the case of individual industries, in cost proportions, i.e., the shares of materials cost, wage and salary cost, and overhead cost in total costs.[13] The forces that bring about a "sharing-around" of the benefits of innovations over the long run appear to be quite strong. Actions of particular interest groups or interventions by the government may temporarily retard or misdirect the process, but they do not seem to be able to affect it permanently.

10.5 External Benefits and Cost of Technological Change

We can interpret the processes we have described in the preceding section in terms of our earlier discussions of the inventor's and innovator's economic motives (see Chapters 6 and 7). There we emphasized the importance of *appropriability* as a driving force for technological progress. Each economic unit's decisions to invest in research, development, innovation, and in the adoption of existing innovations are based on more or less formal evaluations of expected *private benefits and costs*. We also saw, however, that technological change involves *externalities*, i.e., consequences that are not considered in the evaluations of individual units. What we have called the absorption of technological advances by a market economy might then be seen as a development in which the appropriate elements of these advances are gradually eroded by growing external effects. Therefore, we are left, eventually, with a host of intended and unintended consequences, very few of which still have anything to do with the prospects of private gain that goaded innovators to action in the first place.[14]

The vast literature attempting comprehensive assessments of the consequences of technological progress can be summarized by a quotation from the American writer, James Branch Cabell: "The optimist proclaims that we live in the best of all possible worlds; and the pessimist fears this is true."[15] The job of constructing even a sketchy checklist of the social benefits and costs of advances would go way beyond the scope of our explorations. Instead, we want to deal only with a set of problems that have increasingly occupied modern industrial societies—the external costs of environmental damage, of the over-use of renewable resources, and of the hazards for human beings associated with many forms of production and consumption. This still leaves us with a huge task, and we can do no more than to outline some major aspects of these problems.

The theory of externalities has been worked out in great detail by economists. Indeed, one critic has judged that, "By now, the theoretical problems have been explored with the sharpest tools available to economists," but that, ". . . there have been remarkably few attempts to carry the analysis beyond this point."[16] After a brief survey of the theory, we shall turn our attention to some of its practical implications.

10.5.1 *The Theory of Externalities*

Early in this century, the British economist, A. C. Pigou, gave a classic characterization of externalities:

> ". . . the essence of the matter is that one person A, in the course of rendering some service, for which payment is made, to a second person B, incidentally also renders services or disservices to other persons . . . of such a sort that payment cannot be extracted from the benefited parties or compensation enforced on behalf of the injured parties."[17]

In other words, not all the costs or benefits of private economic activity are recorded, or can be recorded, in the market-place. In assembling inputs for producing a certain output with the lowest-cost technique, a firm not constrained by factors other than prices and technology will fail to take into account, for example, the social cost of dumping waste materials into a river. Similarly, the driver who throws an empty beverage can out of his car, because that is the lowest-cost way to dispose of it, does not consider the social cost of a littered roadside.

What causes this divergence of private and social interests? The example of the tossed beverage can provides at least a partial clue: if by accident it had smashed the windshield of another person's car, the thrower would have to face the legal consequences of his action, because he damaged someone else's private property. But the roadside, the air, rivers and lakes are not any one person's property. Therefore, we encounter in this and many other examples what one writer has called "the tragedy of the commons."[18] Although it has been shown that, under certain assumptions, transactions between privately rational parties might avoid the "tragedy",[19] these assumptions are not likely to be met in many real-life situations, under prevailing legal arrangements. Wherever property rights are undefined, or badly defined, the problem of social costs is likely to appear.[20]

Why do not producers and consumers act differently, out of a sense of "social responsibility?" A surprisingly large number of them do, of course, but there is a good theoretical reason why appeals to this sense will be far from one hundred per cent effective. Even if his utility were adversely affected by the unsightliness of littered roadsides, our can-thrower is likely to regard the *marginal* social cost of one more can as negligible. "Everyone is doing it," so why should he incur the inconvenience of acting differently? This is merely the opposite of the so-called "free rider syndrome" in the case of public goods.

A firm in a competitive economy faces a somewhat different problem: if it were to assume the private costs of controlling some *external bad* and its competitors do not, then it would have placed itself at an economic disadvantage. Only if a way can be found to force all firms to internalize these social costs, i.e., to consider them in their calculations of private benefits and costs, will the problem be solved. The reference to the firm in the framework of a competitive economy must not mislead us into thinking that centrally-planned, socialist economies manage to avoid this problem; with private property in the means of production severely limited, they continuously have to confront the tragedy of the commons in its starkest version.

External goods (positive externalities) are created whenever the unit that generated them cannot appropriate all the benefits of its actions. As the above quotation from Pigou suggests their existence can be explained along the same theoretical lines (albeit with opposite signs). *Spill-over effects*, as they are also called, pervade every economy. In part, they consist of the application of new technology to fields for which it was not originally intended and of innovations developed as byproducts of R&D aimed in other directions; in even more important part, they create conditions that help to solve some social problem in perhaps unexpected ways. Thus, there seems to exist general agreement that advances in plumbing, water supply, general living conditions and personal hygiene contributed as much to the eradication of epidemic diseases as did the development of medical technology itself.

Our broad-brush treatment has avoided a number of sticky theoretical problems. One of these has to do with defining the "society" whose interests are at stake. What are we to make, for example, of the situation in a typical one-company town, in which the firm that employs most of the labor force pollutes the air with some unpleasant odors, imposing a clear social cost on the population? If the local people are willing to bear this cost in exchange for continued employment opportunities, is there some other broader social interest that needs to be protected? These are not academic issues. Especially in connection with particular technologies, questions of this type have to be addressed all the time. How far is it in the interest of society to prevent individuals from assuming the risks of, say, riding motorcycles without helmets or flying ultralight aircraft?

10.5.2 *Historical Background*

Resistance to technological innovations because of their real or imaginary social costs is nothing new. Consider, for example, the nineteenth-century writer who argued that the extension of railroads to the Midwest of the United States would "introduce manufactures into the heart of the country, divert industry from primitive healthful and moral pursuits of agriculture, and bring on us the vices and miseries of manufacturing and commercial places."[21] In the face of the new technology's inexorable progress and of the obvious benefits it brought to large segments of the population, such judgments were regarded mainly as the crankish ramblings of romantics and malcontents. Many major innovations, earlier and since, have met up with similar kinds of resistance. It would be difficult to argue that this opposition was always ill-founded. But then as now, expressions of social concern also frequently represented no more than rationalizations by which groups dressed up their opposition to developments that they considered harmful to their private interests.

On balance, however, worries about the social costs of technological progress appear to have played a minor role in the development of the United States. It may well be that a seemingly unlimited supply of land, a highly mobile population, and a social system that tended to spread the benefits of growth rather quickly among various groups, all worked in favor of rapid technological change. Nevertheless, concerns about the effects of industrial growth seem to have focussed first on its implications for the country's resource base. The "conservation movement" may be considered a forerunner of the present-day environmental-protection movement. But until the 1950s, the emphasis was mainly on "the management and wise use of natural assets to prevent their depletion and at the same time produce wealth."[22] Since then, the conceptualization of resources has been broadened steadily, through the development of an integrated, ecological view of the impact of economic activity on the environment.

A second threat of development was formed by growing concerns about the direct physical hazards of new technologies, both for the people working with them and for the public in general. This began in the nineteenth century with the regulation of steam-boiler safety and has found its culmination in public and private efforts to cope with the unprecedented, but largely unknown, risks of nuclear-energy generation. We shall not pursue these developments in any further detail, nor shall we deal with the seemingly accelerating trend to make "consumer protection," in the broadest sense, a part of the public agenda.

One aspect of all these problems has been bothersome, especially from the economist's point of view: efforts to define the physical or biological effects of particular technologies, as well as the assessment of the actual probabilities of harmful externalities, are fraught with so many imponderables that public decision-making has had to rely on what has been called "a kind of adversary proceeding"[23] among scientific and technical experts. Therefore, in trying to estimate the expected benefits and costs of dealing with externalities, economists have been confronted with great difficulties. It is as though engineers said to them, "We cannot yet agree on what this new machine will produce or whether the product will sell, but please tell us what the economic results will be." No wonder that most economists have concentrated on theoretical issues, while public policies have consisted of a hodge-podge of independent and often contradictory measures, promulgated by different agencies, all of them under political or bureaucratic pressure "to do something."[24]

10.5.3   *Policies to Eliminate or Reduce External Bads*

Given the bewildering variety of measures for ameliorating the social costs of production and consumption, we can do no more than to present a rough classification and to make some general judgments about the likely efficacy of each category of policies.

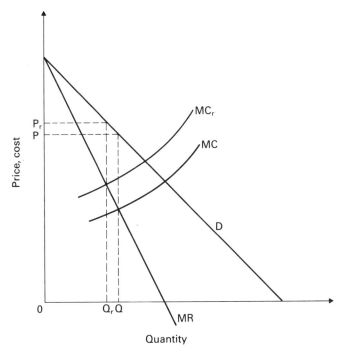

FIG. 10.4 Effect of internalization of social costs on short-run output and prices.

Two points need to be made at the outset. First, to the extent that governmental or quasi-governmental bodies themselves are the source of external bads, even the most cleverly designed policies aimed at private economic units will remain ineffective. And second, whatever means of control are chosen, they will involve an increase in the cost of products and services. This observation would hardly seem worth making, were it not for the fact that industrial leaders frequently try to rally public support against particular pieces of regulation with the, explicit or implicit, threat of price increases on account of the enforcement of such regulations. The economist's answer is: of course, who but the public, as buyers of products or owners of firms, is going to pay for the elimination or reduction of social costs! When firms do not consider these costs, they will produce more of a given product and sell it at a lower price, than if they were forced to internalize them. The proposition is illustrated in Fig. 10.4. The curves labeled D and MR represent current demand conditions. The curve MC reflects the marginal private cost of production; P is the profit-maximizing price, and Q the quantity sold. Internalization will shift the marginal-cost curve to MC_r, with a consequent increase in the price to P_r and a reduction in the quantity produced and sold to Q_r. The only open question is what type of regulation will least impair overall economic efficiency and equity. That the public pays for the amelioration of social costs when programs are financed out of tax funds hardly needs explaining.

In evaluating the various types of public policy, we must realize that their design is governed not only by the economist's criteria, but also be technical and political considerations that frequently violate these criteria. In addition, many issues raise support or opposition on purely ideological grounds.[25] Therefore, it seems all the more important to improve public understanding by pointing up the costs and benefits of particular measures.

(a) *Outright Prohibition.* If a product or process creates what are perceived to be very high social costs, its use may be forbidden altogether. In principle, it is difficult to argue with the prohibition of dangerous drugs or of building materials containing asbestos. At the same time we must recognize a number of practical problems. First, prohibitions tend to be ineffective, and indeed to raise social problems of their own, when the general public refuses to abide by them and enforcement is difficult. The greatest, and least successful, American experiment along these lines, the prohibition of alcoholic beverages, provides persuasive evidence for this point, as do some more recent efforts at outlawing certain other substances. Second, in the absence of full information about a technology, it is politically and bureaucratically safest to prohibit it altogether, regardless of actual benefits and costs. When it was discovered that studded automobile tires caused damage to blacktop roads that are not covered by snow and ice, many states outlawed the use of these tires, simply ignoring the offsetting benefits of greater safety for drivers, passengers, and other vehicles. And third, political pressures for prohibition may not come from a concern with the public good but with the intent of protecting the economic interests of some particular group. On occasion, conflicting pressures produce paradoxical results. Thus, for example, the government is steadily expanding its rules prohibiting smoking in public places (and discouraging it in general), while at the same time subsidizing tobacco-growing by American farmers.

(b) *Prescription of Technology.* A second group of policies attempts to deal with the problem of externalities by specifying the technological means for their reduction or elimination. The static and dynamic inefficiencies resulting from this approach are apparent. From a static point of view, it ignores the differences in the economic implications of compliance for various economic units or products. From a dynamic viewpoint, it eliminates incentives for the development of better technologies. If the air bag were mandated as the only permissible passive-safety device in cars, the effect on the prices of small, inexpensive models would obviously be much greater than the effect on luxury automobiles; and research into alternative solutions would come to a halt. The same arguments apply in all situations where pollution-abatement technology has been prescribed for industry. Needless to say, resistance to such rules tends to make their implementation and enforcement a costly matter to governments as well.

(c) *Setting of Performance Standards.* At first glance, the setting of certain quality or performance standards appears preferable to the prescription of technology. At least it avoids dynamic inefficiencies by leaving it up to individual decision units how they want to meet these standards. But the static problems remain: although the general public may consider it eminently fair that all affected parties should comply with precisely the same standards, this once again ignores differences in the costs and benefits of compliance. Firms with old plant and equipment may find the cost of meeting requirements prohibitive, while a brand-new plant could be built to standards without great additional expense. One can argue as well that the benefits of a dollar spent on air-pollution control in Montana will differ from those in, say, New Jersey. Recognizing this, regulators are frequently forced to issue exemptions or modifications to their rules, so that implementation quickly turns into a political and legal game. The situation becomes even more of a game when compliance depends on factors not directly under the regulated parties' control. The recent shifts in demand toward larger and higher-performance automobiles has led some manufacturers to claim that they are unable to meet "corporate average fuel economy" (CAFE) targets that had seemed reasonable two or three years ago; meanwhile, at least one other firm has insisted on the strict enforcement of CAFE targets, because its product mix enables it to meet these targets.

(d) *Fees and Taxes.* The idea that firms or consumers should be able to "buy off" from some requirement to eliminate or abate externalities has run into a lot of political resistance. Yet, such an approach comes closer to meeting the economist's criteria of efficiency and equity than do other policies. Consider the studded-tire problem once again: instead of prohibiting them outright, would it not be more reasonable for the government to charge those who want to use such tires a fee reflecting the incremental cost of repairing whatever road damage they cause? Then individuals could decide whether the increased safety was worth the extra cost. No doubt many people who have to drive their cars regardless of weather conditions would pay the fee, but many others would rather save the fee and not drive at all when there is ice and snow on the roads.

Not all problems are that simple, even theoretically. In the case of industrial pollution, for example, a decision would have to be made what level of fees or taxes was required to achieve a desirable degree of abatement. One approach, attractive to the economist but obviously abhorrent to politicians, is to conduct an auction for a certain number of licenses to pollute, once tolerable over-all levels of pollution have been decided upon. Presumably, those firms for whom the cost of installing control equipment would be highest will submit the highest bids.

We must not, however, gloss over certain other technical difficulties. For example, if firms are to be charged fees according to the amount of pollution they generate, it must be possible to measure effluents or pollutants. Only then can decision-makers consider the optimal trade-off between the expenditures for environmental control and the payment of fees or taxes. Therefore, even ardent supporters of this type of regulatory scheme realize that some classes of externalities cannot be covered by it.

10.5.4   Concluding Observations

Wherever technologies produce undesirable externalities, they should certainly be regulated by government. As our brief survey has suggested, however, the problems of doing so in an effective way are considerable. If we set to one side the frequently-heard complaints about conflicting rules and about their unreasonable and bureaucratic enforcement,[26] we are left with a number of more fundamental issues.

The first of these concerns our inability to predict all the consequences of innovations. This may lead to either of two types of error—the prohibition or restriction of technologies that later turn out, on balance, to be beneficial, or the unquestioning acceptance of new products or processes that prove to have totally unacceptable side effects. Consider, for example, the story of DDT.[27] Introduced in the 1940s as a miracle pesticide, it was diffused rapidly and worldwide because of its apparent efficacy in eradicating a variety of human, animal, and plant diseases. Only after about two decades was it discovered that DDT also produced irreparable ecological damage. By that time, a host of economic interests had grown up around the manufacture, distribution, and use of the product. Therefore, new scientific and technical insights were pitted against the resistance of many politically influential groups. Banning, or severely restricting, DDT turned out to be anything but an easy matter. Efforts to avoid such problems through systematic technological forecasting or speculative "technology assessment" have yielded few encouraging results.[28]

A second concern has to do with the seemingly proliferating assumption that all risks of life in a technologically advanced society can be eliminated by appropriate administrative measures. The resulting pressures for government action have led to legislation and regulations that no longer aim at particular technologies or industries, but rather cut across a wide variety of products and processes, thus ignoring the specific benefits and costs of regulation. Somewhat paradoxically, we can observe the simultaneous growth of pressures for governmental intervention based on the assumption that there exist technological fixes for all social and behavioral problems.

Third, and most seriously, we may ask what effects an increasing body of rules and court decisions will have on the incentives for further invention, development, and innovation. Rightly or wrongly, decision-makers may feel so hemmed in by these institutional constraints that they opt for other, less risky and less costly strategies. There can be little doubt that the often-bemoaned slow-down in the innovativeness of American firms must be attributed not only to structural weaknesses and to the conservatism of managements, but also to changes in the social and political environment.

Notes

1. Sampedro, J. L., *Decisive Forces in World Economics* (New York: World University Library— McGraw-Hill, 1967), p. 47.
2. Gold, B., *Productivity, Technology, and Capital* (Lexington, MA: Lexington Books— D. C. Heath, 1979), pp. 19–22.
3. U.S. Department of Commerce, Bureau of the Census, *Long-term Economic-Growth, 1860–1965* (Washington, DC: U.S. Government Printing Office, 1966), Part II.
4. For a survey and critical evaluation of these models, see Baird, R. N., "Production Functions, Productivity, and Technological Change," in Gold, B. (ed.), *Research, Technological Change, and Economic Analysis* (Lexington, MA: Lexington Books—D.C. Heath, 1977).
5. Ayres, R. U., *The Next Industrial Revolution* (Cambridge, MA: Ballinger, 1984), p. 70.
6. Gold, B., "Industry Growth Patterns: Theory and Empirical Findings," *Journal of Industrial Economics*, November 1964.
7. Adapted from Gold, B., "Proposed Conceptual and Analytical Improvements," in Gold, B., (ed.), *op. cit.* (1977), pp. 197–8.
8. Terborgh, G., *Business Investment Policy* (Washington, DC: Machinery and Allied Products Institute, 1960), p. 52.
9. For an interesting example, see Mantel, S. J., Tipnis, V. A., Watwe, U. and Ravignani, G. L., "Economic Evaluation of Potential Process Innovations," *Omega*, 11/1 (1983).
10. Gold, B., Rosegger, G. and Boylan, M. G., *Evaluating Technological Innovations: Methods, Expectations, and Findings* (Lexington, MA: Lexington Books—D. C. Heath, 1980), Chapter 8.
11. Gold, B., "Research, Technological Change, and Economic Analyses: A Critical Evaluation of Prevailing Approaches," *Quarterly Review of Economics and Business*, Spring 1977.
12. Resistance to innovations does not, of course, have to be founded on economic interests alone but may be rooted in cultural and social factors. This broader framework of attitudes is surveyed in Rogers, E. M., *The Diffusion of Innovations*, 3rd edn. (New York: The Free Press, 1983), esp. Chapters 7–9.
13. Empirical evidence on this point, for a large number of industries, can be found in Gold, B., *Explorations in Managerial Economics: Productivity, Costs, Technology and Growth* (New York: Basic Books, 1971).
14. The interactions between private incentives and longer-term effects form the basis for an interesting theory of economic change proposed in Klein, B. H. *Dynamic Economics* (Cambridge, MA: Harvard University Press, 1977).
15. Cabell, J. B., *The Silver Stallion* (New York: McBride, 1926), p. 129.
16. Mills, E. S., "Economic Incentives in Air Pollution Control," in Wolozin, H. (ed.), *The Economics of Air Pollution: A Symposium* (New York: Norton, 1966).
17. Pigou, A. C., *The Economics of Welfare*, 4th edn. (London: Macmillan, 1932), p. 183.
18. Hardin, G., "The Tragedy of the Commons," *Science*, December 13, 1968.
19. Coase, R. H., "The Problem of Social Cost," *The Journal of Law and Economics*, 3/1 (1960).
20. For a collection of work on this subject, which includes excerpts from the articles cited under 18 and 19, above, see Ackerman, B. A., *Economic Foundations of Property Law* (Boston, MA: Little, Brown & Company, 1975).
21. Quoted by Stern, J., "Circumventing the Inventor," in Ward, H. (ed.), *New Worlds in Science* (New York: McBride, 1941).
22. From a 1938 declaration of the U.S. Department of the Interior; cited in Fainsod, M., Gordon, L., and Palamountain, J. C., *Government and the American Economy*, 3rd edn. (New York: Norton, 1959), p. 705. The theme is repeated in President's Materials Policy Commission, *Resources for Freedom* (Washington, DC: U.S. Government Printing Office, 1952).
23. Grad, F. B., Rathjens, G. W., and Rosenthal, A. J., *Environmental Control; Priorities, Politics, and the Law* (New York: Columbia University Press, 1971), esp. pp. 13–28.
24. When agencies pursue conflicting objectives, compliance with all rules becomes an obvious impossibility. Thus, for example, the Occupational Safety and Health Administration (OSHA) requires plastic liners in hospital wastebaskets, in order to protect employees from contamination; the Department of Health and Human Services forbids the use of plastic liners, because they are a fire hazard. Peirce, W. S., *Bureaucratic Failure and Public Expenditure* (New York: Academic Press, 1981), p. 120.
25. In the mid-1950s, indisputable evidence had accumulated that adding trace elements of

fluoride to drinking water provided protection against dental caries. But opponents of this public-health measure portrayed the fluoridation of city water supplies as a Communist plot to poison the American people. Thomas, L., *The Youngest Science* (New York: Viking Press, 1983), pp. 139–40.

26. See, for example, the discussion of pesticide regulation in Peirce, W. S., *op. cit.* (1981), Chapter 10.

27. A detailed account can be found in Woodwell, G. M., "Broken Eggshells," *Science 84*, November 1984. The story of DDT is also used as a prime example in Drucker, P. F., "New Technology: Predicting its Impact is Perilous and Futile," *New York Times*, April 8, 1973. Professor Drucker argues that "technology monitoring," i.e., the continuous surveillance of the external effects of new technologies, is the only economically and socially justifiable activity.

28. Congressional concern with "the need for new approaches to establishing a base of knowledge to anticipate the consequences of technology" led to the passage of the Technology Assessment Act of 1972, which established a permanent Office of Technology Assessment (OTA). See Coates, J. F., "Technology Assessment," in Teich, A. H. (ed.), *Technology and Man's Future*, 2nd edn. (New York: St. Martin's Press, 1977), for a detailed discussion. While the OTA has published a number of interesting studies, its forecasting record is not notably better than that of other, private and public, agencies.

Appendix

The Ripple Effects of Technological Change: A Case Study*

In this chapter we stressed the fact that the economic effects of major technological innovations make themselves felt not only at the point of immediate application, but that they tend to permeate the overall structure of firms, industries, and adjacent sectors of the economy. The concept of "ripples" of effects describes this process very well, and the study whose results are summarized here provides a particularly clear and illustrative example. The innovation analyzed is the pelletizing of low-grade iron ore, a process that has brought about revolutionary changes in the American iron and steel industry.

A.1 *The Innovation*

For many decades, the high-grade natural iron ores of Minnesota, centered mainly in the Mesabi Range, were the prime source of metallic input for the iron and steel industry. However, these ores were being exhausted quite rapidly, and after World War II the industry had to confront the problem of tapping alternative sources. One approach was to place increased reliance on imported iron ore; American firms began to invest heavily in mining operations in northern Canada, Latin America, and Africa. The alternative was to develop a technique for utilizing the plentiful deposits of Minnesota taconite—a very hard rock of roughly 25 to 30 per cent iron content, which had been by-passed in the exploitation of the then-rich natural ore mines.

*Adapted from Peirce, W. S., "The Effects of Technological Change: Exploring Successive Ripples," in Gold, B., ed., *Technological Change: Economics, Management, and Environment* (Oxford: Pergamon, 1975).

In order to be technically useable, and economically attractive, taconite had to be beneficiated (i.e., its iron content raised) and put into suitable form for blast furnace consumption. The technical solution, for which research had been going on since the 1920s, was to grind the ore into a very fine powder, to suspend it in water, to extract the iron-bearing particles with magnets, and then to agglomerate the resulting concentrate into spherical pellets of 60 to 62 per cent iron content. These pellets then had to be hardened in a kiln, in order to prevent their deterioration.

Development of the process to the point of commercial feasibility required a number of innovations, ranging from the "jet piercing" of blast holes into the very hard taconite rock (mechanical drills of requisite hardness being prohibitively expensive at the time) to the construction of large-scale "balling drums" in which the concentrate could be agglomerated. The fact that taconite was located in the same region as the natural ore was an obvious economic advantage: development avoided major disruptions there, and commercialization provided continued employment, could rely on existing water transportation arrangements, and did not threaten the location of the ore-consuming firms, most of them in the lower Great Lakes area.

Nevertheless, the discovery of plentiful supplies of cheap natural ores abroad, during the period between the initial decision to build full-scale pelletizing facilities and the first definitive tests of their commercial feasibility, provided critics with ample evidence on the basis of which to question the wisdom of investing in taconite development. Simultaneously, several major iron and steel producers built entire new plants in the Atlantic coastal region, in order to take advantage of foreign ore. Doubts about the innovation's economic success were fueled by extremely high costs of the required facilities: the first plant of roughly four million tons annual capacity, which began operations in the early 1950s, involved an outlay of $187 million; and the vast bulk of this reflected investments that did not have to be made at all if natural ores were used.

A.2 Immediate Effects

The full-scale production of taconite pellets proved an immediate technical success; however, its commercial pay-off remained in doubt for some time. Capital requirements were high (cautious estimates put them at $30 per ton of annual capacity for a plant, not counting transportation and other facilities) and the process consumed prodigious amounts of energy. Thus, pellet prices ended up about 25 per cent higher than those of natural ore.

Steel producers turned out to be quite ready to pay a premium price for pellets, however, because these made a superior blast furnace feed. Although this fact was far from established when the first taconite plant was built, the new input material proved itself advantageous on several counts. Its uniform size and structure, together with a high iron content (compared to the approximately 52 per cent iron in natural ore), greatly increased blast furnace output: for example, a charge consisting of half pellets and half natural ore resulted in an output increase of about 50 per cent; and an all-pellet charge produced an increase of 110 per cent. Here, then, we have an example where an investment in a backward-integrating innovation raised the capacity of a subsequent facility, through the use of an improved input.

At the same time, the new material also resulted in savings of coke and fluxes, the other two main inputs. What had initially been looked at as a defensive innovation, produced economic benefits well beyond expectations. As soon as these results became firmly established, diffusion proceeded quite rapidly, despite high, and rising, investment costs, which were further burdened by increasingly stringent requirements for the installation of environment control devices and for the safe disposal of the tailings (i.e., the non-iron-bearing waste materials). By 1970, pellet production in the Mesabi Range exceeded 45 million tons and made up 66 per cent of total output in the Lake Superior region—and this is in the face of a continuing expansion of foreign natural-ore supplies.

Another beneficiary was the State of Minnesota. Not only did the innovation assure employment opportunities in an area confronted with the prospect of steadily shrinking natural ore operations; taxes levied on taconite also brought in about $100 million of additional revenues each year, and the state receives some royalty income from mining on public lands. Thus, what might have become an economically depressed region requiring governmental subsidies, rather than providing taxes, had got a new lease on life. However, the innovation did not just produce these immediate effects.

A.3   *The First Ripple*

The surprisingly favorable results achieved with pellets, and the great increases in blast furnace productivity, helped to strengthen the continuing dominance of the blast furnace process in the smelting of iron ore. Interest in the development of alternative techniques, all of them involving the so-called "direct reduction" of ore, waned, even though a number of significant inventions had been made. Several companies continued experiments along these lines, and a few small-scale, direct-reduction plants were built, but these inventions certainly did not receive the "big-push" which had been predicted for them in the early 1950s.

The continued availability of ore from the Lake Superior region also avoided a serious disruption of the steel industry's locational pattern. Increasing reliance on foreign ores would have meant a distinct advantage to plants located along the coasts. Large bulk carriers could not have navigated the St. Lawrence Seaway, only water access to the traditional steel-making centers. Taconite pellet supplies assured that the Great Lakes steel firms could obtain materials on a basis that did not impair their competitiveness with the coastal plants.

This beneficial effect was further accentuated by the existence of a transportation network from the mines to the steel centers. Pellets were able to withstand the handling and stockpiling required, without excessive physical degradation. Furthermore, the higher iron content of pellets gave the existing transport facilities a greater effective capacity.

In short, even these secondary impacts of the innovation were non-disruptive; in fact, they strengthened the traditional ways of doing things. Thus, the first ripple served to prevent major changes that had threatened the fundamental structure, and a large part of past investments, of one of the country's key industries.

A.4   The Second Ripple

Despite its essentially conservative nature, the innovation produced a second ripple of effects through removing barriers to some significant changes, especially in the technology of transportation. The handling qualities of pellets differ from those of natural ore in two respects: first, pellets can be moved easily on conveyor belts, whereas the lumpy natural ore cannot; and second, pellets flow freely even in extremely cold weather, whereas natural ores freeze solid.

Thus pellets opened the door to another innovation—the self-unloading ore carrier. This type of vessel has a full length set of conveyors under the cargo hold, which serve to unload the ship speedily, and without any external equipment, such as bucket cranes. Therefore it became possible to build much larger ships, whose economic attractiveness so far had been limited by the extremely long turn-around times required at unloading points. Because of this development, the United States Government decided to undertake major investments in the enlargement of the Sault St. Marie locks, which had so far prevented the passage of larger vessels along the traditional ore route.

The easy handling of pellets in freezing weather, together with the need to recover more rapidly the substantial investment in the new large carriers, also affected the shipping season on the Great Lakes. Instead of having to keep ships idle during the freezing period, companies can now transport iron ore as long as the Lakes are not frozen solid.

An alternative discussed for some time has been the substitution of large unit trains for vessels; with freezing in the cars no longer a problem, such trains could operate throughout the year, thus avoiding any investment in stockpile inventories at both ends of the shipping route. However, so far the economic advantages of this alternative have not been convincing enough to cause any serious development efforts. Besides, the construction of many large ore vessels in recent years seems to preclude any heavy investment in railroad capacity for some time to come.

A.5   Further Ripples

While we are still in the midst of the second ripple of effects, further implications are emerging already. One of these has to do with the scale of production units in the United States iron and steel industry. Many blast furnaces currently produce less than one million tons per year, while newer units elsewhere in the world produce as much as 3.5 million tons. If a new plant in the United States were to include a minimum of two pellet-based furnaces of proven large scale, this would imply (including scrap utilization) an effective steel-making capacity of ten million tons annually. Such a plant appears well beyond any one American company's ability to raise the necessary capital; meanwhile, plants of that size account at least in part for the cost competitiveness of certain foreign producers, who do not have such ready access to the essential raw materials.

A further problem arises, because it is becoming clear that existing ports are too small to accommodate vessels of the large scale now economically attractive. While the current stock of older, smaller boats appears adequate for some time to come, plants such as the ones at Cleveland, for example, would face a growing cost disadvantage due to their inaccessibility by large ore carriers. The technological alternative would be to unload these ships along the shore and move pellets by conveyor to the blast furnace sites; but this would require further substantial investments—directly traceable to the pellet innovation.

Meanwhile, the economies of scale inherent in pipeline transport have led to suggestions that the ultimate solution for pellet hauling was to do away with pelletizing at the mine sites altogether. Instead, taconite slurry would be pumped to the blast furnaces and pelletized there.

Experiments with so-called "pre-reduced" pellets, i.e. material so high in iron content that it can be fed directly into electric steel-making furnaces as "synthetic scrap," have proved economically attractive under certain conditions. There is no reason why this and other techniques for by-passing the blast furnace process could not be expanded in the future. Thus, while the development of pellets initially helped to preserve traditional technology, it may ultimately lead to its obsolescence.

Two other effects unforeseen at the time of the innovation have assumed great importance since. The first has to do with the environmental consequences of processing large amounts of ore and disposing of the waste materials. The innovating company, which dumped these materials (in the form of talcum-like, chemically inert powder) into Lake Superior, with the full approval of state and federal authorities, has recently been confronted with a protracted court action. Like the later adopters, it now has to invest in on-land disposal facilities, whose longer-term environmental effects are also far from clear. The second consequence turned out to be entirely beneficial, both from the firms' and society's viewpoint: had the direct reduction technology been developed more rapidly, it would have confronted great economic problems ever since the "energy crisis" of the early 1970s. Direct reduction processes require large amounts of natural gas; the rising prices of this energy source and growing public resistance to its industrial use would have rendered these facilities economically unattractive under most conditions. In this sense, the success of pelletizing prevented a serious, if probably unforeseeable, mistake.

A.6 *Concluding Observations*

From this case study, it should be obvious that no one set of measures of *the* effect of technological innovations could have captured the wide and significant impact of pelletizing. Yet it is exactly in the assessment of such successive ripples of effects that the economist can come to grips with those problems that are most likely to require action on the part of individual firms and of public authorities. In the very act of defining an innovation as "major," one establishes the presumption that its economic consequences will reach beyond a narrow and immediate area of impact. The fascination of technological changes lies in the fact that they produce adjustments, adaptations, and complementary or compensating changes elsewhere in the economic system.

But the study illustrates another point: Even careful assessments and forecasts of the likely economic effects of major innovations are bound to be wide of the mark to the extent that they produce totally unpredictable technical and social results, or changes in public attitudes. It is more a measure of the economic system's resilience than of our ability to make accurate forecasts and appropriate preparations, that major technological changes do get absorbed without too-great disruptions. Our inability to trace the effects of minor and incremental changes, even *after* the fact, is probably mitigated by the fact that these effects are more likely to occur within a reasonably narrow technological and economic context.

CHAPTER 11

The Effects of Technological Change, II

In the preceding chapter, we briefly discussed the aggregate impact of technological advances on economic growth and then turned to a more detailed examination of their microeconomic effects. In this chapter, we want to deal with two further questions: (1) Does the evolution of basic technologies sow the seeds of their own eventual stagnation and decline? And (2) What have been the effects of technological evolution on employment and on the conditions of work?

Both these questions have been discussed extensively by economists, and at times they have also attracted the general public's attention. They are obviously related; if technological evolution determines the fortunes of industries, then we would expect sectoral employment and the nature of work to be affected in a fundamental way. In the face of major technological advances reaching across many branches of industry, there has even been worry about effects on *aggregate* employment. Predictions by some experts that the assembly line, automation, computerization, and other major innovations would lead to massive, economy-wide unemployment typically have accompanied the introduction of these technologies. No wonder, then, that the issue is of more than academic interest, and that it has aroused the periodic concern of business people, labor leaders, and politicians. Furthermore, such changes might also be expected to have an impact on an economy's position in global competition; this, however, is a subject that we shall investigate in the next chapter.

11.1 The Evolution of Basic Technologies

If we want to examine whether there are some "laws" of technological evolution that govern changes in the characteristics of industries and markets over time, we must first establish what we mean by *basic* technologies. In Chapter 1, we defined primary or basic innovations as those which generate clear discontinuities in an existing industry or which give rise to whole new industries and a host of derivative and incremental innovations. Although one can always argue about classifications at the margin, this definition does help us to identify mainstreams of technological change: It would be difficult to argue that such

innovations as the steam engine, railroads, large-scale electric power generation, the automobile, the electronic computer, or plastics have not been
"basic" in terms of their socioeconomic effects. But many less spectacular
innovations have formed the foundations for the birth and development of
branches of industry, and these, too, would fall within out concept. Thus, for
example, there can be little doubt that the advent of the small, electronic
calculator produced a fundamental change for the slide-rule and the electro-
mechanical calculator industries. Although these industries may not have
weighed heavily in terms of aggregate output or employment, the owners,
managers, and employees of affected firms certainly would have seen the
revolution in the market for calculating devices as a basic change.

   The fact that technologies undergo substantial changes over time, and that
these affect firms, industries, and the operation of markets, is widely recognized. And furthermore, there is agreement that most of these changes are
self-generated, i.e., that they occur as a result of firms' technological responses
to changing competitive conditions. Here as elsewhere, we use the construct of
identifiable stages in this evolution as a somewhat artificial aid in analysis.[1]

11.1.1   Infancy and Early Development

Characteristic of the infancy of basic technologies is the appearance of many
competing versions of products or processes. Although addressing the same set
of problems or opportunities, these versions frequently represent quite different functional approaches. As we pointed out in Chapter 9, slow rates of
diffusion at this stage may be explained by the uncertainty of potential adopters
as to which of these competing versions will ultimately emerge as superior.
Since there is little or no compatibility among the different approaches, a
"wait-and-see" strategy may be preferred by many to an early commitment.
Indeed, pioneers in adoption frequently play an important role in testing and
in working out bugs, thus contributing in an important way to evolution.

   At this stage, one typically finds many firms competing in an undeveloped
market. The total output of any one firm is small, and production is carried on
with general-purpose capital equipment, requiring high levels of know-how
and skill. Other inputs are not yet product-specific, producers having to make
do with generally available parts and materials, or having to integrate backward
themselves in order to provide the required characteristics for inputs.

   Competition being based mainly on *technical performance in relation to price*,
prices as such are not an important competitive weapon. Such characteristics
as an innovation's sheer technical capability to perform the task for which it is
intended, its reliability, ease of maintenance and repair, availability of service
and spare parts, figure most prominently in buyers' evaluations. Therefore,
the thrust of technical effort by producers is in the direction of solving
problems connected with these criteria. Frequently, products or process
equipment are custom-made to the requirements of a specific customer.

Not too surprisingly, the rate of turnover of competing firms tends to be high. Some fail because of their products' technical inadequacies, others because they are simply unable to market the product successfully, and yet others because they are unable to establish adequate facilities for larger production runs. These problems are often caused, or at least aggravated, by the fact that the persons in charge have strong technical backgrounds but lack managerial and sales experience. But given the unsettled state of the basic technology, there are always new firms entering the industry, even as the unsuccessful ones depart.

Eventually, however, technological conditions tend to stabilize, and the competitive turbulence created by uncertainty is reduced. This is so either because one of the contending technical versions emerges as clearly superior or because the members of the industry cooperate in establishing certain basic parameters for their products and agree to set common standards for materials inputs and key components.

Historical examples of the problems and opportunities that exist during a basic technology's infancy abound. One of the best contemporary illustrations is provided by conditions in the small-computer industry.[2] Here we see all the phenomena discussed above: Competing, and incompatible, technical approaches on the hardware side; software that is frequently unreliable and not "user-friendly;" difficulties in production, marketing, and distribution; customer complaints about maintenance and service; and, perhaps most important, great uncertainty about the range of applications for these new products. Industry spokesmen have begun to call for the setting of some common standards as a means of introducing greater stability. Meanwhile, failure rates have been high, and there are at least some signs of the emergence of superior technical solutions. But there seems to be agreement among experts that the industry has a way to go before it will move out of infancy.

11.1.2 *Consolidation and Rapid Growth*

As technological uncertainty is removed and the opportunities for radical product innovations decline, competitive conditions change. Success or failure of firms will now be determined mainly by their ability to make the transition to the high-volume manufacture and marketing of products whose essential technical features have become stabilized. Therefore, the surviving firms' strategies will be aimed mainly at *major process innovations* (mass production) and *product differentiation*. The range of prices at which the innovation is available will tend to narrow, compared to the earlier stage.

Economies of scale and learning that follow the increasing stabilization of basic design will lead to steady, and sometimes even spectacular, reductions in unit costs. The consequent drop in product prices will tend to open up new markets. And this, in turn will stimulate further technological efforts to appeal to these markets. Thus, for example, in the short span of a decade the small electronic calculator went from being a high-priced item bought only by people whose demand was very price-inelastic to a product so cheap that one can find it in the hands of everyone who occasionally has to add, subtract, multiply, or divide.

In the process, the nature of the surviving firms also changes. Their plant and equipment becomes increasingly product-specific and therefore less flexible. Machinery now is supplied by industries specialized in meeting the requirements of a smaller number of large customers, with only minor technical modifications necessary to allow for differences in these requirements. At the same time, some materials and component suppliers will want to benefit from a growing market by tailoring their output to the new, but now firmly established, branch. And in addition, clusters of firms may appear that provide a variety of services at prices below the in-house costs of their customers. In other words, the growth industry benefits increasingly from *external scale economies*. As a result, we typically find elaborate networks of supplier-customer relationships developing at this stage of a basic technology's evolution.

Human inputs into production also undergo change. The successful running of organizations depends more and more on skills other than those of the engineer or technician. The ability to coordinate and manage complex production activities, to deal with the market, to maintain internal financial controls, and to market and distribute products becomes the dominant criterion for success. Quite frequently, R&D efforts are aimed mainly at minor improvements in existing products or at bringing out new versions based on the same basic technology. With the increasing technical specificity of the existing plant and equipment, major innovations tend to be regarded as too risky and too costly. And as long as such perceptions exist among all firms in the industry, they become self-fulfilling prophecies and therefore determine the nature of competition.

The transition to mass production also means that the skill requirements for labor are reduced. With equipment highly product-specific, mechanized, and perhaps even automated, there is less need for experienced workers. Since individual tasks are specialized, covering but a small step of an operation, new laborers can be trained relatively quickly. At the same time, the introduction of further process innovations frequently means that the skills, and with them the status, of long-time employees are depreciated.

11.1.3 *Maturity and Stagnation*

Eventually, technologies—and markets—evolve to the point where, it is often said, their products have become "commodity-like." This is meant to suggest that the output of the (relatively few) large producers has become increasingly homogeneous, with attempts at even minor product differentiation bumping up against technical and organizational barriers. At this stage, straightforward *price competitiveness* becomes the main criterion for survival. Therefore, the technological efforts of the survivors are directed mainly at those minor process innovations that promise to shave a few more pennies off the unit costs of their products.

From a broader perspective, it could also be said that the potential of a basic technology for further improvement has been exhausted, and that the benefit-cost ratio for investment in major technical advances has declined so sharply that there seems to be little that could be done to generate genuine breakthroughs. Dr. Richard N. Foster, of McKinsey & Co., has coined the picturesque term, "clipper ship syndrome," for this stage in the evolution of a technology. He points out that the famous late-nineteenth-century clippers were the epitome of sailing-vessel design but at the same time represented a dead end as far as further advances were concerned. Even relatively crude steam vessels could out-compete them in speed, capacity, and ease of operation—not to mention the new technology's independence from wind force and wind direction. A number of detailed studies of the evolution of basic technologies provides support for the hypothesis that this exhaustion of potential is a pervasive phenomenon.[3] What one observes, then, is the more or less rapid displacement of an old basic technology by a newer one that satisfies not only the same basic requirements, but also meets additional needs and opens up entirely new opportunities, thus starting the evolutionary cycle over again. It would be an oversimplification, of course, to interpret this displacement as just a process of substitution of one basic technology for another. When one considers the network of new economic structures and relationships created by each of them, it quickly becomes clear that steam propulsion was not just a substitute for wind power, that the motor vehicle was not just a substitute for the horse-drawn carriage, or that the jet-propelled aircraft is not simply a faster type of plane than the propeller-driven one.

Returning to the level of the individual firm, we observe that at the mature stage of a basic technology, any number of strategies appear to be more promising than that of investing a lot of resources in R&D. The achievement of marketing superiority, an emphasis on "scientific management" and on what one critic has called "paper entrepreneurialism",[4] as well as the quest for special treatment by the government ("rent-seeking"), often form the main targets of corporate strategy. Ultimately, the sense that the technological opportunities for further cost reduction *and* the potential benefits of these other strategic moves have been exhausted, may cause firms to relocate their entire operations to a region or country with lower input costs.

11.2   Are Industries Tied to Technological Evolution?

So far, we have described the stages of development through which basic technologies appear to go in terms of their *effects* on firms and industries. This raises the question whether these effects are inevitable, whether—no matter what they do—industries are bound ultimately to rise and decline through the life cycle of a particular technology.

The evidence at this level of aggregation is far from clear-cut. In part, the problem may result from the way in which our official industrial statistics are constructed: once a firm has been assigned to a particular category in the Standard Industrial Classification (SIC) scheme,[5] it remains there, regardless of whether it is at the technological frontier or barely hanging on without adopting major innovations. Thus, an old American industry group—like SIC 354, Metalworking Machinery—may show stagnation or decline in the aggregate, even though some firms in the group are among the pioneers in the development of radically new technologies for the cutting and forming of metals, and indeed of whole advanced manufacturing systems.

Even when we set these difficulties to one side, however, there remains the fact that the growth rates of industries show considerable variations over time and that we can observe branches of the economy rising and declining in relative, if not in absolute, significance.[6] A persuasive case for the existence of a life cycle of industries was made by Professor Simon Kuznets in a classic paper, "Retardation of Industrial Growth".[7] He cites three main reasons for stagnation and decline:

"1. Technical progress slackens, changes in methods of production being more numerous in the early period.
2. Slower growing industries exercise a retarding influence upon the faster growing complementary branches.
3. One nation's industry may be retarded by the competitive influence of a branch of the same industry emerging later in another country."

Although Kuznets's article was published in 1929, these explanations certainly have a contemporary ring to them. It is important to recognize, however, that they do not attribute changes in the fortunes of industries to technological evolution alone. Thus, the second of the above reasons is derived from the interdependence of industries in complex networks of relationships. It may well be that technological stagnation in one of them acts as a brake on the growth of others, but it would be difficult therefore to blame the affected industries for their failure to be innovative. The point becomes obvious when we think, for example, of how many suppliers of goods and services are dependent on the fortunes of the motor vehicle industry, without having any direct influence on that industry's performance.

With respect to the rise and decline of whole branches of the economy in international competition, the case has been made that technological factors are but one set in a wider array of determinants of competitiveness.[8] The general conclusion seems to be that success is dependent on the innovativeness of an industry's members, but that this must be understood in the sense of "doing things in a new and different way," and not just in terms of technological advances.[9]

These observations leave us with a somewhat unsatisfactory state of affairs. While it is no doubt true that, in a very long-run perspective, technology is what one observer has called the "driver of change and economic growth",[10] the managers of firms in a particular industry have to deal with a variety of problems and opportunities in formulating enterprise strategies. There may well be times when they perceive that radical changes in products or processes rank relatively low in the hierarchy of possible strategies. Decision-makers are not, after all, concerned with the very long run but rather with the performance of their businesses over a more limited planning horizon. They may turn out to have been right or wrong, but this we can tell only with the wisdom of hindsight.

Once we recognize these facts, we may well come to the conclusion that for the purpose of tracing the effects of technological evolution, an industry, as traditionally defined, does not provide a very useful level of analysis. Given the heterogeneity of firm structures and of firm behavior within a given industry, it would seem more productive to focus attention on the way in which individual enterprises respond to the different conditions created by the transition of basic technologies from infancy, through rapid growth, to maturity.

A persuasive number of case studies at this level suggests that there is nothing inevitable about the impact of the basic-technology life cycle upon the fortunes of firms. Some manage to make the transition to new technological bases for their existing business, or to new kinds of business, whereas others fail to do so. When we look at the early entrants into the emerging automobile industry, for example, we find that a surprisingly large number of manufacturers came from branches that were declining, such as the production of horse-drawn carriages and bicycles. To the extent that large, modern corporations pursue a deliberate strategy of diversifying their lines of business across many products and technologies, one would further expect them to have life cycles more or less independent from those observed for the several industries they may belong to.[11]

We conclude, then, that the question that stood at the beginning of this section can be answered sensibly only if we make a clear distinction: The fortunes of industries, as we define them in our official statistics, and therefore in our economic models, are tied to the evolution of basic technologies. *But* we must not conclude from this that the fortunes of individual firms are. Those with "vision in managing technology"[12] will survive the changing challenges of this evolution, while those that fail to do so will drop out of the game. The dynamics of market economies derive from the sorting-out of winners and losers in the game of competition. And competition in such a setting is among enterprises, not among "industries" or other analytical constructs.

Joseph Schumpeter put the relationship between technological evolution and economic evolution in a free-enterprise system in perspective:

"[The] evolutionary character of the capitalist process is not merely due to the fact that economic life goes on in a social and natural environment which changes and by its changes alters the data of economic action; this fact is important and these changes (wars, revolutions, and so on) often condition industrial change, but they are not its prime movers . . . The fundamental impulse that sets and keeps the capitalists' engine in motion comes from new consumers' goods, the new methods of production or transportation, the new markets, the new forms of industrial organization that capitalist enterprise creates."[13]

11.3   The Long-Wave Hypothesis

Looking beyond the relationship between basic innovations and the life cycles of individual industries, some economists have attempted to discover whether there are technological advances so fundamental in their effects that they produced observable, cyclical swings in aggregate economic activity. Since, starting with the first industrial revolution, virtually every measure of activity exhibits a rising long-term trend, those who want to demonstrate the existence of such swings, or long waves, must rely on evidence that shows some systematic deviations from these trends.

Of necessity, this enterprise is beset by great definitional and statistical difficulties. First of all, agreement has to be reached on what is meant by major or basic innovations. Second, appropriate quantitative indicators of waves around trends have to be decided upon: total output, industrial output, prices, investment, profits, and employment are but some of the candidates. And third, it has to be established that there exists a cause-and-effect relationship between innovations and aggregate economic behavior. This requires isolating the impact of other events, such as wars, political and institutional transformations, changes in resource availability, and so on, which form "noise" that distorts all statistical time series. No wonder, then, that the "long-wave problem" has caused considerable controversy.

Although he had several predecessors, the Russian economist N. D. Kondratieff is generally regarded as the pioneer of the long-wave hypothesis.[14] His work, published in the 1920s, stimulated great interest among a number of researchers. The Great Depression of the 1930s quite naturally raised the question whether this cataclysmic event could be due to some endogenous, historical phenomena, rather than to shorter-term factors. Kondratieff proposed that economic development since the late eighteenth century had been marked by swings of 45 to 60 years' duration. Joseph Schumpeter linked these swings with specific technological events[15] and thus provided a congenial explanation. And Professor Simon Kuznets attempted to construct a chronology of Kondratieff cycles.[16] According to him, the first of the waves, lasting from 1787 to 1842, was triggered by the effects of innovations in cotton textile manufacture, iron-making, and steam power. The second wave coincided with railroad development and extended from 1842 to 1897. This was followed by a third wave, identified with the development of electricity and of the automobile.

Many other investigators contributed to the long-wave literature in the 1930s and 1940s, but then interest in the subject seemed to wane. Post-World War II recovery and the industrialized world's rapid growth in the following two decades diverted economists' attention to other problems. The 1970s, however, saw a revival of the long-wave controversy. No doubt the "oil crisis," structural shifts in the world economy, and the stagnation experienced by virtually all industrial countries contributed to this renewed interest. One of the most interesting contributions came from Professor Gerhard Mensch. The title of his widely-discussed book, *Stalemate in Technology*,[17] catches the essence of his thesis: When existing technologies have reached maturity, economic activity declines, but depressed conditions (the stalemate) are precisely the breeding ground for a new wave of basic innovations. Mensch defines innovations as basic when they are "the source from which new products and services spring and in turn create new markets and new industrial branches to supply them." They are followed by improvement innovations until the potential of prevailing technology has once again been exhausted.

These events will result in "waves" only it it can be shown that basic innovations do indeed occur in clusters, during certain identifiable periods. Mensch provided evidence that such a clustering occurred roughly in 1770, 1825, 1885, and 1935, and he argued that the stagnation of the late 1970s will set off another cluster in the foreseeable future. The fundamental inventions that will trigger the long-term revival are presumed to exist already, and prevailing conditions will provide the stimulus for development and innovation on a large scale.

While many have found the thesis congenial, and while a host of follow-up studies have attempted to intensify the force of Mensch's arguments by placing them into the framework of the older long-wave literature,[18] his findings have not gone unchallenged. Criticism has focussed on the definition and identification of basic innovations, as well as on the underlying economic mechanism proposed by Mensch to explain long swings in activity.[19] Alternative hypotheses have been constructed, focussing, for example, on the speed with which innovations are diffused, rather than on the bunching of innovations themselves.[20] Large-scale simulation models have shown also that swings of the type postulated by technology-oriented explanations might as plausibly be caused by other systemic changes.[21] It is probably fair to say, however, that the majority of economists remains at least agnostic with respect to the existence of long waves, perhaps only because many of them still think of technological change as exogenous to the economic process.

For our purposes, it may be best not to think of the long-term effects of basic innovations in terms of "waves," "swings," or "cycles." These words probably suggest too much: a self-generated, self-repeating sequence of fluctuations, whose shapes and turning points are subject to some invariant "laws." The enormous economic impact of the last two centuries' major advances in technology needs no substantiation. But each of these advances—steam power, mass-produced steel, railroads, electric power, motor vehicles, aircraft, computers, and so on—occurred in its own historical context. Although the search for common characteristics in their economic, social, and political ramifications is essential if we want to draw some useful lessons from the past, neither the empirical evidence nor our present theoretical understanding appear strong enough to support a general theory of cyclical, long-term evolution. Certain themes seem to recur in the processes whereby innovations exert their effects, but—as we have implied all along—these themes are probably best pursued at a microeconomic level, rather than in grand aggregates.

11.4 Technological Evolution and Employment

Over the past two centuries, the rise and decline of basic technologies has been accompanied by a persistent public concern about the effects of innovations on employment. This concern has taken two main forms: worries about the displacement of human labor and the consequent unemployment, and worries about the implications of technological advances for the conditions of work. We shall deal with these issues in order.

11.4.1 *Technological Advances and Aggregate Employment*

Most easily refuted is the notion that, on balance, technological progress has reduced the aggregate demand for labor, i.e., total employment in industrialized countries. Predictions that the diffusion of innovations will result in economy-wide reductions in job opportunities are at least as old as the introduction of the first mechanized techniques for spinning and weaving, and they have persisted ever since. Despite the evidence that none of the past major advances did produce the feared mass unemployment, experts could always be found who were willing to predict that the *next* set of new technologies would be different.

Consider the prediction made in the early 1950s by Professor Norbert Wiener, one of the fathers of the electronic computer, that the impending development of automation would replace most human labor altogether:

> "The automatic factory and assembly line without human agents are only so far ahead of us as is limited by our willingness to put such a degree of effort in their engineering as was spent, for example, in the development of the technique of radar in the Second World War . . . There is no rate of pay at which a pick-and-shovel laborer can live which is low enough to compete with the work of a steam-shovel as an excavator. The modern industrial revolution is similarly bound to devaluate the human brain, at least in its simple and more routine decisions . . . [In] the second revolution . . . the average human being of mediocre attainments or less has nothing to sell that is worth anyone's money to buy".[22]

More than a decade later, in 1964, Professor Crossman of Oxford University predicted that "unemployment due to automation will grow steadily over the next few decades, perhaps centuries, and in the end is likely to reach a very high figure, say 90 per cent of the labor force, unless radical changes are made in the present pattern of working".[23] Such pessimistic forecasts by persons regarded as disinterested experts led others, with a more direct stake in the matter, to voice their concerns and to call for governmental action. Thus, for example, George Meany, President of the AFL-CIO during the 1960s, expressed the fear that anywhere from 400,000 to 4 million job opportunities would be eliminated each year by the progress of automation and that ultimately all the goods needed by society could be produced by a fourth of the present labor force.[24]

In response to these public concerns, the President of the United States appointed a National Commission on Technology, Automation, and Economic Progress. In its voluminous 1966 report,[25] the Commission found little to support the notion that past technological advances had reduced total employment in the economy; nevertheless, it proposed a number of governmental measures aimed at mitigating the likely effects of automation on total employment in the United States. Since then, civilian employment has grown from 73 million to over 105 million, and even manufacturing employment in 1984 stood at about 20 million, roughly the same as in 1966.

In the face of the long-run empirical evidence, economists have tended to dismiss forecasts of doom. The following assessment is typical:

"Past experience shows no reason to believe that technological innovations lead to a decrease in the global volume of employment. On the contrary, it suggests that such innovations, while they may cause declines in some areas of employment, lead in the long run to an expansion of employment by creating increases in other areas".[26]

There are sound theoretical reasons for the proposition that technological progress stimulates the overall demand for labor by increasing the consumption of new products and by creating opportunities for investment in new processes and facilities. The idea that there is only a finite amount of work to be done in an economy and that there are limits to the amount of goods "needed" by society has no support in what we know about the working of economic systems.

11.4.2   Changes in the Structure of Employment

The eighteenth-century French *saboteurs* who used their wooden shoes (*sabots*) to smash the machines that threatened their jobs; the British *Luddites* who rioted against mechanization in nineteenth-century Lancashire; and modern labor unions who are trying to protect their members' positions through featherbedding rules and other devices—these special groups are not likely to derive comfort from economists' sanguine conclusions about the effects of innovations on global employment. When people are confronted with technological changes that affect their incomes and their status in society, they are likely to resist with all means at their disposal. And when the affected branches are large, or when they are heavily concentrated geographically, the problems created by shifts in employment assume great political importance. We need only consider the competitive difficulties of the so-called "smokestack industries" in the Great Lakes region of the United States to get a picture of the economic, social, and political effects of major structural transformations. Indeed, calls for governmental protection against such changes and for general "industrial policies" to alleviate their effects, have become a common feature of all advanced democracies.[27]

An evaluation of the soundness of such measures and of their chances for long-term success would go beyond the scope of our current interest. We are concerned with a basic feature of technological evolution: as technologies mature, for whatever reason, in some branches, demand for labor will be reduced in the affected firms and industries; meanwhile, the growth of other types of activity will lead to increased demand for labor there. To the extent that labor is immobile in the short and medium term, and to the extent that worker skills are mis-matched with new job opportunities, structural unemployment will result.

In recent years, public concern has focussed not only on shifts within the manufacturing sector and on their consequences, but even more on the role of manufacturing in the economy at large. It has become fashionable to speak of ours as a "post-industrial society." Aside from whatever social and cultural consequences this state of affairs is meant to have, the impression is frequently created that industrial production and employment have been declining steadily, in relative if not in absolute terms. Concurrently, it is often implied that the United States is becoming a "service economy."

In order to examine the validity of such claims, we present in Table 11.1 employment data, by major sectors, for selected years since 1900. First and foremost, these figures show that the number of persons employed in manufacturing has risen steadily. Whatever shifts among branches may have occurred, there has been none of the absolute decline in jobs that might be inferred from much of the talk about post-industrialism. Nor can we observe any precipitous drop in the share of manufacturing in total civilian employment. Any claims about the demise of American manufacturing, as a whole, would have to be based on predictions about the future structure of employment. So far, the revolution has not taken place.

If the twentieth century has seen a revolution, it has been on account of technological advances in agriculture. In 1900, well over one-third of all people were employed in the production of agricultural commodities, with forestry and fisheries making up but a small proportion of the totals shown in the Table. By 1940, the absolute number of persons employed had dropped already, and their share in total employment had been halved. In 1980, the 3.5 million workers in the agricultural sector produced over twice the total output of the 9 million workers in 1940.[28] No other major sector of the American economy can match this performance.

The apparent transformation of farming also provides us with an opportunity for reflecting on the extent to which our statistics tend to exaggerate the implications of such trends. The decline in agricultural employment was due

TABLE 11.1 *Structure of U.S. civilian employment, selected years 1900–1980* (1,000 employees and percentages of total)

Category	1900		1920		1940		1960		1980	
	Number	%	Number	%	Number	%	Number	%	Number	%
Agriculture, forestry, and fisheries	10,920	37.6	11,400	27.4	9,140	17.1	5,723	9.5	3,470	2.6
Mining	760	2.6	1,230	3.0	1,110	2.1	709	1.2	940	1.0
Manufacturing	6,340	21.8	10,880	26.1	11,940	22.4	16,762	27.9	21,593	22.2
Construction	1,660	5.7	2,170	5.2	3,150	6.8	2,882	4.8	6,065	6.1
Transportation and public utilities	2,100	7.2	4,190	10.1	4,150	7.8	4,017	6.7	6,393	6.6
Trade, finance, and real estate	2,760	9.5	4,860	11.7	8,730	16.4	14,096	23.5	25,587	26.3
Other	4,530	15.6	6,880	16.5	14,720	27.6	15,881	26.4	33,222	34.2
Total employment	29,070		41,610		53,300		60,070		97,270	

Sources: U.S. Department of Commerce, Bureau of the Census, *Historical Statistics of the United States, Colonial Times to 1957* (Washington, DC: U.S. Government Printing Office, 1961); and *Statistical Abstract of the United States*, 1961 and 1981.

not only to technological progress and scale increases, but also to changes in what farmers do. At the turn of the century, the typical American farm still provided its own transportation (horses, mules, etc.), it produced the energy sources for these means of transport (feed), at least partly processed its products, brought them to the market, and in many instances still served as its own wholesaler or retailer. To be sure, the advent of railroads had already transformed large portions of the agricultural system, but it was only in the course of subsequent developments that farming was able to shed many of the activities that traditionally had been parts of internal operations. As a consequence, a substantial portion of the decline in agricultural employment was offset by a concomitant increase of jobs in such sectors as food processing, transportation, marketing, the manufacture of tractors and machinery, and a whole host of others. Thus, if we were to trace all employment related directly or indirectly to agricultural production, we would get a more accurate picture of structural change.

These observations help us to put into perspective the two other trends apparent from the data in Table 11.1—the rapid rise in trade and finance, and the increasing share of employment accounted for by "other" activities, mostly a variety of services. Just as in the case of agriculture, a substantial portion of these changes is due to the transformation of the character of manufacturing industries. In good measure, the new jobs in what has been called our growing "service economy" are attributable to this transformation. Increasingly, manufacturing companies rely on outside organizations to provide them with services previously performed in-house, as well as with new services requiring special expertise. To the extent that changes in the structure of employment are due to changes in the nature of the work performed within the traditional groupings established by our statistics, only a careful tracing of these networks of effects can provide useful answers to the question: How has the evolution of basic technologies affected sectoral shifts in employment?

11.4.3 *Technological Change and Working Conditions*

Today, most people will accept the view that ". . . a factory performs two major functions: the economic one of producing goods and the social one of creating and distributing human satisfaction among the people under its roof".[29] How best to fulfill these functions is a matter of considerable debate, despite the widespread recognition that working conditions and worker attitudes have a profound effect on industrial performance. Indeed, the Japanese industries' success in global competition has often been attributed to their seemingly unique ability to achieve high rates of technological change in a climate of all-round cooperation. Whatever the real causes of this success, it has served to focus attention on the problem in all industrialized economies.

In historical perspective, we can discern several phases of development, from the paternalistic patterns of employer-employee relations in nineteenth-century factories to the present-day recognition that worker satisfaction contributes directly to the attainment of a firm's objectives.[30] Obvious as this contribution may seem to us, recognition of the fact was gained only slowly and by a circuitous route. Early views of the employer's responsibility toward his workers represented a curious mixture of indifference to the effects of long working hours and to the typical factory's hazards for life and limb, with a great concern for the moral well-being of employees. Working under the close discipline of "mechanical manufacture" was seen as a means of improving both, the laborers' economic lot and their human worth, at least as perceived by the educated classes. In 1884, the historian Arnold Toynbee (uncle of the better-known Arnold J. Toynbee) perfectly summarized this spirit in reflecting on the impact of industrialization:

> "Turning to the moral condition of the workpeople, we find an improvement even greater than in their material progress. When we see or read of what goes on in the streets of our great towns, we think badly enough of their morality; but those who have had most experience in manufacturing districts are of the opinion that the moral advance, as manifested, for example, in temperance, in orderly behavior, in personal appearance, in dress, has been very great. For the improvement in the inner life of workshops as early as 1834, take the evidence of Francis Place . . . He told the Committee [of the House of Commons] that, when he was a boy, he used to hear songs, such as he could not repeat, sung in respectable shops by respectable people; it was no longer so, and he was at a loss how to account for the change."[31]

Whatever else might be said about factories in the last century, they surely were far from realizing the full economic potential of the great innovations in manufacturing because not much attention was paid to relevant worker attitudes or, for that matter, to using human labor efficiently and in tune with modern process technologies. In the 1890s an American, Frederick W. Taylor, believed that he had found the secret of extracting optimal performance from man-machine combinations: it lay in the scientific study of work performance, in the breaking-down of specific human operations into their machine-like component tasks, and in arranging and controlling these tasks in the most minute detail. He became the father of time-and-motion study and of the profession of industrial engineering. His theories found widespread application and made for a clear break with the past, much more haphazard, utilization of human labor in a mechanized environment.

Much to the chagrin of Taylor, who simply could not understand that people might be interested in things other than productive efficiency, workers responded poorly to his new system. Instead of appreciating the fact that many of their physical tasks had been eased, they railed against the total standardization of their jobs and the regimentation of strictly-timed performance. Their complaints were not even mitigated by the higher economic rewards of piece-work pay. "Taylorism" regarded workers as components of a system that performed best under conditions of uniformity and repetition. Personal identification with jobs and personal satisfaction did not enter into the equation.

As the development of mass-production techniques progressed, the amount of skill and experience required of workers decreased. Nimbleness and endurance in the performance of quickly-learned tasks were the main characteristics desired. Even otherwise enlightened employers paid little attention to the potential benefits of recognizing and treating workers as individuals. In this climate, which had become typical of industry in the 1920s, some experimentally-minded engineers made an interesting discovery: no matter how routine and dull their tasks, workers still responded favorably to a working environment that left them with some feeling of personal involvement, initiative, and responsibility.[32] Recognition of this fact led to an entirely new approach: the field of industrial psychology developed and made many contributions to a better understanding of what constitutes a satisfactory job, from the employee's point of view.

Neither the state of the labor market during the Great Depression nor the all-out production efforts of World War II provided a setting favorable to experimentation based on these new perspectives on human performance. The struggles for the unionization of mass-production industries and the rallying of resources for the conduct of the war shaped dominant attitudes in labor-management relations. After 1945, therefore, the climate had changed radically. On the one hand, labor unions had gained great strength and were seen as effective institutions for translating workers' economic and non-economic demands into industrial reality. And on the other hand, a growing recognition that day-to-day worker attitudes played a direct part in the performance of even the most mechanized industries, led managements to explore and exploit the insights gained by industrial psychology.

Attention to these matters varied greatly from industry to industry. In some of the older branches, traditional relationships between "bosses" and workers continued virtually unchanged. But in many others, the beneficial results of a new approach reinforced the search for further improvements. Interest was no doubt fueled by a concern about the additional upheavals in industrial relations that, according to the predictions of experts, would result from the progress of automation. In the view of many observers, problems were likely to be aggravated by the fact that in an affluent society, in which most industrial workers had achieved middle-class status, pressures for further economic improvement were replaced by a quest for greater job satisfaction. Alleviation of these concerns would seem to require a compromise between the regimentation seemingly imposed by modern production technology and the freedom promised by higher real incomes and increased leisure time.

In all of this, the spirit of Taylor continued to prove more congenial to the implications of technological change than the tenets of the "human-relation-in-industry" experts. In the 1950s, John Diebold expressed a criticism that could just as easily have been stated several decades earlier, or three decades later: "Many of the human problems of today are the result of the attempts to adjust the worker to the machine that paces him and, in a broader way, of the mechanistic concepts of the function of workers in mass production."[33] In order to overcome these problems, some pioneering firms have experimented with systems that uncouple human contributions to production from the pace of machines. Thus, for example, the Swedish automobile manufacturer, Volvo, has assigned the building of engines to small teams of workers who take full responsibility for the division of labor among themselves as well as for the quality of the product. Yet others have argued that such efforts at reform are mere palliatives in the face of long-term trends that presage a shift of all manufacturing based on traditional, mass-production techniques from the advanced economies to the so-called "newly industrialized countries." In the meantime, however, industrial firms in North America as well as in Europe are continuing their search for better ways of realizing the full potential of the human input into production—not necessarily from an increased sense of social responsibility, but because the pressures of international competition force them to do so.

So far, none of these efforts at innovation has brought conclusive results. Perhaps the only thing that has been learned with any certainty is that one cannot simply lift the institutions and mechanisms of labor-management relations out of one socio-cultural context and transfer them to another. Thus, except for certain external features, the "Japanese model" has proven largely irrelevant for the American setting. In a world in which basic innovations are diffused rapidly and widely, and in which therefore the conditions of production would seem to converge, differences in *how* societies come to terms with these technologies have emerged in sharp contours. This observation should make us skeptical of the frequently-heard view that the demands of modern technology ruthlessly homogenize social and cultural traits across the globe. Different societies clearly find different ways of reconciling the tension between having to work within the requirements imposed by technology on the one hand, and the ill-defined and heterogeneous desires of people for something more than a decent income from their jobs, on the other.

Notes

1. By now, there exists a copious literature on the stages of industrial evolution. One of the most concise discussions can be found in Abernathy, W. J., and Utterback, J. M., "A Dynamic Model of Process and Product Innovation," *Omega*, 3/6 (1975).
2. Kneale, D., "The Unfinished Revolution," *The Wall Street Journal*, September 16, 1985, Section 3, "Special Report: Technology in the Workplace."
3. See, for example, Abernathy, W. J., *The Productivity Dilemma: Roadblock to Innovation in the Automobile Industry* (Baltimore, MD: Johns Hopkins University Press, 1978).
4. Reich, R. R., "The Next American Frontier," *The Atlantic Monthly*, March 1983.
5. See Note 9, Chapter 3, above, for a brief description of the SIC system.
6. A comprehensive survey can be found in Gold, B., "Industry Growth Patterns: Theory and Empirical Results," *Journal of Industrial Economics*, 13/1 (1964).
7. Kuznets, S., "Retardation of Industrial Growth," *Journal of Economic and Business History*, August 1929. Reprinted in Kuznets, S., *Economic Change* (New York: Norton, 1953).
8. Gold, B., "Technological and Other Determinants of the International Competitiveness of U.S. Industries," *IEEE Transactions on Engineering Management*, EM-30/2 (May 1983).

9. Hayes, R. H., and Abernathy, W. J., "Managing Our Way to Economic Decline," *Harvard Business Review*, July–August 1980.

10. Ayres, R. U., *The Next Industrial Revolution* (Cambridge, MA: Ballinger—Harper & Row, 1984), Chapter 3.

11. Miller, D., and Friesen, P. H., "A Longitudinal Study of the Corporate Life Cycle," *Management Science*, 30/10 (October 1984).

12. Foster, R. N., "A Call for Vision in Managing Technology," Business Week, May 24, 1982.

13. Schumpeter, J. A., *Capitalism, Socialism, and Democracy*, 3rd ed. (New York: Harper & Row, 1950), pp. 136–7.

14. A thorough review of the state of the art in long-wave research can be found in Van Duijn, J. J., *The Long Wave in Economic Life* (London: Allen & Unwin, 1983).

15. Schumpeter, J. A., *Business Cycles* (New York: McGraw-Hill, 1939).

16. Kuznets, S., "Schumpeter's Business Cycles," *American Economic Review*, XXX/2 (June 1940).

17. Mensch, G., *Stalemate in Technology: Innovations Overcome Depression* (Cambridge, MA: Ballinger—Harper & Row, 1979).

18. See, especially, Kleinknecht, A., *Innovation Patterns in Crisis and Prosperity; Schumpeter's Long Cycle Reconsidered* (Amsterdam: Free University, 1984).

19. For an example of such criticisms, see Mansfield, E., "Long Waves and Technological Innovation," *American Economic Review, Papers and Proceedings*, 73/2 (May 1983).

20. Freeman, C., Clark, J., and Soete, L., *Unemployment and Technical Innovations* (London: Pinter, 1982).

21. The best known work along these lines was done by the Systems Dynamics Group at Massachusetts Institute of Technology. Representative of the Group's research is Forrester, J. W., "Innovation and the Economic Long Wave," *The McKinsey Quarterly*, Spring 1979.

22. Quoted in Kranzberg, M., and Gies, J., *By the Sweat of Thy Brow: Work in the Western World* (New York: Putnam, 1975), p. 182.

23. Quoted in Mansfield, E., *The Economics of Technical Change* (New York: Norton, 1968), p. 135.

24. Quoted in Kranzberg and Gies, *op. cit.*, p. 183.

25. *Studies Prepared for the National Commission on Technology, Automation, and Economic Progress* (Washington, DC: U.S. Government Printing Office, 1966).

26. "Impact of Technological Progress on Labor and Social Policy," in U.S. Department of Labor, Bureau of Labor Statistics, *Impact of Automation*, Bulletin No. 1278 (Washington, DC: U.S. Government Printing Office, 1960), p. 16. The same conclusions are reached by Browne, L. E., "Conflicting Views of Technological Progress and the Labor Market," *New England Economic Review*, July/August 1984.

27. For a comprehensive, and critical, summary see Roe, A. R., *Industrial Restructuring: Issues and Experiences in Selected Developed Economies*, World Bank Technical Paper No. 21 (Washington, DC: The World Bank, 1984).

28. Council of Economic Advisers, *Economic Report of the President* (Washington, DC: U.S. Government Printing Office, 1985), p. 339.

29. Stuart Chase, quoted in Kranzberg and Giese, *op. cit.*, p. 167.

30. One of the best historical surveys is Kranzberg and Gies, *op. cit.*

31. Toynbee, A., *The Industrial Revolution* (Boston, MA: Beacon Press, 1956), pp. 120–1.

32. The best-known experiments along these lines were carried out by Elton Mayo at the Hawthorne Works of the Western Electric Company. He summarized his findings in *The Human Problems of Industrial Civilization* (New York: Macmillan, 1933).

33. Diebold, J., *Automation* (New York: Van Nostrand, 1952), pp. 160–1.

CHAPTER 12

International Aspects of Technological Change

Technology plays an ever more important role in international economic relations. Merchandise trade among nations has become dominated by the exchange of manufactured goods whose production involves sophisticated technologies, and most of these goods move between the advanced, industrial economies. The steadily-growing volume of international direct investment, i.e., the setting-up of operations by a corporation in another nation, involves massive transfers of technology. And the governments of all countries seem to be concerned about the consequences of technology transfers, inward or outward. It is appropriate, therefore, that we conclude our survey of the economics of technological change with a brief foray into the international arena.

12.1 Foreign Trade and Technological Change

The traditional theory of international trade had little to say about the role of technology. Technological knowledge was assumed to be a free good, equally accessible to all countries. Differences in the production techniques actually utilized by national economies were attributed to variations in the availability, and in the relative prices, of the factors of production—land (natural resources), labor, and capital. In general, the theory concluded that each country will export those goods in whose production it makes intensive use of its (relatively) most abundant factor. If, for example, capital is plentiful relative to natural resources and labor, the prediction would be that the country will export products requiring capital-intensive production techniques.[1]

Obviously, such a prediction is based on the assumption that each country has a free choice among techniques. It also assumes that inputs within each country are not sector-specific, i.e., that they can move freely from one branch of the economy to another. Adjustments in the economy's product mix are taken to occur by having the branches in which factors are most productive bid these factors away from other branches. If these adjustments were carried out fully, the theory would predict two non-obvious results:

249

(1) Under conditions of free trade, i.e., without tariffs or other obstacles to exchange, international differences in factor incomes (wages, interest, rents) will tend to disappear; and

(2) since all countries are assumed to have free access to technology, trade in commodities is a perfect substitute for the international movement of labor and capital. Technological innovations as such will not affect these results, because such innovations would once again be equally available to all countries.

Efforts to test the theory's predictions have brought mixed success. Relative factor endowments frequently did explain patterns of trade between any two nations, and they also gave some broad indications of trends in the development of trade among all industrial countries. But the theory also failed to account for two trends that have become ever more apparent in post-World War II international economic relations. First, there has been a steady increase in trade involving the movement of the same industries' products in both directions—countries both importing *and* exporting automobiles, for example. And second, growing trade did not turn out to be a substitute for the international movement of capital. On the contrary, the countries—and even the individual corporations—that were particularly successful in exporting a certain group of products often also were the biggest investors abroad. Add to this the fact that some nations developed industries and became major exporters, even though they seemed to have none of the essential inputs for these industries within their borders, and it is not surprising that economists began to search for better explanations of what they were observing in the real world of trade and investment.

Several so-called "new theories" of trade were developed. At this point, they have not been tested adequately and are far from universally accepted. But they are of interest to us, because they explicitly recognize *technology as a separate factor of production*, which is no more freely accessible to a given country than another country's natural resources or capital. Furthermore, they recognize that technological innovations have the unique ability to make all the other factors more productive, and that therefore countries not only have an incentive to innovate, but also to try to appropriate the results of innovations. In this view, then, the movement of technologies across the international boundaries would confront most of the same incentives and obstacles encountered by other factors of production. The following discussion is not meant to be anything like a comprehensive survey of the new theories. Instead, we want briefly to describe just two representative versions.

12.1.1   *Technology Gaps and Changing Trade Patterns*

Economic historians have long observed that major innovations in a particular branch of a country's industry tend to be followed by a spurt in that branch's exports. Such observations led to further investigations into the possible causes of this phenomenon, which obviously could not be explained by the traditional theory of trade. The country's factor endowment could not have anything to do with it, because it did not change. On the other hand, the supply of technical entrepreneurship, the mobility of a high-quality labor force, access to risk capital, and the existence of receptive domestic markets appeared to foster spurts in innovation, even in cases where the underlying inventions were more generally accessible.[2]

As a consequence, trade patterns among economies would reflect the existence of *technology gaps* that resulted from such major advances. Innovations create disturbances in the structure of trade, because after the profitability of a new process or product has been established in the innovators' home markets, they will look to exports as a means for gaining additional net revenues (quasi-rents). Trade will adjust itself to production, and not the other way round. The innovating country's exports will grow as long as it has a technological lead in the industry concerned. Eventually, however, the innovation's international diffusion or the development of even better substitutes for it elsewhere will tend to close the technology gap. At this point in time, the assumptions of traditional theory (similar production functions in all countries) may once again prevail, until the next disturbance comes along.

12.1.2 *Product Life Cycles, Trade, and Foreign Investment*

A related, but more comprehensive, explanation has been suggested by Professor Raymond Vernon in his product cycle hypothesis.[3] He agreed that initial export spurts are the result of technology gaps but then added a model that accounts for the international diffusion of innovations and the resulting longer-term changes in the structure of trade and investment.

The model's outlines are familiar from our discussion in the preceding chapter. According to Vernon, during their infancy innovations require technical skills and know-how as crucial inputs; furthermore, their introduction is accompanied by high levels of uncertainty about market reaction. As technology matures, the originating country will enjoy a temporary competitive advantage. But then the innovation will tend to be diffused to countries having a technological standard similar to that of the innovator, each of these countries making adaptations and incremental improvements. Eventually, in maturity, products and techniques will be standardized to the point where many more countries can take them up successfully.

As a product goes through these stages in its life cycle, international competition will intensify, simply because the number of producers has increased. The innovating country's position as a leading exporter will be eroded, and it may even be forced out of the world markets altogether, becoming an importer of the product instead. Note that the model as such says nothing about *who* does the producing in the follower-countries. It may well be that a firm domiciled in the leader nation decides to abandon production there and to move operations to other economies. In fact, one of the major reasons for the growth of international direct investment is that the owners of mature technologies want to exploit their proprietary strength as widely as possible. With further investment in R&D promising only minor improvements, and with the potential economies of scale more or less exhausted, a strategy aimed at the "internationalization of production" may be the best vehicle for extracting further benefits.

Studies of the product cycle in individual industries give strong support to the hypothesis, although it can explain only a part, albeit a significant one, of observed trade patterns. In the case of the United States, for example, the evolution of textile and shoe-making technologies to a high level of mechanization and automation enabled low-skill, low-wage countries to take up production and to become the dominant suppliers in world trade. Meanwhile, the U.S. turned into a net importer and domestic production declined sharply. More recently, the contours of similar developments have begun to appear in iron and steel, in standard machine tools, and even in automobiles.

12.1.3 The Product Cycle and International Competitiveness

If the product cycle hypothesis is generally valid, we would expect innovation-originating countries to lose their competitive advantage as technologies are transferred to the rest of the world. This raises the question whether economies that once enjoyed economic positions are predestined to lose these positions as key industrial technologies mature. Is the rise and decline of nations in international competition pre-programmed through technological evolution?

In an article suggestively entitled, "An American Economic Climacteric?,[4] Professor Charles Kindleberger examines the histories of Germany, Britain, the United States and Japan and raises the possibility that there may be an aging process for economies as well as for people. On the basis of the historical evidence, he concludes that "lulls in commercial technological achievement" as well as a "decline in personal savings habits" [and therefore in capital formation] appear to be responsible for old industrial countries' difficulties in maintaining their competitive position. It seems clear, however, as Kindleberger himself argues elsewhere,[5] that there is no reason why technological leadership as such should produce stagnation and decline. Rather, it appears as though seemingly unassailable leads in technical and economic development are responsible for changes in attitudes and institutions that lower static and dynamic efficiency. This interpretation of history is supported strongly by the work of Professor Mancur Olson,[6] who carries the argument one step further by showing that the root cause of stagnation and decline cannot be found in the economy alone, but rather in the transformation of political arrangements and decision-making processes in the once-leading nations.

Needless to say, views such as these have received wide attention in recent years, as the United States and Western Europe had to face the challenge of

Japan and of other newcomers to global competition. Refusing to accept the notion that decline is pre-programmed and therefore inevitable, writers have asked questions like the following: Which of the technologies and products currently in their infancy are most likely to serve as the sources of renewed vigor in the old industrial economies? What changes in enterprise strategy and in the traditional ways of managing innovation and production are required to bring about a revival of competitive strength? And what is the role of governments in providing an environment that does not get in the way of a new spurt of technology-based expansion?[7]

Answers to these questions are far from easy to come by, and even a cursory survey of the discussion would go beyond the present chapter's scope. Therefore, we want to conclude this section with an observation based on simple arithmetic: If the rate at which existing technologies are diffused across the globe is higher than the rate at which the leading countries produce new technologies, a *convergence* of industrial performance levels, and therefore of real incomes, among the affected economies is the inevitable result. At the same time, this process would obviously raise serious concern among those less-developed nations which for a whole host of political, social, and economic reasons feel that they have been left behind in the game. It is no wonder, then, that they have called for a "new international economic order",[8] in which they could benefit more widely from the advances generated by the leaders.

12.2   Technology Transfer—Mechanisms and Likely Effects

12.2.1   *General Considerations*

By what means is technology transferred from one country to another? Before trying to answer this question, we must remind ourselves of our definition of technology: it is human knowledge *applied* in production. It follows that the mere transmission of information about techniques is a necessary, but not a sufficient condition for technology transfer.[9] The point is worth making, because it is frequently ignored in discussions of the subject. To be sure, innovations in international communication and transportation have greatly improved the speed with which new knowledge is diffused. But knowing about technology is not the same as using it. If there has been acceleration of the rate of transfer, this was due not so much to faster communication but, as we shall argue below, to changes in the institutional arrangements for transfer.

A second point should be made at the outset: the great bulk of all transfers has taken place among the industrialized economies. Although we have no unequivocal quantitative measure for the phenomenon, we are probably not too far off the mark if we estimate that only about one quarter of the transfers of industrial technology has been to the developing countries. If we were to include other innovations, especially those in agriculture and health care, the proportion would be substantially higher.

12.2.2 Transfer Modes

Let us turn to a listing of some of the most important modes of technology transfer, together with some speculation about their likely effectiveness:

1. Scientific knowledge and a lot of generalized technical knowledge are in the nature of public goods. Although we have argued above that the spread of information alone does not constitute technology transfer, we must recognize that some of this knowledge is an essential part of an economy's technological infrastructure. Being in tune with the requirements of advanced production methods requires a "feel for technology" that may be difficult to acquire, even though it seems to be readily available. A simple example will illustrate the point: By the time they enter the labor force, typical American teenagers will be thoroughly familiar with the operation, and most likely with the inner workings, of a motor vehicle. Although they probably will not work in jobs involving internal-combustion engines, they nevertheless possess a "feel" for things mechanical. How does one transfer this kind of knowledge into an environment in which ownership of cars is restricted to the upper classes? Even much more elementary notions of speed, mass, and energy may be missing in such environments. Since these kinds of knowledge are taken for granted in the developed nations, it is not surprising that the transfer of proprietary technology confronts fewer problems.

2. It is generally recognized that the movement of people with expert knowledge is one of the keys to transferring technology. Not only can they be the sole factors in the introduction of disembodied technology (e.g., new engineering or management methods) in another country, but they will also frequently provide the expertise and know-how necessary for the successful transfer of capital equipment. Their effectiveness may well depend, however, on the specific context of their movement. Consider, for example, the chances of achieving productive results in the case of a consultant who is brought in to solve a technical problem in starting up a new plant, as against the situation confronted by an expert who was invited by a government to "improve the productivity of industry." Recognizing the importance of people with specific technical skills and know-how, governments have occasionally tried to restrict the emigration of such persons, in order to prevent or slow the outward transfer of technology. Most of these efforts have been signally unsuccessful.

3. Proprietary technology can be sold internationally in arm's-length transactions. Most obviously, established industries in one country can acquire licenses to utilize inventions patented by a corporation in another country. Needless to say, such contracts do not assure an effective transfer, since the recipient firm still has to make all the moves necessary for successful production. It is not surprising, therefore, that these transactions have been most common among businesses already operating at a reasonably similar technological standard.

4. Transfers may occur through the conscious imitation of another country's technology. In many instances, this is done in the interest of import substitution, i.e., in a deliberate effort to replace foreign products with domestically-produced ones. Rightly or wrongly, firms in some countries have acquired a reputation for placing *one* order for a new product and then proceeding to copy it. Acrimonious situations have arisen when these firms then attempted to export the product to the originating country. Thus, there has been evidence that manufacturers in Southeast Asia built very good imitations of American-made small computers and proceeded to offer them in the world market. Before World War II, the Japanese were known mainly as producers of cheap copies. This image stood them in good stead during their postwar efforts to establish global dominance in a variety of industries. They still ranked low as major inventors and innovators and therefore lulled a number of technological leaders into a false sense of security. But by making substantial improvements to existing products and by developing cost-effective process technologies, Japanese firms managed to establish strong competitive positions in a variety of markets. Thus, Japanese cameras have replaced German ones as high-quality products, and Japanese motorcycles have forced British and American manufacturers out of business. It is important to recognize, however, that the original "imitation" often occurred on the basis of quite legitimate licensing transactions, but that thereafter the innovative strategies of firms together with appropriate government policies enabled Japanese industries to spurt ahead.

5. New technology may be transferred through the movement of capital equipment, or of whole plants, to another country. The effectiveness of this kind of transfer will depend, once again, on the underlying transactions. We may usefully distinguish three basic types:

  a. Sales of plant and equipment to a purchaser in the recipient country. In such transactions, effectiveness may be influenced by who initiated the transfer and who financed it. Private entrepreneurship and commercial financing of an undertaking create a different set of incentives from, say, projects financed through a governmental program or through an international agency. Failures, or at least questionable results, of the latter kind of transfer have not been restricted to developing countries but have occurred even in industrialized economies.

  b. International movement of equipment, proprietary technology, and know-how may result from the setting-up of joint ventures between firms in two countries. Although such arrangements face all the well-known risks of partnerships (the relationship may be dissolved because of disagreements, but the transfer cannot be reversed), they are often the only feasible way of transferring technology. They are, for example, the most common form of cooperation between firms in capitalist countries and the state-owned enterprises in the Soviet-type economies.

c. Transfers of physical capital may occur in connection with a corporation's establishment of controlled operations in another country, either through the purchase of an existing facility or through the building of a new one—in other words, through direct foreign investment. Firms that have expanded internationally through this type of arrangement have become known as multinational (or transnational) corporations. Their activities and their economic as well as social and political effects have met with mixed reactions, in both their home countries and their host nations.[10] But their defenders and their critics seem to agree on one thing: multinationals have proven to be the most efficient institutions for the transfer of technology. Therefore, the development of international direct investment deserves separate discussion.

12.3   Multinational Firms as Agents of Technology Transfer

The list of transfer modes in the previous section suggests why multinational corporations (MNCs) have played such an important role in technology transfer: The answer lies in their ability to *internalize*, within one decision-making and organizational framework, all the various means for moving information, people, and capital across national boundaries. The reasons why firms establish operations abroad may differ, but technology will inevitably accompany them, whether they are engaged in manufacturing, banking, trade, or any other line of business.[11]

12.3.1   *The Development of Foreign Direct Investment*

The worldwide stock of direct foreign investment has increased roughly tenfold in the last quarter-century. Table 12.1 shows the current distribution of this stock's value among the major source countries, and the direction of inward and outward flows from 1965 to 1981. It will be seen that the United States and the countries of Western Europe are the main investors, followed by Japan and Canada. The developing countries account for but a minor portion of total investment. According to one source,[12] American MNCs operate close to 10,000 affiliates across the globe. The United Kingdom is next, with about 7,000; the German Federal Republic (2,900 affiliates) and France (2,000 affiliates) follow in the rankings. While the definitions of what constitutes a direct foreign investment for statistical purposes vary somewhat from country to country, the dominance of the leading industrial economies is obvious.

When we look at the outward and inward flows of direct investment, we find that most of these are accounted for by the advanced economies as well. To be sure, the developing countries were hosts for over one quarter of all new investment, with more than half of this concentrated in the Western Hemisphere (Latin America). But more interesting, for our purposes, is the fact that

TABLE 12.1 *Foreign Direct Investment Positions, by Country of Origin, 1981, and Direct Investment Flows, 1965–1981*

Country	Stock of D.F.I. $ billion	%	Outward flow [% of total]	Inward flow [% of total]
All countries	545.6	100.0	100.0	100.0
Developed countries	528.0	96.8	98.4	73.7
U.S.A.	226.4	41.5	47.5	27.3
European Community*	114.7	21.0	21.2	27.1
United Kingdom	65.5	12.0	14.2	9.9
Canada	25.6	4.7	5.2	5.2
Japan	37.0	6.8	6.0	0.7
Other dev. countries**	58.8	10.7	4.1	3.4
Developing countries	17.6	3.2	1.6	26.3
OPEC countries	n.a.	—	1.0	1.8
Western Hemisphere	n.a.	—	0.1	15.4
Africa†	n.a.	—	—	2.0
Asia†	n.a.	—	0.2	7.1

* Belgium, France, German Federal Republic, Italy, Luxembourg, the Netherlands.
** Includes Australia, New Zealand, South Africa.
† Excludes flows from OPEC countries, shown separately above.
Source: U.S. Department of Commerce, International Trade Administration, *International Direct Investment: Global Trends and the U.S. Role* (Washington, DC: U.S. Government Printing Office, 1984).

the bulk of MNC activity involved an increasing interpenetration among economies which, on the face of it, appear to have quite similar technological standards. Trade among these economies also accounts for most of world trade. Furthermore, investment and trade—in both directions—tend to take place to a large extent in the same industries. Apparently there exist a host of subtle differences in embodied and disembodied technology that account for the success of MNCs in global competition. No wonder that a recent study of intra-industry foreign investment referred to MNCs as "mutual invaders".[13]

12.3.2 *Attitudes toward Multinational Corporations*

As we suggested already, attitudes about the effects of MNCs have been ambivalent, in their home countries as well as their host economies. When a corporation engages in direct foreign investment, labor union officials and political leaders often consider this an "export of jobs." But such a judgment is based on the assumption that the corporation could have made the same investment at home and exported its products to the rest of the world. In fact, however, the largest MNCs also tend to be their home countries' largest exporters. Even more frequently one hears the objection that MNCs take technology and know-how abroad, thus undermining whatever leads the home country might have enjoyed. Where (actually or potentially) defense-related technologies are involved, governments even have acted to stop transfers via direct investment. On the whole and over the long run, such restrictions have not proven particularly effective. The development of a "global marketplace," a declared objective of international political efforts since World War II, probably has been carried further than ever before in modern history. One of the consequences has been an increase in technology-based competition that has made it very difficult for any one country to retain a monopoly position for very long.

Host countries generally have welcomed inward direct investment as a source of new technology, employment, and income. At the same time, however, they often have expressed strong reservations about the effects of foreign-owned firms on traditional ways of doing business and, indeed, on cultural and social values. Furthermore, it is claimed that although MNCs bring their technological and managerial knowledge into an economy, they may also retard indigenous technological development by continuing all of their R&D operations in their home countries. These objections have by no means been restricted to less-developed countries. In the 1960s, for example, Western European observers regarded the "American challenge"[14] as a serious threat to the survival of their own businesses. The manufacturing methods of U.S. MNCs, their managerial philosophy, and their approaches to marketing were seen as undermining existing economic and social relationships. More recently, the reception given to foreign firms in the United States has been far from uniformly cheerful. To be sure, the regions where Japanese and European corporations established subsidiaries considered the newly-created jobs and tax revenues a blessing. But the domestic firms confronted by these aggressive new competitors understandably were more dubious about the benefits of international transfers of technology.

In historical perspective, the rapid evolution of MNCs as international carriers of technology can be seen as the culmination of a process that began with the growth of large, mass production-based firms in the industrial countries. In the United States, the growth of "national corporations" in the late nineteenth and early twentieth century was accompanied by discussions about their benefits and costs that resemble those more recently heard in connection with the evaluation of international business. What MNCs appear to have done on a global, rather than just on a domestic or interregional, scale is to undermine the economic significance of (largely immobile) resource endowments. In their pursuit of worldwide business, whether by trade or through direct investment, these corporations have demonstrated that embodied and disembodied technological knowledge is the single most important factor of production.

Seen in this way, the activities of MNCs fit very well into Schumpeter's concept of "creative destruction" through innovations. Such an interpretation also explains why some critics, while not denying the effectiveness of MNCs as vehicles for technology transfer, have expressed reservations about the wider-ranging economic, political, and cultural implications of their activities. Just as the convergence of income levels, consumer tastes, and market structures led to a greater uniformity of life *within* the advanced industrial countries, so the international spread of technology-based businesses appear to be producing a similar convergence among countries.

12.4   The Role of the United States in Technology Transfer

Until the 1940s, the United States had a reputation mainly for its genius in the development of foreign innovations so as to meet the requirements of efficient mass production. Process, rather than product innovation was thought to be the strength of American industry, and Henry Ford's automotive assembly line stood as a symbol of this strength. Justified or not, this image seemed to dominate European attitudes toward the United States as a competitor in the world market. This country was seen as a source of technologies whose characteristics derived primarily from the existence of a large, relatively high-income, domestic economy.

12.4.1   *Developments since World War II*

World War II and its aftermath marked a change in this picture. Aside from America's leadership in the development of nuclear power and in a number of other war-induced technologies, the country was to become the prime innovator in what has been called the "materials revolution," in electrical and electronic products, in military and commercial aircraft, in chemicals and pharmaceuticals, and in a variety of other fields.[15] The United States' position of leadership was no doubt accentuated by the fact that virtually all other industrialized nations had suffered the direct ravages of military action and were preoccupied with the reconstruction of their capacities, rather than with venturesome forays into unknown technological territory.

Some investigators have suggested that a technology gap between the United States and the rest of the world had existed for a long time.[16] Be that as it may, the immediate postwar era saw a rapid transfer of American capital and know-how to other countries, especially to their traditional, large companies. To the extent that these transfers were financed by the U.S. government, as was the case in the European Recovery Program, the emphasis on rebuilding the mass-employment industries also had a political rationale: it seemed to be the safest short-cut toward assuring urban populations of jobs and thus inducing them to resist the blandishments of Communist propaganda. Reconstruction was spectacularly successful, in economic and political terms. Government-to-government transfers of technology and capital seemed a relatively easy method for triggering economic growth. That Europe had all the necessary infrastructure in place tended often to be overlooked.

In his inaugural address of 1949, President Truman expressed the desire of the United States to ". . . make available to peace-loving people the benefits of our store of technical knowledge."[17] Through the famous Point Four Program, technology transfers were to bring the less-developed countries the same benefits that had just set the European economies on the path to growth and political stability. But except for some successes in the eradication of endemic diseases and in agriculture, Point Four resulted in few real advances—least of all in industrial development. Even when supplemented by massive financial aid, attempts to inject modern technology into economies that lacked most of the prerequisites for effective absorption had less than spectacular results.

The frustration of policy-makers had an ideological component as well: the recipients of technology and capital had to engage in some sort of industrial planning in order to identify opportunities and set priorities for development. In the absence of an entrepreneurial class in most of the countries, governments of necessity had to take on this task. But the United States wanted to encourage the growth of private enterprise and free markets, and so it confronted an apparent dilemma. In a speech in 1955, President Eisenhower suggested a shift in emphasis:

> "The whole free world needs capital; America is its largest source. In that light, the flow of capital abroad from our country must be stimulated and in such a manner that it results in investment largely by individuals or private enterprise rather than by government."[18]

Increasingly, the American government withdrew from massive involvement in technology and capital transfers, leaving the field to the fast-growing multinational corporations. Responding to the shock of Sputnik, the Soviet Union's first satellite, the United States shifted to a heavy commitment of public resources to the competition with Russia in space technology.

This development had two important consequences: (1) Through direct innovation and through the application of so-called "spin-offs" from the space programs in some industries, the technological lead of the United States tended to lengthen in those branches, while eroding in others: and (2) American firms responded by aggressively looking for opportunities abroad, either in order to take advantage of growing markets or to find lower input costs. The most efficient method for doing so appeared to be the establishment of fully-controlled operations abroad. Thus, multinational corporations became the prime vehicles for technology transfer.

The figures in Table 12.2 illustrate the rapid expansion of U.S. direct investment abroad over the last three decades. While the bulk of this growth occurred in the developed economies, the developing economies still account for roughly one quarter of the total. Investment in manufacturing made up approximately 30 per cent at the beginning of the period and grew to over 42 per cent by the middle 1970s; its share has stagnated since then. Other major foreign holdings by U.S. corporations are in petroleum, in the service industries, and in banking.

12.4.2   *The Era of Technological Convergence*

While the worldwide success of American business in the 1960s and early 1970s was generally attributed to a technology gap in many industries, this period

TABLE 12.2   *U.S Direct Investment Position Abroad, by Area*
(selected years, $ millions)

Area, country	1950 Amount	%	1966 Amount	%	1982 Amount	%
World total	11,788	100.0	51,792	100.0	221,343	100.0
Developed countries	5,696	48.3	35,290	68.1	163,076	73.3
Canada	3,579	30.4	15,713	30.3	44,509	20.1
Europe	1,733	14.7	16,391	31.6	99,877	45.1
United Kingdom	847	7.2	5,421	10.5	30,785	13.9
E.C. (6)*	637	5.4	7,256	14.0	43,032	19.4
Other Europe	248	2.1	3,714	7.2	26,059	11.8
Japan	19	0.2	731	1.4	6,872	3.1
Australia, New Zealand	226	1.9	1,965	3.8	9,305	4.2
South Africa	140	1.2	490	0.9	2,513	1.1
Developing countries	5,736	48.7	13,866	26.8	53,157	24.0
Latin America	4,577	38.8	9,752	18.8	33,039	14.9
Africa	146	1.2	1,344	2.6	5,069	2.3
Asia	1,013	8.6	2,770	5.3	15,050	6.8
Middle East	692	5.9	1,462	2.8	2,703	1.2
Far East	321	2.7	1,308	2.5	12,347	5.6

* Belgium, France, German Federal Republic, Italy, Luxembourg, the Netherlands.
Source: U.S. Department of Commerce, International Trade Administration, *International Direct Investment: Global Trends and the U.S. Role* (Washington, DC: U.S. Government Printing Office, 1984).

also proved to be the high-water mark of U.S. leadership. For during this period a number of countries managed to develop their industries on the basis of new technologies and in many instances to leap-frog previous American advantages. Outstanding among them was Japan, but Western European economies also achieved spectacular successes. And in the last decade, global manufacturing competition was joined by a number of entries from the less-developed world, among them South Korea, Taiwan, Brazil, and Mexico. These so-called "newly industrializing countries" (NICs) proved especially adept in absorbing many of the mature manufacturing technologies and in capitalizing on the lower labor and other input costs. In this respect, the directions of their expansion conformed to Vernon's life-cycle hypothesis.

What we have seen, then, in recent years is the emergence of very similar technological standards among a large number of countries and a concomitant decline in the United States' relative position in the world economy. Indeed, in many areas this country is now the recipient, rather than the originator, of innovations. There has been a lot of soul-searching among business and government leaders about the reason for this apparent loss of competitive positions. Looked at in a longer-term perspective, the development could be regarded as the quite natural outcome of global technological evolution. Among the factors contributing to the shifting patterns of competition the following appear to have been particularly important:

(1) Many customers, suppliers, and direct competitors of American firms abroad were able to advance their own technology because of *demonstration*

effects in production. More than copying the methods and products of U.S. industries, they managed to push basic technologies ahead through their own innovative activities.

(2) The very success of technology-based multinational companies has stimulated many host countries to intensify their own R&D and production efforts, motivated in many instances by governmental encouragement and subsidies. Industrialization and the development of "high-technology" capabilities frequently have become explicit policy goals in these countries, with the ultimate objective not only a reduction of their dependence on the world market for manufactured products, but entry into this market.

(3) To the extent that foreign industries were started up virtually from base zero, they could embody the most up-do-date equipment, while many U.S. (and Western European) branches were burdened with an older capital stock. One may well ask why firms did not simply scrap their obsolete plants and themselves switch to the new techniques. In part, this may well be due to a certain conservatism, for which American top managers have been upbraided by many critics. In part, however, it is also the result of a vicious cycle: firms that have fallen on hard times in competition have great difficulty raising capital for replacement, as long as investors perceive chances for higher rates of return in other, seemingly more dynamic, industries; but without the massive renewal of plant and equipment in the traditional sectors, the expectation of their decline becomes a self-fulfilling prophecy. It is frequently claimed that such sectors need "temporary" protection from foreign competition or governmental subsidies, but the results of such policies have been unimpressive.

(4) Perhaps most significant has been the worldwide diffusion of American techniques in management, production logistics, and marketing. Again, countries like Japan have probably improved on these techniques, but the basic organizational methods for running the large-scale, complex production systems that are a prerequisite for success in international competition were developed in the United States. In this connection, it is worthy of note that American consulting firms joined the ranks of multinational business early on, acting as effective transfer agents for these techniques.

12.4.3   *Indicators of the Changing U.S. Position*

A number of quantitative indicators for the closing of the technology gap between America and the rest of the industrialized world could be cited. Perhaps the most telling is the rapid growth of foreign direct investment in this country. As Table 12.3 shows, this has more than quadrupled in the past decade. Although foreign multinational corporations had a number of motives for establishing operations in the United States, such as avoiding the likely effects of protectionist legislation, the fact remains that these strategic moves were based on confidence in the firms' technological parity or superiority. The

TABLE 12.3   *Foreign Direct Investment Position in the United States, by Area*
(selected years, $ millions)

Area, country	1950 Amount	%	1966 Amount	%	1974 Amount	%	1982 Amount	%
All countries	3,391	100.0	9,054	100.0	25,144	100.0	101,844	100.0
Canada	1,029	30.3	2,439	26.9	5,136	20.4	9,823	9.6
Europe	2,228	65.7	6,274	69.3	16,756	66.6	68,514	67.3
United Kingdom	1,168	34.4	2,864	31.6	5,744	22.8	23,334	22.9
E.C. (6)*	†	†	2,144	23.7	8,266	32.9	37,670	37.0
Other Europe	725	21.4	1,266	13.9	2,747	10.9	7,507	7.4
Japan	†	†	103	1.2	345	1.4	8,742	8.6
Latin America‡	†	†	195	2.2	2,598	10.3	9,197	9.0
Other areas	134	4.0	43	0.5	310	1.2	5,568	5.5

* Belgium, France, German Federal Republic, Italy, Luxembourg, the Netherlands.
† Negligible (less than 0.5%).
‡ Including other Western Hemisphere.
Source: See Table 12.2.

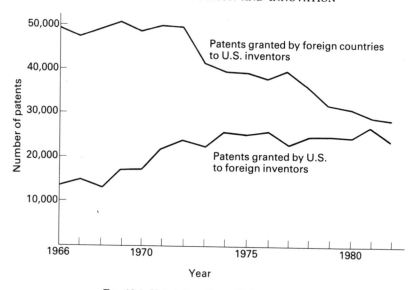

FIG. 12.1 *United States Patent Balance, 1966–82.*
Source: National Science Board, *Science Indicators 1982* (Washington, DC: U.S. Government Printing Office, 1983).

competitive success of companies like Michelin, Honda, Sony, and many others has borne out this confidence.

The narrowing of the gap is also suggested by trends in *international patenting*. The number of patents granted to American inventors abroad has declined since the early 1970s, while patents obtained by foreigners in the United States have been on the rise (see Fig. 12.1). We have pointed out on a number of occasions the shortcomings of patent statistics as indicators of technological change. They do no more than to reflect the generation of new ideas considered worthy of protection by the originators. Whether these ideas have been, or will be, converted into operational innovations is not evident from the statistics. Furthermore, to the extent that patenting strategies differ among countries and industries, the numbers may overstate or understate the actual significance of technological leads and lags.

Another measure of the United States' changing position is the *international balance on royalties and fees*, shown in Table 12.4. These data indicate receipts and payments on account of "patents, techniques, processes, formulas, designs, trademarks, copyrights, franchises, manufacturing rights, management fees, etc."[18] They suggest a continuing strong lead by American firms, with the ratio of inflows to outflows almost ten to one. It must be recalled, however, that these figures reflect pay-offs from past performance rather than current accomplishments and that they include transfers made from the foreign subsidiaries of U.S. multinationals to their home corporation, which in fact account for almost four-fifths of the total.

TABLE 12.4   *U.S. Receipts and Payments of Royalties and Fees, 1966–81*
($ millions)

Year	Receipts	Payments	Ratio Receipts/ Payments
1966	1,515	140	10.8
1967	1,516	166	9.1
1968	1,683	186	9.0
1969	1,842	221	8.3
1970	2,143	225	9.5
1971	2,375	241	9.8
1972	2,566	294	8.7
1973	3,021	385	7.8
1974	3,584	346	10.3
1975	4,008	473	8.5
1976	4,084	482	8.5
1977	4,503	434	10.4
1978	5,312	610	8.7
1979	5,747	764	7.5
1980	6,617	762	8.7
1981	6,917	693	10.0

Source: National Science Board, *Science Indicators 1982* (Washington, DC: U.S. Government Printing Office, 1983).

None of these generalized indicators is very satisfactory. What matters in international competition, after all, is how individual firms and industries perform with respect to technological innovation. Spectacular American achievements in many fields of "high technology" have been counter-balanced in recent years by the stagnation and decline of a number of traditional industries. At the same time, several countries have demonstrated that no one has a monopoly on the generation of major technological advances. The absolute dominance of the United States, across virtually all fields of industrial technology, is definitely a thing of the past. As one prescient observer of the changing scene put it, a decade ago: "It is clear that the technological competence of other countries will continue to increase and that the United States should view foreign technology as a resource which should be tapped to help stimulate our own technological innovation."[19]

The only conceivable obstacle to this desirable state of affairs would be the imposition of restrictive policies by the government. While ostensibly aimed at preserving jobs and regional economic stability but in fact sheltering industries against foreign competition, such laws and regulations involve a considerable cost to American consumers. To the extent that restrictive measures, often disguised as parts of "industrial policy," reflect the political pressures exerted by special-interest groups, they will tend to violate the tenets of dynamic efficiency and prevent the adjustment of firms to the changed climate of international rivalry. Even observers who do not oppose governmental intervention in principle have been sceptical about the long-term effectiveness of such policies. They tend to conclude that the government can play a role in supporting basic research and technological experimentation, but that beyond this the best public strategy may well be not to get in the way of market forces and only to mitigate some socially or politically undesirable outcomes, such as the displacement of workers.[20] These are, of course, problems with which all the older industrial nations have to wrestle as they confront the arrival of vigorous newcomers to global competition in technology.

12.5 Technology and the Developing Countries

There is general agreement that the development of the world's low-productivity, low-income economies requires that their indigenous technological base be supplemented by imports of technologies from the industrial nations. The big issue is whether these economies should borrow the latest available techniques and products or whether it would be more advantageous for them to rely on simpler technologies of the kind that are now largely obsolete in the advanced countries.

12.5.1   *The Question of Appropriate Technology*

As is so often the case in economics, the "appropriate technology debate," as it has become known, has to do primarily with one's perspective. In a static sense, i.e., referring to a country's relative endowment with factors (inputs) and to its economic and social infrastructure, most members of the so-called Third World are not ready for modern technology. But from a dynamic viewpoint, unless a country imports some advanced techniques that can serve as seeds for further development, it could be condemned to continue at low levels of output and income.[21]

Additional disagreement may arise because the debate frequently is carried on strictly in terms of the labor-intensity or capital-intensity of available techniques. Since virtually all developing economies are rich in labor and poor in capital, and since most advanced industrial techniques are regarded as rigidly capital-intensive, appropriateness seems to imply the importation of techniques requiring large amounts of unskilled workers. But, argues the other side, how can these countries enhance the quality of their investment in human capital without providing the proper technological setting?

The problem is often compounded by considerations of market size versus the minimum efficient scale of production with modern techniques. Are the large factories that have sprouted in many small, developing countries merely monuments to their leaders' political ambitions, or are they necessary components of "modernization," even if they require continuing infusions of public subsidies? Should poor countries welcome multinational corporations, even if these form enclaves of modern technology, aimed at utilizing cheap labor in production for export rather than for domestic consumption? Obviously, such questions are difficult to answer in general terms, without regard to the characteristics of particular economies and technologies. And answers have not been made any easier by the astonishing success of the NICs, about many of whom these questions were asked only a short time ago.

12.5.2   Indigenous Technology Development

In abstract terms, nomadic agriculture represents as legitimate a technological response to an abundance of land and a shortage of water as does the development of an irrigation scheme. From this unexceptional premise, it is sometimes argued that poor countries would be best off if they worked out their own technological innovations in ways that are fully responsive to local input availabilities and the potentials of local markets. At least in the case of agriculture, the argument also receives some support from actual experience. Thus, for example, any number of critics have claimed that the efforts by Western European countries to load off their surpluses of wheat and dairy products in the form of aid to their former African colonies have distorted agricultural development, as well as aggravating malnutrition and hunger. Having acquired a taste for these products, which were not previously part of their diet, the recipients of this largesse gave up growing traditional foodstuffs and attempted to raise European crops. In this, they were further encouraged by aid in the form of farm machinery, tractors and trucks. Most of these efforts resulted in massive failure, and then the people had neither their customary food, raised by well-established techniques, nor enough of the new kinds of nourishment. Clearly, they would have been better off if, instead of distorting their way of life, the advanced countries had encouraged them to improve existing agricultural technology.

The issue is much less clear-cut, however, when it comes to industrial techniques. We have seen how costly and risky development and innovation are even in the advanced countries with their plentiful resources for R&D. How much greater must be the difficulties in an environment lacking most basic inputs into industrial innovation! To be sure, there have been some examples of successful development of indigenous techniques, but these are few and far between. Incremental improvements in handicrafts or in textile-weaving are not what most of these countries have in mind when they speak of industrial development. And for them to re-invent and re-develop the older techniques of the advanced economies would surely be wasteful.

The very existence of a technology gap suggests that it might be more useful for developed and developing countries jointly to scan available techniques and products, and to select those seemingly most adaptable to local conditions. In this effort they may well be aided by a fact that tends to be overlooked in the debate about appropriate technologies: most modern techniques are much less rigid in terms of their capital–labor ratios and scale requirements than is often

assumed.[22] In some industries, such as petroleum refining or chemical manufacture, advanced technology may indeed dictate strict proportions of capital
and labor. But in many others, modern processes allow for considerable leeway
in the trade-off between basic inputs.

Consider, for example, just the methods whereby a seemingly "capital-
intensive" plant may be built: In a labor-scarce setting, this will be done by
machinery, but where construction workers are cheap, that plant will already
contain much more labor input than it would have in an advanced economy.
Similarly, varying degrees of vertical integration provide choices as to which
production stages a firm might first engage in. And finally, there is nothing
unusual about the co-existence of more and less advanced techniques in a given
production system. The most important rule is to deploy the scarce factor,
capital, most intensively in those stages of production where its contribution to
the quantity and quality of output is greatest, and to rely on labor-intensive
methods at other stages. There exists, in other words, much more flexibility in
adaptation than would be suggested if one thinks about the problem only in
terms of neatly-defined production functions.

12.5.3   *Importation of Advanced Technology*

In the case of modern technologies, whether imported through an internation-
ally-financed project or via direct investment, concerns about capital intensity
and general appropriateness appear largely irrelevant. Since the financial
resources would not have been available for any other purpose, their opportunity cost to the host country is zero. However, observers of development
sometimes express a concern about the possible consequences of creating a
so-called *dual economy*, i.e., one in which the enclaves of advanced technology
remain segregated from the traditional economic system. There is little
evidence, however, that such islands of modern production persist over the
longer run. As long as people are free to move back and forth between the two
economies, spill-over effects are bound to occur. Moreover, even lower and
middle-level management may be an important breeding-ground for native
entrepreneurial talent, people who later start their own firms on the basis of
what they have learned in their work with advanced methods of production.

In day-to-day practice, most of the purely economic arguments about the
suitability of advanced technologies for developing countries quickly run afoul
of a host of political influences, as do all other strategies formulated only in
terms of efficiency criteria. For the political leaders of less-developed nations
confront a genuine dilemma. On the one hand, they regard the importation of
best-practice technology as an essential symbol of advancement, and they
refuse to be fobbed off with technologies considered obsolete by the industrialized countries. On the other hand, they are fully aware of the fact that
major technological changes are challenges to political and social stability and
thus may undermine existing arrangements, including their own status as

leaders. There is nothing surprising, then, about the frequent animosity of developing countries' ruling classes against what they call "modernism." Leaders who want to modernize their economies have to walk a tightrope, and the resolution of tensions is more often played out in the political arena than in the impersonal marketplace. On the surface, the clash between competing interests is often conducted in terms of ideological slogans— "socialism" in various guises on one side, "capitalism" on the other. In the process, both designations tend to lose all precise meaning. But as a result the debate over the importation of modern technology frequently has little to do with questions of economic efficiency, but rather with matters of status and control in society.

In all of the resulting turmoil, there remains one dominant theme: despite the pronouncements of "no-growth" advocates in the high-income countries, the people in the less-developed nations regard technological progress as the most important source of improvement in the conditions of life. None of them wants to settle permanently for the primitive, pastoral existence that seems to look so attractive to romantics satiated with the material benefits of the industrialized world. For most of the world's population, the debate on technology transfer is about means, not about ends.

Notes

1. A survey of the traditional theory of trade can be found in any text on international economics. One of the best is Lindert, P. H., and Kindleberger, C. P., *International Economics*, 7th edn. (Homewood, IL: Irwin, 1982).
2. For a discussion of these matters see Ergas, H., *Why Do Some Countries Innovate More than Others?* (Brussels, Belgium: Centre for European Policy Studies, 1984).
3. Vernon, R., "International Investment and International Trade in the Product Cycle," *Quarterly Journal of Economics*, May 1966.
4. Kindleberger, C. P., "An American Economic Climacteric?" *Challenge*, January–February 1974.
5. *Cf.* Lindert and Kindleberger, *op. cit.*, pp. 102–4.
6. Olson, M., *The Rise and Decline of Nations* (New Haven, CN: Yale University Press, 1982).
7. A collection of articles dealing with strategies for technological revival can be found in Tushman, M. L., and Moore, W. L., eds., *Readings in the Management of Innovation* (Boston, MA: Pitman, 1982). The potential role of government is explored in Federal Reserve Bank of Kansas City, *Industrial Change and Public Policy: A Symposium* (Kansas City, MO: The Federal Reserve Bank, 1983).
8. See Bhagwati, J. N., ed., *The New International Economic Order* (Cambridge, MA: M.I.T. Press, 1977), and Cline, R. W., ed., *Policy Alternatives for a New International Economic Order* (New York: Praeger, 1979).
9. A wide-ranging survey of issues can be found in Samli, A. C., ed., *Technology Transfer: Geographic, Economic, Cultural, and Technical Dimensions* (Westport, CT: Quorum Books, 1985).
10. Useful treatments are Vernon, R., *Sovereignty at Bay* (New York: Basic Books, 1971), and Kindleberger, C. P., ed., *The International Corporation* (Cambridge, MA: M.I.T. Press, 1970).
11. The general theory of direct investment is outlined in Lindert and Kindleberger, *op. cit.*, Chapter 25. See also Rosegger, G., "Multinational Corporations and Technology Transfer: The Need for a Fresh Look," in Sichel, W., ed., *The Economic Effects of Multinational Corporations* (Ann Arbor, MI: University of Michigan, 1975).
12. Samli, *op. cit.*, p. 161.

13. Erdilek, A., ed., *Multinationals as Mutual Invaders: Intra-Industry Direct Foreign Investment* (London: Croom Helm, 1985).

14. Servan-Schreiber, J. J., *The American Challenge* (New York: Athenaeum Press, 1968).

15. For a historical review, see Rosenberg, N., *Technology and American Economic Growth* (New York: Harper, 1972), esp. Chapter V.

16. See, for example, Nelson, R. R., "The Technology Gap: Analysis and Appraisal," Clearinghouse for Federal Scientific and Technical Information, December 1967 (mimeo.).

17. Cited in Krause, W., *Economic Development* (San Francisco: Wadsworth, 1961), p. 305.

18. National Science Board, *Science Indicators 1982* (Washington, DC: U.S. Government Printing Office, 1983), p. 223.

19. Gee, S., "Foreign Technology and the United States Economy," *Science*, February 1975.

20. *Cf.* Roe, A. R., *Industrial Restructuring: Issues and Experiences in Selected Developed Economies*, World Bank Technical Paper Number 21 (Washington, DC: The World Bank, 1984).

21. A careful evaluation of the appropriateness controversy can be found in Kindleberger, C. P., *Economic Development*, 2nd edn. (New York: McGraw-Hill, 1965), Chapter 14.

22. See, for example, the empirical evidence presented in Rosegger, G., "On 'Optimal' Scale and Technology in Industrialization: Steel-Making," *OMEGA*, January 1975.

Selected Bibliography

This list of books represents no more than a small sample of the large, and rapidly growing, literature on the economics of industrial production and innovation. The only criterion for the selection of items was that they deal with subjects discussed in the preceding chapters. Much additional work can be found in general economics and management journals, as well as in periodicals specializing in topics related to technological change, such as *Technology and Culture, Technovation, Technological Forecasting and Social Change, American Heritage of Inventions & Technology, Technology Review, R&D Management* and *The Journal of Product Innovation Management*.

Abernathy, W. J., *The Productivity Dilemma: Roadblock to Innovation in the Automobile Industry* (Baltimore, MD: Johns Hopkins University Press, 1978).

Ayres, R. U., *The Next Industrial Revolution: Reviving Industry through Innovation* (Cambridge, MA: Ballinger, 1984).

Baier, K., and Rescher, N., eds., *Values and the Future* (New York: Free Press, 1969).

Capron, W. M., ed., *Technological Change in Regulated Industries* (Washington, DC: Brookings Institution, 1971).

Caves, R. E., *Multinational Enterprise and Economic Analysis* (London: Cambridge University Press, 1983).

De Gregori, T. R., *A Theory of Technology: Continuity and Change in Human Development* (Ames, IA: Iowa State University Press, 1985).

Eilon, S., Gold, B., and Soesan, J., *Applied Productivity Analysis for Industry* (Oxford: Pergamon Press, 1976).

Erdilek, A., ed., *Multinationals as Mutual Invaders: Intra-Industry Direct Investment* (London: Croom Helm, 1985).

Federal Reserve Bank of Kansas City, *Industrial Change and Public Policy: A Symposium* (Kansas City, MO: The Federal Reserve Bank, 1983).

Freeman, C., *The Economics of Industrial Innovation* (Baltimore, MD: Penguin Books, 1974).

Freeman C., Clark, J., and Soete, L., *Unemployment and Technical Innovation* (London: Pinter, 1982).

Gold, B., *Foundations of Productivity Analysis* (Pittsburgh, PA: University of Pittsburgh Press, 1956).

Gold, B., *Explorations in Managerial Economics: Productivity, Costs, Technology, and Growth* (New York: Basic Books, 1971).

Gold, B., ed., *Technological Change: Economics, Management, and Environment* (Oxford: Pergamon Press, 1975).

Gold, B., ed., *Research, Technological Change, and Economic Analysis* (Lexington, MA: Lexington Books—D. C. Heath, 1977).

Gold, B., *Productivity, Technology, and Capital* (Lexington, MA: Lexington Books—D. C. Heath, 1979).

Gold, B., Rosegger, G., and Boylan, M. G., *Evaluating Technological Innovations: Methods, Expectations, and Findings* (Lexington, MA: Lexington Books—D. C. Heath, 1980).

Gold, B., Peirce, W. S., Perlman, M., and Rosegger, G., *Technological Progress and Industrial Leadership: The Growth of the U.S. Steel Industry, 1900–1970* (Lexington, MA: Lexington Books—D. C. Heath, 1984).

Gruber, W. H., and Marquis, D. G., *Factors in the Transfer of Technology* (Cambridge, MA: M.I.T. Press, 1969).

Hamberg, D., *R&D: Essays on the Economics of Research and Development* (New York: Random House, 1966).

Jewkes, J., Sawers, D., and Stillerman, R., *The Sources of Invention*, 2nd edn. (New York: Norton, 1969).

Kamien, M., and Schwartz, N., *Market Structure and Innovation* (London: Cambridge University Press, 1980).

Kindleberger, C. P., *Economic Development*, 2nd edn. (New York: McGraw-Hill, 1965).

Klein, B. H., *Dynamic Economics* (Cambridge, MA: Harvard University Press, 1977).

Kranzberg, M., and Gies, J., *By the Sweat of Thy Brow: Work in the Western World* (New York: Putnam, 1975).

Kuznets, S., *Economic Change* (New York: Norton, 1953).

Mansfield, E., *Industrial Research and Technological Innovation* (New York: Norton, 1968).

Mansfield, E., *The Economics of Technological Change* (New York: Norton, 1968).

Mansfield, E., *et al.*, *Research and Innovation in the Modern Corporation* (New York: Norton, 1971).

Mansfield, E., *et al.*, *Production and Application of New Industrial Technology* (New York: Norton, 1977).

Meadows, D. H., *et al.*, *The Limits to Growth* (New York: Universe Books, 1972).

Mensch, G., *Stalemate in Technology: Innovations Overcome the Depression* (Cambridge, MA: Ballinger, 1979).

Mishan, E. J., *Technology and Growth: The Price We Pay* (New York: Praeger, 1969).

Morison, E. E., *Men, Machines, and Modern Times* (Cambridge, MA: M.I.T. Press, 1966).

Nabseth, L., and Ray, G. F., *The Diffusion of New Industrial Processes: An International Study* (London: Cambridge University Press, 1974).

Nelson, R. R., ed., *The Rate and Direction of Inventive Activity* (Princeton, NJ: Princeton University Press, 1962).

Nelson, R. R., Peck, M. J., and Kalachek, E. D., *Technology, Economic Growth, and Public Policy* (Washington, DC: Brookings Institution, 1967).

Nelson, R. R., and Winter, S. G., *An Evolutionary Theory of Economic Change* (Cambridge, MA: Harvard University Press, 1982).

Nordhaus, W. D., *Invention, Growth, and Welfare* (Cambridge, MA: M.I.T. Press, 1969.

Olson, M., and Landsberg, H., eds., *The No-Growth Society* (New York: Norton, 1973).

Pavitt, K., and Wald, S., *The Conditions for Success in Technological Innovation* (Paris: Organization for Economic Cooperation and Development, 1971).

Peirce, W. S., *Economics of the Energy Industry* (Belmont, CA: Wadsworth, 1986).

Pratten, C. F., *Economies of Scale in Manufacturing Industry* (London: Cambridge University Press, 1971).

Rogers, E. M., *Diffusion of Innovations*, 3rd edn. (New York: Free Press, 1983).

Rosenberg, N., ed., *The Economics of Technological Change* (Baltimore, MD: Penguin, 1971).

Rosenberg, N., *Technology and American Economic Growth* (New York: Harper & Row, 1972).

Rosenberg, N., *Perspectives on Technology* (London: Cambridge University Press, 1976).

Salter, W. E. G., *Productivity and Technical Change*, 2nd edn. (London: Cambridge University Press, 1969).

Samli, A. C., ed., *Technology Transfer, Geographic, Economic, Cultural, and Technical Dimensions* (Westport, CT: Quorum Books, 1985).

Scherer, F. M., *Industrial Market Structure and Economic Performance*, 2nd edn. (Chicago, IL: Rand McNally, 1980).

Schmookler, J., *Invention and Economic Growth* (Cambridge, MA: Harvard University Press, 1966).

Schumpeter, J. A., *The Theory of Economic Development* (Cambridge, MA: Harvard University Press, 1934).

Schumpeter, J. A., *Capitalism, Socialism, and Democracy* (New York: Harper & Row, 1942).

Science Policy Research Unit, *Project SAPPHO: A Study of Success and Failure in Industrial Innovation* (Brighton: University of Sussex, 1971).

Stoneman P., *The Economic Analysis of Technological Change* (Oxford: Oxford University Press, 1983).

Tushman, M. L., and Moore, W. L., *Readings in the Management of Innovation* (Boston, MA: Pitman, 1982).

van Duijn, J. J., *The Long Wave in Economic Life* (London: Allen & Unwin, 1983).

Weiss, L. W., *Case Studies in American Industry*, 2nd edn. (New York: Wiley, 1971).

Name Index

Subject Index

The Economics of Production and Innovation

An Industrial Perspective

2nd Edition

Gerhard Rosegger, Case Western Reserve
University, Ohio, USA

The role of technology and innovation in increasing the competitiveness
of firms and industries in domestic and international markets is of major
concern to both economists and industrial managers. Professor
Rosegger, Frank Tracy Carlton Professor of Economics at Case Western
Reserve University in the US, surveys some important topics in the
economics of production and technological change, exploring
innovation, in the broadest sense, as an economic activity, from an
industrial perspective.

This book is a well-integrated and comprehensive study of knowledge to
date in this important area, using theoretical models and providing a
generous selection of empirical illustration. Emphasis is on knowledge
useful to students of economics, engineering and management.

In this new edition, every chapter has been rewritten to take account of
updated statistical evidence, to add new empirical data or to reflect
changing emphases of scholarship.

0 08 033959 X